Academic Discourse

English in a Global Context

THE UNIVERSITY OF
WINCHESTER

Continuum Discourse Series

Series Editor: Professor Ken Hyland, Institute of Education, University of London.

Discourse is one of the most significant concepts of contemporary thinking in the humanities and social sciences as it concerns the ways language mediates and shapes our interactions with each other and with the social, political and cultural formations of our society. The *Continuum Discourse Series* aims to capture the fast-developing interest in discourse to provide students, new and experienced teachers and researchers in applied linguistics, ELT and English language with an essential bookshelf. Each book deals with a core topic in discourse studies to give an in-depth, structured and readable introduction to an aspect of the way language in used in real life.

Other titles in the series:

Metadiscourse: Exploring Interaction in Writing
Ken Hyland

Using Corpora in Discourse Analysis
Paul Baker

Discourse Analysis: An Introduction
Brian Paltridge

Spoken Discourse: An Introduction
Helen de Silva Joyce and Diana Slade (forthcoming)

Media Discourse
Joanna Thornborrow (forthcoming)

Professional Discourse
Britt-Louise Gunnarsson (forthcoming)

An Introduction to Critical Discourse Analysis
Carmen Rosa Caldas-Coulthard and Malcolm Coulthard (forthcoming)

and writing to bring out the dynamics and conventions which pattern particular social situations and (ii) those which have a more social theoretical orientation and consider the institutionalized ways of thinking which define our social boundaries. Discourse, in other words, spreads between two poles giving more-or-less emphasis to concrete texts and institutional social practices.

i. Texts and life-worlds

There is a long tradition of treating discourse in linguistic terms, informed by both pragmatics and a maturing, activity-centred linguistic perspective on language. This take on discourse recognizes 'language-in-use' as a legitimate object of analysis and sets out to discover grammatical and structural features of language operating at levels higher than the sentence (Blommeart, 2005). Many different frameworks have been developed for this purpose, crossing a number of disciplines and drawing on a broad variety of assumptions and analytical methods. They all, however, regard linguistic signalling and organization patterns as potential resources for interpreting text meanings and as contributing to our understanding of how texts are produced and used.

Many social scientists, on the other hand, particularly those influenced by Foucault (1972), pay very little attention to textual features. Instead they focus on the 'socially constructive effects' of discourse, or on the ways it functions to create social, cultural and institutional developments and to influence how we understand the world. This is what we might describe as discourse as form-of-life: the stuff of our everyday world of activities and institutions which is created by our routine uses of language, together with other aspects of social practices. It is through discourses, for example, that we build meanings for things in the world such as lectures, presentations, meetings and research; it is the ways that we construct identities for ourselves and relationships with others; it is how we distribute prestige and value to ideas and behaviours; and it is the ways we make connections to the past and to the future.

This difference is neatly encapsulated in Gee's (1999) distinction between 'big D' and 'little d' discourse. Gee defines discourse (with a little 'd') as 'language-in-use', that is, language as we use it to enact our identities as teachers, discourse analysts, taxi drivers or particle physicists and how we get things done in the world. Discourse (with a big 'D'), on the other hand, is a wider concept involving both language and other elements. It highlights the fact that our displays of who we are and what we are doing when we act as members of particular groups, always involves more than just language. As Gee observes:

> It involves acting-interacting-thinking-valuing-talking in the 'appropriate way' with the 'appropriate' props at the 'appropriate' times in the 'appropriate' places. Such socially accepted associations among ways of using language, of thinking, valuing, acting, and interacting in the 'right' places and at the 'right' times with the 'right' objects (associations that can be used to identify oneself as a member of a socially meaningful group or 'social network'), I will refer to as 'Discourses' with a capital 'D'.
>
> (1999: 17)

Discourse, then, is a way of being. It is the institutions, activities and values which we constantly recreate through discourse as members of social groups.

ii. Agency and social structure

Fairclough, like Gee, is just one among many analysts who see no opposition between these two views of discourse and its analysis. He observes that:

> Text analysis is an essential part of discourse analysis, but discourse analysis is not merely the linguistic analysis of texts. I see discourses analysis as 'oscillating' between a focus on specific texts and a focus on what I shall call the 'orders of discourse', the relatively durable social structuring of language which is itself one element of the relatively durable structuring and networking of social practices.
>
> (2003: 3)

For Fairclough, then, this 'oscillation' between texts and the structures which support them is needed to understand how language is used to conduct interactions and how it is embedded in social and cultural practices.

What Fairclough calls 'orders of discourse' are the relatively stabilized configurations of discourse practices and conventions found in particular social domains or institutions. These are Gee's 'Big D' discourses; the genres and styles used for creating meanings in particular areas. In Higher Education, the research, pedagogic and assessment genres of the university and the formal expectations which surround them offer frames for interaction among participants. But they also carry symbolic value because they are linked to, and by repetition reinforce, the values and beliefs of dominant groups. Academic orders of discourse, then, are ideologically shaped by those who exercise authority, the powerbrokers and gatekeepers of the field. The analysis of academic discourses needs to take both these dimensions of discourse into account.

The point here is that we don't only use discourse to express our attitudes, ideas and understandings, but that these are themselves shaped by discourse. Authorized and valued ways of using language make certain possibilities available to us and exclude others, thereby constraining what can be said and how it can be said. The topics we discuss, how we approach them and the ways we see the world are all influenced by the language we have available to us. Since the late 1970s, work by Kress and Hodge (1979), Fairclough (1989), Van Dijk (1997) and others has pointed to the need to consider these broader social, political and ideological forces that influence many professional and public texts.

This research, however, suggests that the connection between our social arrangements and our discourses is not a deterministic, one way process. We are not simply moulded by the texts we produce and encounter, but also act on these over time so that there is a balancing of human agency and social structure. Put another way, social practices both shape discourses and are themselves shaped by discourses. Giddens (1984) refers to this as the *duality of structure*: social structures (or 'orders of discourse') make social action possible and at the same time social action creates those structures. It is the repetition of the routine acts of individual agents in day-to-day life, including the routine uses of discourses, which reproduces the structure. This, in turn, also creates the possibilities for change. The traditions, institutions, moral codes and established practices which constitute social structures can be transformed when people reproduce them differently by combining different genres or developing them in new ways (Faiclough, 1989).

iii.   Writing and speech

In addition to distinctions of text and context and of agency and structure, the term discourse analysis has also been used to refer to different kinds of analyses in two separate contexts: multiple-source, dialogic spoken environments and single-source, monologic written contexts. There are clearly differences between these modes and we often recognize speech to be more highly contextualized, far more dependent on a shared situation, more reliant on immediate feedback and involving more real-time monitoring and less planning. Such differences are generally attributed to the distinct functions that speech and writing have evolved to perform (e.g. Halliday, 1989), or to the degree of detachment and reflection that each permits (e.g. Tanen, 1982).

23

These different conceptions of speech and writing have, moreover, led to the emergence of different analytic techniques. Studies of spoken discourse have tended to focus far more on the local management of participation such as turn-taking, politeness, utterance sequencing and the sensitivity of interaction to situational and cultural differences. Written discourse analysis, in contrast, has looked more closely at discoursal patterning and contextual factors operating outside the moment of production. We find conversation analysts, speech act philosophers and ethnographers of communication exerting a greater influence on analyses of spoken discourse, and the tools of Systemic Functional Linguistics, text linguistics and Critical Discourse Analysis brought to bear on written texts.

Attempts to identify clear-cut dichotomies between the features of speech and writing, however, have to be treated with caution. It is all too easy to attribute differences to the channel used, rather than to conventions which are specific to particular genres and contexts. This broad distinction thus oversimplifies a more muddied reality. It is often the case that formal written discourse tends to be more lexically dense (with a higher ratio of content words to grammatical words), to have greater nominalization (where events are presented as nouns rather than verbs) and to be more explicit (with clear signalling of semantic relations), but these depend on the purpose of the text and are not absolutes. Such differences are often overstated as a result of focusing on extreme cases such as face-to-face conversation and expository prose, for example, and neglect the considerable diversity of spoken and written genres. In fact, no single dimension of comparison can separate speech and writing and differences should be seen on a continuum rather than as polar opposites of mode.

Comparisons will necessarily reflect differences in the register, purpose and formality of the particular genres studied. Some genres of academic speech, such as supervisory meetings, poster discussions and seminars for example, are closer to casual conversation in their relative informality and spontaneity, blending interactivity with transactional purposes (Biber, 2006). Other genres like prepared lectures and conference presentations, on the other hand, are usually scripted to be delivered orally and are consequently more tightly organized and patterned, while still carrying something of the provisionality and time-constraints of speech (Swales, 2004). We might also note here the complicating role of multimodal semiotics in spoken presentations of various kinds, further undermining a direct spoken–written split in communicative features. The non-verbal dimension of academic speech (and writing) in both structuring talk and conveying information of various kinds is substantial, Kress *et al.* (2001), in fact, argue that meaning is not created by linguistic means alone but by both linguistic and visual modes acting jointly.

Technological and social changes further blur folk divisions of speech and writing, with new discourse forms increasingly important in the continuous evolution of research and instructional contexts. Much has been written about the potentially dramatic impact of electronic research communications such as e-journals, for example, although we still await their full flowering into new layered, multimodal and hyperlinked documents. More immediate are the changes that electronic media have brought to instructional genres, particularly for online feedback on students' written work, peer conferencing and computer-mediated distance pedagogies. Not only are such genres reshaping teaching, but the absence of physical co-presence seems to be changing our conceptions of what counts as appropriate communication forms by grafting a simulated conversational style onto a written mode.

Having raised a number of issues in how discourse and its analysis are understood, I now turn to describe some of the principal investigative tools employed, grouping them in terms of three main orientations: Textual, contextual and critical.

2.2 Textual approaches

At the beginning of this chapter I suggested that approaches to discourse analysis spread between two poles of a cline, either tending to an emphasis on language or context. The goal of describing and explaining academic discourse means that analyses must ultimately incorporate both dimensions to show how we actively create a world of activities, identities, relationships and institutions through discourse. The notion of *text*, in other words, should be seen as a spoken or written instance of *system*, or the general communicative resources which are available to a particular community. Here, I begin with textual approaches and the ways individuals employ language to structure and express their ideas, identities and communities, focusing on genre, corpora and multimodality.

i. Genre analysis

Like *discourse* itself, *genre analysis* is a broad term embracing a range of tools and attitudes to texts, from detailed qualitative analyses of a single text to more quantitative counts of language features. We can, in other words, examine the actions of individuals as they create particular texts, or we can examine the distribution of different genre features to see how they cluster in complementary distributions across a range of texts. The first emphasizes the decisions of particular writers while the second steps back to reveal collections of rhetorical choices rather than specific encounters. Different types of genre analysis also draw on different understandings of language and its relationship to social contexts. It is possible, therefore, to identify perspectives influenced by Systemic Functional Linguistics, English for Specific Purposes and New Rhetoric (Hyon, 1996; Hyland, 2004c) with the first two of these taking a more explicitly linguistic approach, largely to inform teaching practice.

Nor is there agreement on the concept of genre itself. It is, for example, seen as *typified rhetorical action* by Miller (1984), as *regularities of staged, goal oriented social processes* by Martin (1993), and as *shared sets of communicative purposes* by Swales (1990). In the most general terms we can follow Bhatia (2002: 22) in saying that 'genre analysis is the study of situated linguistic behaviour in institutionalized academic or professional settings'. But Swales (2004: 61) despairs of pinning down genres more clearly as definitions generally fail to hold true in all cases and often prevent the recognition of new genres. Instead, he suggests that we regard genres metaphorically, and perhaps the most productive metaphor might be to see them as frames for social action which offer users guiding principles for achieving particular recognized purposes by means of language. In other words, genres are schema. From all the possible ways of using language we make a relatively narrow selection and employ this selection repeatedly and routinely to both understand and demonstrate competence in a particular community.

Genres thus provide an orientation to action for both producers and receivers, suggesting ways to do things using language which are recognizable to those we interact with. This ability to see texts as similar or different, and to produce or respond to them appropriately, is possible because communication is a practice based on expectations: our chances of interpreting the writer's (or speaker's) purpose are increased if the writer takes the trouble to anticipate what the we might be expecting based on our previous experiences with texts. Hoey (2001) likens readers and writers to dancers following each other's steps, each assembling sense from a text by anticipating what the other is likely to do by making connections to prior texts. We know immediately, for example, whether a text is an essay, a joke or a lecture and can respond to it and perhaps even construct one of our own, given sufficient practice.

Genres are often associated with recurring rhetorical contexts as we draw on familiar resources to address routine communication needs, but they also permit expert users a certain leeway and opportunities for innovation. In other words, like dancing, established patterns can form the basis of variations and creativity. This kind of variation is important in creating new forms and genres can be 'sites of contention between stability and change' (Berkenkotter and Huckin, 1995: 6). But genres are not completely open and fluid and such variations are typically circumscribed with limited effects. Expectations for particular conventions of layout and language imply some constraint on choice and so tend towards conformity among genre users which leads to some temporary genre stability. Choice, in fact, is actually defined by constraint and there can be no meaning without it. Devitt (1997) refers to these constraints as a language standard of what is socially and rhetorically appropriate, and while these change over time, there are rewards for playing the game and, as students tend to discover, often consequences for violation.

The genres of the academy represent an enormous assortment which Swales (2004) refers to as a 'constellation' of academic discourse, some of which are shown in Figure 2.1.

Many of these genres interact with, draw on and respond to others in webs of *intertextuality* (Bakhtin, 1986), Useful here is Fairclough's distinction between *manifest intertextuality*, where quotes, paraphrase, citation, and so on signal traces of earlier texts, and *constitutive intertextuality* (or '*interdiscursivity*') where a texts is shaped by borrowing generic or rhetorical conventions from other genres, as in the use of biography in some qualitative research articles, thus merging what may be originally distinct orders of discourse to create new discourses. Genres are also related to each other in clusters of dependence which help construct a particular context. The idea of 'genre set' that Devitt (1991), for example, refers to is the full array of texts a particular group is likely to deal with, so that textbooks, lab reports and lectures may form a set for many science students while 'genre chains' refer to how spoken and written texts can cluster together in a given social context.

Written genres		Spoken genres	
Research articles	Book reviews	Lectures	Student presentations
Conference abstracts	PhD dissertations	Seminars	Office hour meetings
Grant proposals	Textbooks	Tutorials	Conference presentations
Undergraduate essays	Reprint requests	Peer study groups	PhD defences
Submission letters	Editor response letters	Colloquia	Admission interviews

Figure 2.1 *Some academic genres*

In sum, despite some terminological and conceptual uncertainties, genre analysis is the major instrument in the text analyst's toolbox.

ii. Corpus analysis

Corpus analysis is 'the study of language based on real life language use' (McEnery and Wilson, 1996: 1), but unlike more qualitative variants of genre analysis it draws on evidence from large databases of electronically encoded texts. A *corpus* is simply a collection of naturally occurring language samples (often consisting of millions of words) which represent a speaker's experience of language in some restricted domain, thereby providing a more solid basis for genre descriptions. While it does not contain any new theories about language, a corpus provides an alternative to intuition by offering both a resource against which intuitions can be tested and 'a motor which can help generate them' (Partington, 1998: 1). In other words, intuition and data work together to offer fresh insights on familiar, but perhaps unnoticed, features of language use. This assists to reduce any bias introduced by looking at just one text, enables analysts to depict what is usual, rather than what is simply grammatically possible, and helps to suggest explanations for why language is used as it is in academic domains and genres.

Corpus studies are therefore based on both qualitative and quantitative methods, using evidence of *frequency* and *association* as starting points for interpretation.

Frequency is a key idea in corpus studies. If a word, string or grammatical pattern occurs regularly in a particular genre or sub-set of language, then it can be taken to be significant in how that genre is routinely constructed by users. Thus Coxhead (2000), for example, shows that a list of 570 word families covers some 8–10 per cent of running words of academic texts while being relatively uncommon in other kinds of texts. Items such as *analyse, process, function* and *significant* are likely to be encountered by most academic readers. We need to be cautious, however, as such 'semi-technical' words are not evenly distributed across the academic register. Analyses of both writing (Hyland and Tse, 2007) and lectures (Thompson, 2006) reveal considerable disciplinary specificity in such frequencies, indicating clear preferences for lexical choices. Analyses also offer insights into the frequencies of other text features as electronic corpora are often annotated, or 'tagged' with additional information such as part of speech codes or sociocultural characteristics of speakers. Biber (1988), for instance, shows how written academic prose is characterized by bundles of grammatical features such as frequent nouns, long words, attributive adjectives and preposi-tional phrases which function to present densely packed information.

Frequency information is often supplemented by qualitative analy-ses of the ways features associate with each other in collocational patterns. Using concordance data, researchers are able to uncover pat-terns in the surrounding co-text which can suggest clues to the use of target words. Thus analyses can elucidate 'semantic preferences' (Stubbs, 2001) for certain patterns so that, for example, we find the adjective *massive* used in science writing to convey mass, modifying words like *star, planet* and *black hole*, while being used in journalism in the sense of size and collocating with *gamble, profits* and *blow* (Lee in Hunston, 2002: 162).

In addition we find that some words take on particular meanings as a result of their tendency to repeatedly occur in certain semantic envi-ronments, sometimes leading to evaluative connotations in a process referred to as 'semantic prosody'. In general use, for instance, the item *cause* normally implies something negative, as in these examples from the BNC newspaper corpus:

1. And that will cause uproar tonight when the general commit-tee gather to ratify the decision.

   . . . on or before Tuesday, March 2, they conspired at Walford Road and elsewhere to cause an explosion in the UK and with possessing a quantity of Semtex.

   Animal studies have shown dioxins to be carcinogenic and to cause birth defects in rats at very high doses.

The strength of collocation can most easily be seen in the use of differ-ent clusters across registers, with extended collocations like *as a result of, it should be noted that* and *as can be seen* helping to identify a text as belonging to an academic register while *with regard to, in pursu-ance of,* and *in accordance with* are likely to mark out a legal text (Hyland, 2008a).

Corpus analyses thus help provide a grounded basis for discourse studies, highlight unseen patterns and restrict the influence of intuition on research. The pervasiveness of collocations, in fact, has led Sinclair (1991) to propose that grammar is actually the output of repeated collo-cational groupings and Hoey (2005) to suggest that every word is mentally 'primed' for use with other words through our incremental experience of them in frequent associations. Corpus analyses have, however, been criticized for providing only a partial account of language use and for offering a description of text as a product rather than discourse as a process (e.g. Widdowson, 2000a). The fact that corpus data is typically restricted to language at the expense of both non-verbal meanings and the surrounding circumstances of the creation and use of text tends to mean that we are left with rather abstract and disembodied data. While there is something in this, corpus analysis comprises a range of different techniques and these are increasingly used in tandem with other, more qualitative methods to produce a fuller picture of academic discourse.

iii. Multimodal analysis

For many linguists discourse cannot be restricted to linguistic forms of representation alone but comprises all meaningful semiotic activity (e.g. Blommaert, 2005). There has certainly been a shift in our systems of representation away from the purely verbal to the visual in a whole range of genres in domains from advertisements to journalism in recent years, and this trend has also been apparent in research and education. Visuals are often as important as verbal elements in many academic genres and multimodal analyses attempt to offer an integrated perspective to study these developments. Researchers adopting this view consider the specific ways of configuring the world which different modes offer and draw attention to consequent shifts in authority, in forms of meaning and in forms of human engagement with the social and natural world (Kress, 2003; Kress and Van Leeuwen, 2002). Most dramatically, this requires very different semiotic work from the 'reader' as contemporary electronic texts often offer a range of entry points to the 'page' and different reading paths through it when compared with print texts, while involving the reader more actively in filling the relatively 'empty' words with meaning.

Essentially, multimodal analyses seek to describe the potentials and limitations (or 'affordances') for making meaning which inhere in different modes. Considering writing, for example, Kress (2003: 1) argues that writing and image are governed by different logics: writing by time and image by space. So in writing meaning is attached to 'being first' and 'being last' in a sentence, while in a visual it is position which is important, placing something in the centre, for instance, gives it a different significance from placing at the edge, while placing something above can make it 'superior' to what is below. The expansion of genres using new technologies such as e-journals, PowerPoint and digital portfolios in academic contexts thereby hasten and intensify, through their affordances, different potentials for communication, interaction and representation.

Academic written texts, particularly in the sciences, have always been multimodal, but textbooks and articles are now far more heavily

30

influenced by graphic design than ever before. Graphics typically do more than merely illustrate or supplement information and frequently carry the informative and persuasive weight of an argument. Figures, tables and photographs can occupy up to a half of a contemporary science research article, for example, while pedagogic texts are increasingly multimodal, with coloured maps, graphical representations and photographs helping to both represent an objective world and introduce disciplinary ways of seeing. We cannot, in other words, understand written academic discourse by looking at the resources of writing alone. Learning to read and create images has become a central aspect of learning scientific discourse.

The discourses of the classroom and lecture hall also draw on a multiplicity of representational modes. Kress *et al.* (2001), for example, show how school science teachers orchestrate a complex assembly of meaning resources in their discourse, including image, gesture, speech, writing, models, spatial and bodily codes. Different modes are foregrounded at different parts of lessons in a 'shifting hierarchy' to produce a coherent discourse. Visual material plays an equally prominent role in conference presentations, with something like a new slide every 50 seconds in many science presentations (Rowley-Jolivet, 1999). Dubois observed as long ago as 1980 that scientists frequently structured their talk around their slides, and this practice seems to have become ever more widespread, although there is considerable disciplinary variation in the use of visuals (Swales, 2004).

Few discourse analysts, however, have addressed the interaction between these modes and descriptive studies of lectures and presentations still massively privilege speech. Discussing PowerPoint technology, however, Myers (2000) notes the tyranny of bulletization and the blurring of written and visual modes. More importantly, he points to the rhetorical impact of this presentation software in reducing the speaker from author to animator so that the text is the star of the performance supported by the speaker. While this may overstate matters slightly, it reminds us of how much there is still to learn about the effects of visual presentations.

2.3 Contextual approaches

To understand how language works in the academy we need to move beyond the page or screen to see discourses as firmly embedded in the cultures in which their users participate. If we understand discourse as language-in-action, then this means looking more closely at the ways semiotic resources connect with everyday social, cultural and historical patterns. A second broad group of approaches therefore begins by foregrounding contextual elements of discourse. This group is potentially very large, but I have collected a variety of tools under three broad headings, each of which deserves more attention than it can receive in the limited space here. These are analyses informed by the sociology of science, by sociohistorical studies and by ethnography.

i. Sociology of science

Sociologists like to explain the beliefs of human communities by referring to aspects of their social organization, but natural science largely escaped this kind of scrutiny until relatively recently. The alleged objectivity of its methods seemed to give science a unique epistemological status which placed it beyond the bounds of sociological analysis. Quite simply, it was not necessary to examine its methods of persuasion because any claim could be tested empirically. But in the 1960s researchers began to look for more social bases for knowledge, questioning the view that texts are deductive proofs of claims or simply the conduit by which ideas and theories are channelled from one individual mind to another. Medawar (1964 (reprinted in 1990)), for example, argued that the scientific paper was 'fraudulent' as it rhetorically disguises methodological choices and interpretations to misrepresent research as an unproblematic inductive process of discovery. Scientific activity and the everyday processes by which research findings are transformed into scientific knowledge therefore became legitimate areas of inquiry.

Taking a strong social constructionist position (discussed briefly in the last chapter), and adopting techniques such as ethnography, participant observation and conversation analysis, sociologists began to insist on the importance of *context* in the creation of knowledge. At the broadest level of context, sociologists have explored the social structure of science, theoretically constructing how we might understand scientific writing as a social act, embedded in the received knowledge of the academic community. Kuhn (1970), for instance, refers to the practices of normal science, where scientific texts manifest the disciplinary perceptions, styles of speculation and other habits of a settled community paradigm. Similarly Lakatos (1978) proposes that a scientific community shares a research programme comprising methods and rules which define what valid research is.

From these perspectives, a model of science emerges where 'independent creativity is disciplined by accountability to shared experience' (Richards, 1987: 200) as scientific methods and findings are coordinated and approved through public appraisal and peer review. Writers must consider how their research fits with prior work and contributes to that work. The communication system is therefore the basic structural component of the scientific community, and an understanding of knowledge involves an understanding of how it is employed in the social justification of belief. It is the collective agreement of scientists which establishes that a claim has been adequately tested, and it is the verdict of a specially trained audience which is authorized to establish it as knowledge. Research is therefore less a search for truth than a quest for agreement (e.g. Polanyi, 1964: 13), as claims must be critically reassessed by other scientists before they can be regarded as 'well established'.

Studies have also focused on the more immediate contexts of scientific discourse by exploring the connections between writing and research activities. A key work here is Latour and Woolgar's (1979) ethnographic study which suggests that the modern research lab devotes more energy to producing papers than discoveries, and that scientists' time is largely spent in discussing and preparing articles for publication in competition with other labs. They see the lab as a factory where raw materials and labour are processed to produce the marketable products of publications which will enhance the prestige of the lab and attract more funding to continue the process. Other studies have focused on the processes by which research findings gain the status of accredited knowledge through peer review and the uptake of a disciplinary community (e.g. Myers, 1990). Some claims will be ignored or rejected as invalid while others will be recognized through citation and provide support for additional future claims. With time, the successful claim will no longer be referred to but incorporated into arguments as a taken-for-granted assumption. Readers are therefore only fully persuaded when all sources of support have disappeared.

Studies of academic discourse in the sociology of science therefore reveal the ways academic papers are socially situated in institutional and social contexts. They help illuminate how articles are written to provide an account that reformulates research activity in terms of an appropriate, but often contested, disciplinary ideology. This perspective shows us that the scientific writer's purpose is to create a text where a knowledge claim seem unproblematically related to observed data. In part, this involves concealing contingent factors, downplaying the role of social allegiance, self-interest, power and editorial bias, to depict a disinterested, inductive, democratic and goal-directed activity (e.g. Gilbert and Mulkay, 1984).

ii. Sociohistorical approaches

The constructionist idea that things are only true for a particular group at a particular time has generated research into the historical circumstance in which academic discourses emerge and become relatively stabilized in certain periods. These sociohistorical studies trace the evolution of research writing from the advent of modern empirical science in the seventeenth century and adopt methods which span discourse analysis, history and the sociology of science. These studies demonstrate the importance of situating cultural practices in their wider social contexts and represent a significant contribution to how we understand academic discourse. In particular, they show that the writing conventions familiar to us today are not timeless and self-evident means of establishing knowledge but have been consciously developed over time in response to particular social situations.

It is difficult to imagine science in the early Restoration period in England, with its diverse and competing array of cultural practices aimed at describing and controlling the natural world. While the idea of a 'scientific revolution' is now treated with scepticism, there were, nevertheless, large scale attempts to problematize and change classical and medieval beliefs about nature. This period witnessed considerable innovations in ways of identifying, validating and communicating experience; as scientists sought to reject ideas based on trust and authority to find ways of establishing *knowledge*. The concept of knowledge itself, in contrast to an individual's set of beliefs, implies a public and shared commodity, but in the mid-seventeenth century the linguistic practices for establishing the credibility of individual belief and securing its status as knowledge did not exist. It was Robert Boyle and his colleagues at the Royal Society who eventually created rules of discourse which would generate and confirm facts independently of man-made hypotheses, establish conventions of scholarly interaction and create a 'public' for experimental research (e.g. Shapin and Schaffer, 1989).

Essentially, scientific papers evolved as a way of offering a vivid account of experimental performances to distant readers. Although these readers would never see the event themselves, the writer could use the text to create an audience which Shapin (1994) calls 'virtual witnesses'. The reliability of these written accounts crucially depended on two things: (i) the ability to trust in the honesty and incorruptibility of the gentleman scholar within a culture of honour (Shapin, 1994); and (ii) the development of a rhetoric which gave detailed illustrations of experiments and carefully distinguished 'matters of fact' from speculations. Credible knowledge thus emanated from credible persons, and

Robert Boyle was among the most influential of them in creating a scientific rhetoric. His admonishments to avoid a florid style and display personal modesty continues to characterize scientific discourse to this day, but equally important was a probabilistic stance towards natural causes, thus establishing the basis of the experimental programme. Only facts, as discovered rather than invented, could be spoken of assuredly, while opinions as to the causes behind them were to be hedged with utmost caution. Anything else was dogmatism and merely served to undermine both the empiricist model and good manners.

The development of scientific discourse from the 1660s to the present has been traced by Valle (1997) and Atkinson (1999) in analyses of papers in *The Philosophical Transactions of the Royal Society of London*. These analyses show how linguistic practices, particularly those relating to the presentation of experiments, were gradually refined as audiences became increasingly professional, critical and research-motivated. A network of scientists slowly evolved which required institutionalized standards of public argument, and this moved research writing away from scientific reports characterized by narrative structure, personal involvement and author-centred norms of genteel conduct, towards a reporting format with greater emphasis on methodology and experimental description.

The past century has seen further changes, with the de-emphasizing of methods and the substantial expansion of theoretical discussions (Atkinson, 1999; Bazerman, 1988); changes which have probably come about because of the standardization of experimental procedures and the greater need to contextualize work in discipline-recognized problems. Theory and references have increased, with citations now spread throughout the paper as 'common theory has become an extremely strong force in structuring articles and binding articles to each other' (Bazerman, 1988: 157). Visuals have been given greater prominence and have been increasingly integrated into arguments, multiple authorship has increased massively, syntax has become simpler, and sections have become more clearly marked both typographically and stylistically. Titles, abstracts, sub-heads and graphics have developed to foreground novelty and significance in order to accommodate the scanning reading patterns of information-saturated readers searching rapidly for relevance and novelty (Berkenkotter and Huckin, 1995).

The changes noted in these studies demonstrate that the research article is a dynamic textual product strongly responsive to changing disciplinary norms and practices. The sociohistorical literature reminds us that the means by which arguments are presented, procedures enumerated, literature cited, readers engaged and data discussed can only be seen as persuasive against a broader social canvas. The changing conditions of research, the development of a scientific community, and the creation of ways of talking about nature and gaining assent for knowledge helped to shape the language of scientific presentation we see today.

iii.   Ethnographic approaches

Ethnography is an interpretive and qualitative approach to research based on the study of behaviour in naturally occurring settings. Originating in anthropology and sociology, it sets out to give a participant, or insider, oriented description of individuals' practices by gathering naturally occurring data under normal conditions from numerous sources, typically over a period of time (Ramanathan and Atkinson, 1999). While acknowledging that language is always an important part of such settings, ethnographic studies take a wider view to consider the physical and experiential contexts in which language is used. This perspective therefore gives greater emphasis to what people *do*, locating acts of communication in the behaviour of groups and employing methods which are interpretive, contextualized and respectful of participants' views.

Ethnographic methods are based on 'watching and asking' and so include participant and non-participant observation, in-depth interviews, surveys, focus group discussions, diaries and biographical histories. While something of an uncertain and contested term, ethnographic research generally requires analysts to use a variety of methods and data sources, to engage in research for long periods of time, and to recycle the results through participant verification and 'member checking'. While criticized by researchers from more positivist traditions for a perceived lack of rigour, imprecision and subjectivity, ethnography claims to offer a richer, first-hand interpretation based on interaction with a local context. For analysts of academic discourse it suggests methods for studying texts in ways which are 'situated', offering an alternative perspective to those discussed in the sections above. Ethnographic methods have been widely used in educational research and in the area of discourse studies have largely been used to inform studies of student writing.

One example is Prior's (1998) study of the contexts and processes of graduate student writing at a US university. Drawing on transcripts of seminar discussions, student texts, observations of institutional contexts, tutor feedback and interviews with students and tutors, Prior provides an in-depth account of the ways students in four fields negotiated their writing tasks and so became socialized into their disciplinary communities. The interplay of these different types of data and various theories of writing allows us to see how the multiple influences of academic practices, peers, mentors and students' own personal experiences and changing goals all contributed to their writing and to the process of becoming academic writers. Writing is therefore seen as mediated by other people and things, by classroom tasks and speech genres, by different discourses and disciplinary practices. But as Prior discovered, this training of graduate students is not the induction of individuals into clearly defined disciplines each with its own neatly configured idea and practices, as is often supposed. Instead it is the complex production of persons whereby 'an ambiguous cast of relative newcomers and relative old-timers (re)produce themselves, their practices and their communities' (Prior, 1998: xii).

While Prior is able to offer a detailed and 'thick' description (Geertz, 1973) of this context to develop an explanatory framework of these students' writing experiences, the generalizability of such accounts is often questioned. Hammersley (2001), however, argues that all generalizations are a matter of degree, especially in social research where there are always a multiplicity of interacting variables, and that 'fuzzy generalizations' can provide valuable descriptions of a situation. Such research can also generate what Glaser and Strauss (1967) call *grounded theory,* where categories generated in the early stages of analysis are developed with multiple methods to provide frameworks which may have explanatory relevance beyond the specific local situation investigated.

In this way, Ivanic's (1998) study of the tensions experienced by mature students in coping with the literacy demands of a UK university helped illuminate Lillis' (2001) qualitative research into the experiences of another group of student writers. Detailed investigation of students' accounts of their literacy histories, discussions about university essay writing, and analyses of their essays informed both studies and helped to show how students' values and beliefs shaped their approaches to writing assignments. Ethnographic studies have also been of a larger scale. The 'Framing student literacy' project, for instance, analysed a sizable corpus of student assignments and tutor feedback together with accounts from interviews and focus group discussions with tutors and students in various disciplines in four Australian universities (Candlin and Plum, 1998). Analyses of these diverse data sources not only revealed disciplinary differences in literacy practices but provided insights into how Higher Education requires competency in an institutional form of literacy which is neither agreed nor shared by all students and staff.

Ethnographic-oriented studies have also explored the literate cultures of academics themselves. Perhaps the best known of these

37

is Swales' (1998) 'textography' of his building at the University of Michigan. Swales makes greater use of analyses of texts and systems of texts in his approach than many ethnographies, combining discourse analyses with extensive observations and interviews. Together these methods provide a richly detailed picture of the professional lives, commitments and projects of individuals in three diverse academic cultures working in the building: the computer centre, the Herbarium and the university English Language Centre. The study brilliantly captures the different practices, genres and cultures of these disciplines and reveals the intriguing complexity which distinguishes academic activity. Through a variety of qualitative methods we get a sense of the individual voices and the kinds of insights which close observation and detailed analysis can reveal.

2.4 Critical approaches

The final orientation to discourse analysis I want to mention here does not fit neatly onto my text-to-context cline, nor does it necessarily comprise a particular theory or set of methods for analysing data. In fact, it extends the cline and bends it round into a loop, reminding us that the ultimate instance of discourse is not the text but the socially positioned reading it affords: how texts can be read in different ways depending on the subjectivity of readers. Critical approaches are better characterized as an attitude to discourse: a way of approaching and thinking about texts. In this sense, Discourse Analysis is neither a qualitative nor a quantitative research method, but a manner of questioning the basic assumptions of these methods. It shares with other forms of discourse analysis an interest in the ways texts are contextually situated, but it stresses that the most important dimension of social context is the relations of power that exist in it and the ideologies that maintain these relations. There are a number of critical perspectives, but the most relevant to the study of academic discourse are those of Critical Discourse Analysis (CDA) and Academic literacies.

i. Critical discourse analysis

Critical discourse analysis views 'language as a form of social practice' (Fairclough, 1989: 20) and attempts 'to unpack the ideological underpinnings of discourse that have become so naturalized over time that we begin to treat them as common, acceptable and natural features of discourse' (Teo, 2000). CDA therefore links language to the activities which surround it, focusing on how social relations, identity, knowledge and power are constructed through written and spoken texts in communities, schools and classrooms. Discourse is thus a mediator of social life: simultaneously both constructing social and political reality and conditioned by it.

Because of its diverse theoretical concepts and methods, Blommaert (2005) rightly cautions against identifying CDA too clearly as a uniform 'school', but it does provide a label for those adopting a critical stance in accounts of texts. A central aspect of critical views is that the interests, values and power relations in any institutional and sociohistorical context are found in the typical ways that people use language. As one of its leading figures observes:

> By 'critical' discourse analysis I mean analysis which aims to systematically explore often opaque relationships of causality and determination between (a) discursive practices, events and texts, and (b) wider social and cultural structures, relations and processes; to investigate how such practices, events and texts arise out of and are ideologically shaped by relations of power and struggles over power; and to explore how the opacity of these relationships between discourse and society is itself a factor securing power and hegemony.
>
> (Fairclough, 1992: 135)

This overtly political agenda therefore distinguishes CDA from other kinds of discourse analysis.

In terms of theoretical background, it is possible to trace links from CDA to French post-structuralist theory, which emphasizes the centrality of language and discourse. According to Foucault and Derrida, for example, discourses are not transparent or impartial means for describing or analysing the social and natural worlds but work to construct, regulate and control knowledge, social relations and institutions. Everything that exists is expressed in discourse, including scholarship and knowledge. CDA also draws on Bourdieu's argument that textual practices become 'embodied' forms of 'cultural capital' with different exchange values in particular social fields. Particular literacy practices and discourses possess authority because they represent the currently dominant ideological ways of depicting relationships and realities. Discourses that have symbolic value in an institution are ideologically shaped by its dominant groups and access to these valued discourses, and rights to use them, are unequally distributed. Educational institutions can therefore be seen as sites constructed by and through discourses and expressed in texts such as policy statements, curriculum documents, textbooks, student writings and lectures.

To analyse the 'symbolic power' of such texts CDA emphasizes *intertextuality* (the 'quotation' of one text by another), *interdiscursivity* (the use of generic conventions, register and style across texts), and *recontextualization* (how elements associated with particular discourses colonize new contexts). While CDA does not subscribe to any single method, Fairclough (1992, 2003) and Wodak (1989) draw on Systemic Functional Linguistics (SFL) (Halliday, 1994) to analyse concrete instances of discourse. In this model, language is seen as systems of linguistic features offering choices to users, but these choices are considerably circumscribed in situations of unequal power. Young and Harrison (2004) claim that SFL and CDA share three main features:

1. A view of language as a social construct, or how society fashions language.
2. A dialectical view in which 'particular discursive events influence the contexts in which they occur and the contexts are, in turn, influenced by these discursive events' (ibid. p. 1).
3. A view which emphasizes cultural and historical aspects of meaning.

SFL thus offers CDA a sophisticated way of analysing the relations between language and social contexts, making it possible to ground concerns of power and ideology in the details of discourse.

To examine actual instances of texts, CDA typically looks at features such as:

- Vocabulary – particularly how metaphor and connotative meanings encode ideologies.
- Transitivity – how participants, processes and circumstances are represented in a clause which can show, for instance, who is presented as having agency and who is acted upon.
- Nominalization and passivization – how processes and actors can be repackaged as nouns or otherwise obscured.
- Mood and modality – which help reveal interpersonal relationships such as discourse roles, attitudes, commitments and obligations.
- Theme – how the first element of a clause can be used to foreground particular aspects of information or presuppose reader/hearer beliefs.
- Text structure – how text episodes are marked or the turn-taking system employed.
- Intertextuality and interdiscursivity – the effects of other texts and styles or registers on texts – leading to *hybridization*, such as where commercial discourses colonize those in other spheres.

These textual devices reveal a considerable ideological richness in both spoken and written texts.

Research has largely addressed mass media and public discourses, dealing with issues such as racism, gender, and class. Studies in schools have pointed to the fact that classroom talk is a primary medium through which teachers and students construct 'readings' of textbooks, creating authoritative interpretations and shaping what will count as knowledge, legitimate social relations and textual practices. CDA has also looked at representation in language through the concept of commodification, or the creeping expansion of marketing discourses into other domains. An example of this is how universities construct themselves discoursally as corporate bodies selling educational products in response to the shift to a market-driven model of Higher Education (Fairclough, 1995). University prospectuses, brochures, handbooks, job advertisements and programme materials all reflect the fact that the abolition of grants and the introduction of fees have created markets where students are clients in a marketplace of competing institutions.

My own university's homepage, for example (Figure 2.2), constructs the institution as an attractive product through a range of positive associations (age, excellence, diversity, etc), a personalized corporate

Institute of Education
University of London

Founded in 1902, the Institute of Education is a world class centre of excellence for research, teacher training, higher degrees and consultancy in education and education-related areas of social science. Our staff of pre-eminent scholars and talented students from all walks of life make up an intellectually rich and diverse learning community.

Figure 2.2 *Institute of education homepage*

identity (our staff and students, learning community), and a collage of images which link the professional, academic, social and corporate features of the institution.

On a more critical note, CDA has been criticized for cherry-picking both texts and particular features of texts to confirm the analyst's prejudices while reducing pragmatics to semantics in assuming just one possible reading of the text – that provided by the analyst (Widdowson, 2000b). There is a strong tendency in this work to assume certain patterns of power relations as relevant context without pinpointing their realization in text features, and often there is a failure to go beyond the analyst's interpretations to consult participants' understandings. This privileging of the analyst's viewpoint is, as Blommaert (2005) notes, often further reinforced by appeal to an explanatory level of social theory which lies above any analysis of the text itself. This effectively closes all dialogue with the reader and makes interpretation a black box rather than a product of textual analysis. The plausibility of any interpretation of a text ultimately depends on our willingness to accept it, of course, but this is not greatly enhanced by CDA's consistent failure to establish the intentions and interpretations of participants themselves.

But while CDA has generally remained uncritical of its methods, it has encouraged a broader contextual analysis in discourse analysis and encouraged the search for hidden text motivations. It has also underlined a rethinking of pedagogical practices and outcomes, encouraging teachers to assist students to an awareness of how writing practices are grounded in social structures by exposing the ideological assumptions of the prestige discourses that they seek to acquire. This agenda works to shift curriculum development and instruction away from producing workplace and civic competencies towards critical analyses of text-based cultures and economies.

ii.   Academic literacies

An academic literacies perspective implies a different understanding of 'critical' to that advanced by CDA and emerges from very different theoretical premises and practical concerns. It is, in fact, not strictly an approach to *discourse* at all. It is a way of conceptualizing and influencing teaching and learning by radically rethinking *literacy* to take account of the cultural and contextual components of reading and writing. Like CDA, the academic literacies' view frames language as discourse practices, the ways in which language is used in particular contexts, rather than as a set of discrete skills. In so doing it re-establishes the intrinsic relationship between knowledge, writing and identity

(Ivanic 1998, Lillis 2001) and raises issues of relevance and legitimacy in relation to writing practices.

The academic literacies' perspective takes a 'New Literacies' position which rejects

> the ways language is treated as though it were a thing, distanced from both teacher and learner and imposing on them external rules and requirements as though they were but passive recipients.
>
> (Street, 1995: 114)

Instead, literacy is something we *do*. Street characterizes literacy as a verb, an activity 'located in the interactions between people' (Barton and Hamilton, 1998: 3). Because literacy is integral to its contexts, it is easier to recognize the disciplinary heterogeneity which characterizes the modern university. From the student point of view, a dominant feature of academic literacy is the requirement to switch practices between one setting and another, to control a range of genres appropriate to each setting, and to handle the meanings and identities that each evokes. Such experiences underline for students that writing and reading are not homogeneous skills which they can take with them as they move across different courses and assignments.

One problem for participants is that while achievement is assessed by various institutionalized forms of writing, what it means to write in this way is rarely made explicit to students. A failure to recognize that discourse conventions are embedded in the epistemological and social practices of the disciplines means that writing is a black box to students, particularly as lecturers themselves have difficulty in explaining what they mean (Lea and Street, 2000).

The academic literacies approach recognizes that the difficulties students often experience with academic writing are not due to technical aspects of grammar and organization, but the ways that different strands of their learning interact with each other and with their previous experiences. Entering the academy means making a 'cultural shift' in order to take on identities as members of those communities. Gee stresses the importance of this shift:

> [S]omeone cannot engage in a discourse in a less than fluent manner. You are either in it or you're not. Discourses are connected with displays of identity – failing to display an identity fully is tantamount to announcing you do not have that identity – at best you are a pretender or a beginner.
>
> (1996: 155)

Academic success means representing yourself in a way valued by your discipline, adopting the values, beliefs and identities which academic discourses embody. As a result, students often feel uncomfortable with the 'me' they portray in their academic writing, finding a conflict between the identities required to write successfully and those they bring with them.

A central issue here is that writing tends to be viewed as simply the *medium* through which students present what they have learned without consideration of its deeper cultural and epistemological under-pinnings. This separates writing from ways of knowing and the institution's processes and discourses from students' individual histo-ries. Herein lies the critical dimension of this approach:

> The level at which we should be rethinking higher education and its writing practices should not simply be that of skills and effec-tiveness but rather of epistemology – what counts as knowledge and who has authority over it; of identity – what the relation is between forms of writing and the constitution of self and agency; and of power – how partial and ideological positions and claims are presented as neutral and as given through the writing requirements and processes of feedback and assessment that make up academic activity.
>
> (Jones *et al.*, 1999: xvi)

The academic literacy position therefore encourages us to see that writing must be understood as the crucial process by which students make sense not only of the subject knowledge they encounter through their studies, but also how they can make it mean something for them-selves. The varied discourses and expectations of the academy therefore necessitate negotiation between students and teachers rather than accommodation to foreign, and complexly diverse, discourses and literacy conventions.

2.5 Conclusions

This overview of approaches is, I admit, rather brief and inconclusive. Instead of offering a clear way forward to those wishing to adopt a 'best method' for understanding academic discourse, it seems to raise yet more questions. How much context, whether historical, social, dis-coursal or material, do we need in order to gain insights into academic discourses? Is there a single 'best approach' to the study of all academic discourse? How do various textual discourses interact with each other in real contexts of use? How do we resist dominant ideological posi-tions in understanding academic discourses? What kinds of approaches and descriptions are most helpful for pedagogy?

Perhaps the main conclusion to be drawn from all this is that there are various ways of understanding discourse and different approaches to its study. I hope it is clear, however, that there is no single, uniquely right way of analysing academic discourse. On one hand, different approaches, concepts and terminologies obviously connect to particular theoretical orientations and research groups. But while these may be championed as defining the work of such groups or expressing their identity, there may be more overlapping, more opportunities for borrowing, and even more prospect of mixing and matching, than we might initially suppose. On the other hand, different approaches address different questions and fit different issues better than others. No single theory or set of research tools is going to offer the best understanding of discourse in all possible situations, so our interests, needs and specific local objectives will influence the ways we approach discourse and the questions we have about it.

We need, in other words, to make choices in analysing discourse and to draw on the most appropriate methods. This does not mean, however, a marketplace of free options. Any method comes with a theory attached to it, however implicit, and will make certain assumptions about what language is and how people use it. No approach to academic discourse can be divorced from our understandings of either the academy or discourse because we select our methods and conceptual tools thorough the filter of what questions we think are important to ask and where we feel we are most likely to find answers. Methods do not, however, exist in some fixed and isolated world, and researchers often adopt them to their own purposes to some extent, taking what they need to fit their goals and understandings. For this reason we should not oppose labels like 'qualitative' and 'quantitative' or 'genre' and 'ethnographic' but must look for ways that offer evidence for a theory of academic discourse which explains how language works in university contexts.

3 Academic communities

Until fairly recently research into academic discourse mainly concerned itself with describing general contexts of academic life and broad features of the register, exploring academic *discourse* rather than *discourses*. Scientific writing was taken to be the prototype of such discourse and its ability to represent meanings with little reference to people seen as a model of more general principles of academic communication. Influenced by a growing acceptance of social construction and more detailed descriptions of textual practices, however, a more sophisticated appreciation of language variation has emerged over the last decade or so. With doubt cast on the idea that knowledge claims are decided by appeal to self-evident truths or faultless logic, the decision-making of disciplinary groups has been elevated to greater importance. This, then, turns our attention to the concept of *community* and what it might contribute to our understanding of academic discourse.

3.1 The idea of 'discourse community'

As I discussed in Chapter 1, successful academic discourse depends on the individual's projection of a shared professional context. Academic discourses are not, in other words, just regularities of a peculiar kind of formal style or the result of some mental processes of representing meaning. Instead they evoke a social milieu, where the writer activates specific recognizable and routine responses to recurring tasks. Texts are constructed in terms of how their authors understand reality. These understandings are, in turn, influenced by their membership of social groups which have objectified in language certain ways of experiencing and talking about phenomena. Academic discourse is therefore a reservoir of meanings that give identity to a culture. Assumptions about what can be known, how it can be known, and how certainly it can be known all help shape discourse practices, but while the notion of community has informed a great deal of work into academic discourse, it is by no means a settled and accepted concept, as I discuss in this section.

i. Basis of the concept

As early as the mid-1960s Del Hymes (1966) cautioned against relying on abstract rules of communication and encouraged us to focus instead on understanding the cultural assumptions and practices of social groups. More recently, this sensitivity to a community-oriented view of literacy has emerged through ideas such as *communicative competence* in applied linguistics, *situated learning* in education and *social constructivism* in the social sciences. In particular it follows Faigley's (1986: 535) claim that writing 'can be understood only from the perspective of a society rather than a single individual' and Geertz's (1973) view that knowledge and writing depend on the actions of members of local communities.

The concept of community draws attention to the idea that we do not use language to communicate with the world at large, but with other members of our social groups, each with its own norms, categorizations, sets of conventions and ways of doing things (Bartholomae, 1986). The value of the term lies in the fact that it offers a way of bringing writers, readers and texts together into a common rhetorical space, foregrounding the conceptual frames that individuals use to organize their experience and get things done using language. It is therefore the basis of communication for without such schema we would not be able to effectively interpret each others' discourses.

Theoretically, the concept is informed by Bakhtin's (1981) influential notion of *dialogism* which stresses that all communication, whether written or spoken, reveals the influence of, refers to, or takes up, what has been said or written before while at the same time anticipates the potential or actual responses of others. He points out that all utterances exist 'against a backdrop of other concrete utterances on the same theme, a background made up of contradictory opinions, points of view and value judgements (Bakhtin, 1981: 281). As we noted in the last chapter, in engaging with others we enter into a community of shared belief or value concerning what is interesting or worth discussing and through our language choices we align ourselves with, challenge, or extend what has been said before. The notion of community therefore seeks to offer a framework within which these actions occur and so characterize how speakers position themselves with and understand others. It is a means of accounting for how communication succeeds.

So, in pursuing their personal and professional goals, academics attempt to embed their talk and writing in a particular social world which they reflect and conjure up through discourses which others expect and anticipate. The ways we communicate with each other, exchange information, and work together will vary according to the groups we belong to, and such rhetorical practices also reflect wider, non-linguistic aspects of community. Specific linguistic realizations like the avoidance of personal pronouns and the embedding of research in previous literature, for example, index common ideologies such as 'objectivity' and the view that knowledge emerges in a linear step-wise fashion in scientific practice. Community conventions are therefore also a means of fostering group mythologies, solidarity and social control, helping to ring-fence communities by identifying their users as insiders and excluding others.

This approach therefore asks us to accept a certain homogeneity in the practices of social groups. Each discipline might therefore be seen as an academic tribe (Belcher and Trowler, 2001) with its particular norms and practices which comprise separate cultures. Within each culture students and academics gradually acquire specialized discourse competencies that allow them to participate as group members. Wells sets these out as:

> Each subject discipline constitutes a way of making sense of human experience that has evolved over generations and each is dependent on its own particular practices: its instrumental procedures, its criteria for judging relevance and validity, and its conventions of acceptable forms of argument. In a word each has developed its own modes of discourse. To work in a discipline, therefore, it is necessary to be able to engage in these practices and, in particular, to participate in the discourses of that community.
>
> (1992: 290)

Essentially, the idea of *community* draws together a number of key aspects of context that are crucial to how spoken and written discourse is produced and understood. Cutting (2002: 3) describes these as:

- the *situational context*: what people 'know about what they can see around them';
- the *background knowledge context*: what people know about the world, what they know about aspects of life and what they know about each other;
- the *co-textual context*: what people 'know about what they have been saying'.

Community thus provides a principled way of understanding how meaning is produced *in interaction* and so is useful in identifying how we communicate in a way that others can see as 'doing biology' or 'doing sociology'. In the academic world, these community conventions both restrict how something can be said and authorize the writer as someone competent to say it.

ii. Conceptions of community

But while the notion of *community* occurs frequently in the study of discourse, it lends itself to many different readings. Swales (1990), for instance, sets out criteria which see communities as groups which use language to achieve collective goals or purposes, while other writers have suggested a weaker connection, arguing that common interests, rather than shared goals, are essential (Johns, 1997). Barton, on the other hand offers us a much looser association of individuals engaged in either the reception or production of texts, or both:

> *A discourse community is a group of people who have texts and practices in common, whether it is a group of academics, or the readers of teenage magazines. In fact, discourse community can refer to the people the text is aimed at; it can be the people who read a text; or it can refer to the people who participate in a set of discourse practices both by reading and writing.*
>
> (1994: 57)

It is not surprising then that, as Bazerman (1994: 128) observes, 'most definitions of discourse community get ragged around the edges rapidly'. To avoid a lengthy citation list, we might instead, with Kent (1991), see these definitions as spreading across a spectrum from *thick* to *thin* formulations:

> On one end of the spectrum are thick formulations that depict a community as a determinate and codifiable social entity, and on the other end are thin formulations that depict a community as a relatively indeterminate and uncodifiable sedimentation of beliefs and desires.
>
> (1991: 425)

In other words, it is possible to see communities as real, relatively stable groups whose members subscribe, at least to some extent, to a consensus on certain ways of doing things and using language. On the other hand, community can be regarded as a more metaphorical term for collecting together certain practices and attitudes.

Perhaps the best known attempts to pin down the concept of discourse community is that of Swales (1990 and 1998) who emphasizes its heterogeneous, socio-rhetorical nature, focusing on collectivities which share occupational or recreational goals and interests and which employ particular genres to do so. This is a very different notion to that of speech community found in the sociolinguistic literature as it gives less emphasize to geographic proximity and attends to what people *do* rather than what they *are*. Swales puts it like this:

> In-group abbreviations, acronyms, argots, and other special terms flourish and multiply; beyond that, these discourse communities

49

> evolve their own conventions and traditions for such diverse verbal activities as running meetings, producing reports, and publicizing their activities. These recurrent classes of communicative events are the genres that orchestrate verbal life. These genres link the past and the present, and so balance forces for tradition and innovation. They structure the roles of individuals within wider frameworks, and further assist those individuals with the actualization of their communicative plans and purposes.
>
> (1998: 20)

While Swales goes on to acknowledge that matters may be a little more complex than this, the notion of discourse community does have significant explanatory potential, allowing us to locate individuals in particular social contexts and to identify how their rhetorical strategies are dependent on the purposes, setting and audience of a discourse (e.g. Bruffee, 1986). Bizzell (1982: 217), for example, has discussed communities in terms of 'traditional, shared ways of understanding experience' including shared patterns of interaction, and Doheny-Farina (1992) refers to the 'rhetorical conventions and stylistic practices that are tacit and routine for the members' (p. 296). Communities are therefore constraining systems which focus on both texts and surrounding activities and which affect the manner and meaning of any message delivered within it.

iii.   The local and the global

One difficulty with the term has been reconciling what might be seen as the *local* and the *global*. This refers to how the idea of large, amorphous and dispersed groups of like-minded individuals defined by common bonds of discourse practices and conventions can be squared with groups who typically work together and subscribe to common practices of work and patterns of communication. How, in other words, do we concretize the ghostly 'invisible colleges' that focus on fairly specialized textually encoded knowledge and span the globe through webs of journals, symposia, informal contacts and pre-print circulations? When we do turn to local systems, how do we define membership and draw boundaries? Do we look for communities in universities, departments, classrooms or all of these?

Gee (2004) responds by arguing that we can avoid most of these difficulties by focusing on 'affinity spaces' rather than communities, beginning with the places (whether physical or virtual) where people interact through shared practices in a common endeavour. Porter's (1992) solution is to see local manifestations of wider communities in its *forums* or approved channels of discourse such as publications, meetings and conferences. This view cuts across social and institutional boundaries to emphasize local discourses which carry traces of the community's orientations, methodologies and practices.

Killingsworth and Gilbertson (1992) see a similar connection here, and distinguish local groups of speakers and writers who habitually interact in departments, research units, or labs, and global communities 'defined exclusively by a commitment to particular kinds of action and discourse' (p. 162) irrespective of where they work. This seems to capture neatly the often fraught tension in academic communities between local working practices, comprising the pressures of teaching, supervision, research and administrative practices, with the wider pressures of publishing, networking and conference attendance. Killingsworth and Gilbertson themselves comment on the conflicts often produced by participating in these different dimensions of community, arguing that 'global communities' now dominate the lives and activities of Western academics. Killingsworth and Gilbertson (1992: 169) believe that 'membership in global communities tends to be regulated exclusively by discourse-governed criteria (writing style, publication in certain journals, presentations at national conventions, professional correspondence, and so forth)'. Local communities, however, have largely been characterized in terms of shared *practices*, or the engagement of individuals around some project which fosters particular beliefs, ways of talking and power relations.

Attention to local communities shifts the focus from either language or social structure to the situated practices of individuals acting in communities strongly shaped by a collective history of pursuing particular goals within particular forms of social interaction. Swales (1998) endorses a similar view in his idea of *Place Discourse Communities*, drawing attention to groups who regularly work together and have a sense of their common roles, purposes, discourses and history. But this is not to say that all our endeavours in various groups constitute participation in discourse communities. Clearly we are all members of numerous temporary collectives such as student study groups or promotion committees, but not all demand equal degrees of commitment and not all impact on our self-perceptions and ways of being in the world. Professional and occupational communities are far more likely to both absorb our time and attention and help define our sense of self than many other, perhaps more temporary, engagements.

Whether we choose to focus on local or more general communities, the concept moves us from a concern with the abstract logicality and lofty ideas expressed in academic discourses to worlds of concrete practices and social beliefs. It takes us closer towards an explanation of how writers and readers make sense to each other in shorthand

(and often seemingly obscure and tortuous) ways; it suggests how communication often seems more awkward with members of other groups and relatively effortless among those we know; it shows how heterogeneous classes of undergraduates might come to form a successful unit; how conflicts arise and are resolved (or not); how newcomers may be initiated and apprenticed into full membership; and how the discourses of different disciplines may be distinguished and understood. It short, the notion of community puts individual's decision-making and engagement at centre-stage and underlines the fact that academic discourse involves language users in constructing and displaying their roles and identities as members of social groups.

3.2 Critiques and responses

Despite these positives, the concept of community has not found universal favour. Harris (1989), for example, argues that we should restrict the term to specific local groups, and labels other uses as 'discursive utopias' which fail to state either their rules or boundaries. We just don't know how to identify them or get any sense of where they begin or end and this means the idea reduces to a nebulous assortment of conventions. Canagarajah (2002), Pennycook (1994) and Prior (1998), among others, more pointedly view the term as altogether too structuralist, static and deterministic, giving too much emphasis to a stable underlying core of shared values which removes discourse from the actual situations where individuals make meanings. Nor is it readily apparent how communities come into being or how they develop and change; the ways they shed redundant genres and practices to take up new ones; and how they replace established members with young blood. Such criticisms alert us to the dangers of viewing communities as stable, rule-conforming groups which adhere to a collection of values and uphold a consensus concerning ways of doing and communicating.

i. Conformity and power

The attractiveness of the concept is, to a large extent, its power to explain conformity and diversity in social and discourse practices, but critics point out that this often means stressing sameness and modelling compliance. An emphasis on conformity therefore both ignores the extent of diversity within communities and can prevent critical inquiry into the power relations which support it, failing to unpack *whose* language is being shared and *what* functions this serves. Such questions raise issues of power and identity which are often glossed over in discussions of discourse communities. We need then, to understand the language using habits of any community as part of a larger pattern of interaction with both other members and the world itself.

Within the group, such conventions are ideologically shaped by those who exercise authority, the powerbrokers and gatekeepers of the field, and serve particular interests within the discipline. Discourses therefore not only negotiate community knowledge and credibility, but help produce and sustain status relationships, exercise exclusivity and reproduce interests which lead to an unequal distribution of influence and resources within communities. Particular literacy practices, discourses, and genres are underpinned by dominant ideological positions and carry the interests and beliefs of the powerful. This raises issues of heresy, of controlling topics of discourse, of defining who might speak with credibility and of establishing who has public authority (Foucault, 1972). Hierarchical relationships within disciplines are then, at least in part, a consequence of the ability to effectively manipulate, exploit and perhaps innovate its generic and rhetorical conventions and as a result academic disciplines are highly stratified.

Turning to interactions with those outside the group, Bourdieu's (1991) notion of symbolic capital I mentioned earlier draws attention to the value attached to particular forms of discourse in social and economic life. The expert use of specialist language defines someone as belonging to an exclusive group which in turn both helps form the individual's identity and excludes others who do not have the same experience and training. This means that our discourses are integrated into wider aspects of our lives, social identities and life-styles, and these are, again, socially evaluated according to the symbolic value attached to them. Power is exercised by restricting access to different discourses and, because a discipline's discoursal resources are not ordinarily available to outsiders, this increases the social distance between members and others. This is a process which clearly works against cooperation and integration and helps contribute to the relentless diversification and specialization of academic niches.

Perhaps it is inevitable that the patterns of integration and membership which accompany the development of groups leads to a division of insiders and outsiders. But there is nothing in the idea of a discourse community which excludes the possibility of differing ideological perspectives, competition or even conflict within them. Any conception of community needs to acknowledge the potentially tremendous diversity and variation which membership can imply. Our own experiences of belonging to communities tell us that they are not monolithic and unitary but potentially disparate and divergent, composed of antagonistic groups and discourses, marginalized ideas, contested theories, peripheral contributors and occasional members. Individuals have diverse

53

experiences, backgrounds, expertise, commitments and influence. Empiricists contest the same ground with phenomenologists, cognitivists with behaviourists, existentialists with Freudians, and relativists with realists. Nobel Prize winners, influential gatekeepers and high-profile proselytizers interact with and use the same texts and genres as student neophytes, research assistants and lab rats. They may, however, use them for different purposes, with different questions and with different degrees of engagement.

In much the same way, participants are likely to subscribe to the various goals of the community to a different extent and emphasis, participate in its diverse activities in different ways, and identify themselves with its conventions, histories and values with different degrees of commitment. Communities are frequently pluralities of practices and beliefs which accommodate disagreement and allow sub-groups and individuals to innovate within the margins of its practices in ways that do not weaken its ability to engage in common actions. Norms help constitute the public worlds in which we operate, but to acknowledge their usefulness does not make us prisoners of them, it simply admits that discourse occurs in a social context and that it is easier to accomplish mutual understanding if we occasionally recognize them.

In sum, the concept of community helps account for what and how issues can be discussed and for the understandings which are the basis for cooperative action and knowledge-creation. It is not important that everyone agrees on everything, but that members are able to engage with each others ideas and analyses in agreed upon ways. Disciplines, then, are the contexts in which disagreement can be deliberated.

ii. Communities and identities

Current conceptions of identity see it as largely forged through discourse as we construct representations of ourselves in particular contexts and places. All of us may therefore have a number of identities, each of which is displayed at different times as we perform and enact a particular persona, establishing who we are in a given context. Almost everything we say or write, in fact, says something about us and the kind of relationship we want to establish with our interactants. As Bloemmaert (2005) observes, however, our identities are only successful to the extent that they are recognized by others, and this means adopting, constructing and transforming recognizable discourses. It follows from this that, because communities privilege particular ways of making meanings, they encourage the performance of certain kinds of professional or student identities. This means that they restrict which rhetorical resources participants can bring from their past experiences and influence what they might take from those made available by the context.

One discourse is likely to be dominant in any context (Wertsch, 1991) and hence more visible, so that writers consciously or unconsciously take up the identity options this privileged discourse makes available. Adopting a voice associated with a particular field of study certainly involves us in aligning ourselves with its knowledge-making practices to some extent, but this doesn't mean undergoing a complete identity transformation. There are always discoursal alternatives which allow us to represent ourselves in different ways (Ivanic, 1998). The fact is that we bring our experiences as members of multiple communities to how we understand our disciplinary participation and how we want to interact with our colleagues in performing an academic identity.

Gender, social class, religion, race and geographical region are the most obvious of these experiences; but other communities like school, family and the workplace also shape our perceptions and understandings. We might usefully look at gender as an example. Tse and Hyland (2006 and 2008), for example, found some evidence to support the view that male academics tend to adopt a more personal, assertive and argumentative stance than females in a study of academic book reviews, but acknowledge that the picture is also more complex than this. Most importantly, their findings caution against seeing a one-to-one relation between either gender or discipline and language as this is likely to exaggerate difference, create a fixed notion of linguistic roles and ignore variations in the social, cultural and situational contexts in which language is used.

Following Cameron (1992) we need to the acknowledge the cross-cutting effects of participants' relative power and status in any interaction, both written and spoken, while recognizing that writers can represent themselves in alignment, or dissonance, with particular discourses (Bakhtin, 1986). New theorizations of gender, for example, have raised alternative conceptions which suggest our identities are more multiple and fluid than we once supposed. Researchers have come to focus on 'plurality and diversity amongst female and male language users, and on gender as performativity – something that is done in context rather than a fixed attribute' (Swann, 2002: 47). These ideas, based on social and linguistic construction, give more respect for individual agency and introduce a notion of both gender and academic identity as constituted through the repeated performance of norms rather than as reflecting essentialized categories of discipline or gender.

Some feminist writers, however, see academic writing itself as a gendered discourse representing a male-dominated academic culture where language encodes male values and which works to exclude female academics and their preferred forms of expression. Robson *et al.* (2002), for example, believe that assertive and conflictual expressions of argument may be a general feature of academic discourse, employed by both men and women. This 'masculinist epistemology' (Luke and Gore, 1992: 205) therefore privileges competition, agnosticism and rationality and enables only a limited range of identity options. It forces both male and female academics to adopt a masculine style of writing, or at least to present versions of themselves in their writing which correspond to imposed gender identities.

Studies of gender-preferential language use have been inconclusive, however, and the view that the use of conventional academic interaction patterns represents a conscious and unwelcome adoption of gender-specific cultural values and practices falls into the 'essentializing' trap I mentioned above. Quite clearly, a preoccupation with bi-polar conceptions of academic writing as either masculine or feminine tends towards a reification of gender difference which encourages us to see individual acts of self-representation as either socially determined or aberrant.

In sum, writers do not construct a self-representation from an infinite range of possibilities, but neither is individual agency eliminated by the authority of teachers, editors, reviewers, examiners and other community gatekeepers. Because discourses are 'ways of being in the world' (Gee, 1999: 23), language choices are always made from culturally available resources and therefore involve interactions between the conventions of the literacy event, the ways that communities maintain their interests, and the values, beliefs and prior cultural experiences of the participants. We draw on a repertoire of voices and make judgments about how far successful communication will involve juggling these voices, subordinating some and foregrounding others. In short, academic communities are human institutions where actions and understandings are influenced by the personal and biographical, as well as the institutional and sociocultural. They are sites where differences in worldview or language usage intersect as a result of the myriad backgrounds and overlapping memberships of participants.

iii. Momentum and change

In addition to questions of power and identity, another criticism often levelled at the idea of discourse community is that it neglects the innovation and momentum that is possible in disciplines and fails to account for change. Atkinson (1999), for example, points out that Swales' (1990) definitional criteria for discourse communities, which emphasize common goals, communication practices, genres, lexis and expertise, refer only to established, mature communities. It is a model which neglects, in other words, how communities emerge and grow, the mechanisms by which members enter and leave and the ways they are inducted through socialization practices. Add to this the fact that academic discourse communities are organized around the production and legitimation of particular forms of knowledge and social practices rather than others, and we can begin to see why communities tend towards the kind of stability and conformity I discussed earlier. Conventional and ideological forces can therefore work to limit our understanding of change.

The emphasis that is often given to the consensual, static aspects of discourse communities is perhaps a consequence of taking an exclusively discoursal perspective at the expense of the wider interactions, activities and practices which sustain them. As we have seen, the discourse conventions which characterize the particular genres and argument forms of academic communities are an institutional response to recurring rhetorical situations. Common collocational patterns, generic structures and grammatical patterns offer community members a coordinated response to the negotiation of knowledge claims, facilitating smooth, shorthand ways of making sense of each others' discourse. But we must also recognize that discourses change too, both historically and incrementally, as genres and the pool of meanings required and generated by a community develop.

As I noted briefly in the last chapter, the carefully machined rhetorical artefact of the research article is a relatively recent development and writers such as Atkinson (1999) and Valle (1997) have documented the considerable changes that have taken place in research writing. Atkinson (1999), for instance notes movement from a comparatively involved and personal discourse in published letters to a highly informational and nominal 'object-centred' style of writing in research articles. More immediately and routinely, academic communities are in a state of constant change driven by the pursuit of novelty and the concern to be newsworthy. As Foucault (1981: 66) observes, 'for there to be a discipline, there must be the possibility of formulating new propositions, ad infinitum', while Kaufer and Geisler (1989: 286) refer to academic communities as 'factories of novelty, encouraging members to plod towards their yearly quota of inspirational leaps'. Finally, where a community has arrived in its evolution provides the social context for the linguistic development of individual members, both newcomers and old hands, as they interact to learn and gradually change these discourses. Writing, in other words, can be seen as a force for intellectual and personal change within relatively stable social communities.

Followers of Vygotsky have proposed an alternative way of understanding expert communities which seeks to avoid the idea of a shared core of rather abstract knowledge and language often assumed in the idea of community. Instead the concept of 'communities of practice' places emphasis on situated activity and 'a set of relations among persons, activity, and world, over time and in relation with other tangential and overlapping communities of practice' (Lave and Wenger, 1991: 98). Texts, then, are part of larger integrated webs of activity, particularly the processes by which novices are admitted and learn the ropes while old-timers are displaced and move on.

Although something of an idealistic perspective, which leaves the notion of participation in such practices rather vague, it helps add a dimension of change often missing in discussions of community. The emphasis on the motivations for socialization and the apprenticeship practices by which members are inducted into given sociocultural groups helps to revitalize the notion of community and refocuses it as a collection of historically evolved and diverse activities. It also reminds us that individuals are members of multiple communities, not all of which will have consistent values, goals and patterns of activity. These differences may not mean much to every individual member, but they might lead to dissonance and fragmentation, precipitating change and adjustments in community practices.

3.3 In search of academic communities

Given the difficulties of conceptualizing and identifying communities, it is worth considering some collectivities of academic participation which help structure and are themselves structured by different discourses. In this section I look briefly at *disciplines, specialisms* and *domains* as representing sites where we make sense of our experience that have evolved over time and which might fulfil the role of academic communities. The differences in addressing and reporting knowledge they adopt and their distinct methods of persuasion offer some understanding of academic discourse communities.

i. Academic disciplines

Academic disciplines would seem to be good candidates as discourse communities. *Discipline* is a common enough label, used to describe and differentiate knowledge, institutional structures, researchers, and resources in the working world of scholarship. Students and academics appear to have little trouble in understanding what a discipline is, placing themselves in one and confidently identifying borderline cases.

Received wisdom also assumes a relatively unproblematic notion of academic disciplines. They are typically seen in terms of their objects of enquiry, so that intellectual criteria are generally employed and disciplines associated with areas of knowledge. Maths, chemistry, Italian and law seem, on the face of it, to be fairly clear examples of disciplines whereas urban studies, peace studies and parapsychology do not.

In fact, it is possible to view disciplines in a range of different ways. They have been seen as institutional conveniences, networks of communication, domains of values, and modes of enquiry. Kuhn (1977) identifies them according to whether they have clearly established paradigms or are at a looser, pre-paradigm stage; Donald (1990) draws on faculty perceptions and Kolb (1981) on learning style differences to provide categories which distinguished hard from soft and applied from pure knowledge fields; Storer and Parsons (1968) oppose analytical to synthetic fields; and Berliner (2003) distinguishes 'hard' and 'easy-to-do' disciplines in terms of the ability to understand, predict and control the phenomena they study.

However, the term discipline needs to be treated with caution as a gloss on the complexity of how research and teaching is socially organized and conducted. While it is convenient to represent disciplines as distinguishable and relatively stable, the boundaries of scholarship are progressively shifting and dissolving. There is considerable room for uncertainty, particularly as they are subject to historical and geographic variation.

Research problems and investigations often fail to respect disciplinary boundaries and the resulting interaction between domains encourages constant change. New disciplines spring up at the intersections of existing ones and achieve international recognition (biochemistry, gerontology), while others decline and disappear (philology, astrology). Similarly, there are cultural and geographic variations among disciplines considered more globally, as the structure of a country's education system, level of economic development, or ideological traits account for further differences (Podgorecki, 1997). Under the challenge of post-modernism, which sees intellectual fragmentation and disciplinary collapse at every turn, and institutional changes such as the emergence of practice-based and modular degrees, the idea of discipline is increasingly questioned (e.g. Gergen and Thatchenkery, 1996). It is, however, important to recognize that centripetal as well as centrifugal forces are at work, with increased global information flows and resource networks counteracting the influence of nation-states and local cultural practices.

Although disciplines are often associated with broad domains of knowledge, the extent to which these are blessed with the label of *discipline*, rather than, say, *method* or *approach* largely depends on institutional recognition. International currency is a key criterion, particularly the extent to which leading universities recognize the independence of an area and give it the status of a department with professorial chairs, budgets, and degrees; whether a distinct international community has appeared around it with the professional paraphernalia of conferences, learned societies, and specialist journals; and whether the wider international community generally perceives it to have academic credibility and intellectual substance.

Clearly then, disciplines are not monolithic knowledge-generating institutions but contextually contingent, dependent on local struggles over resources, recognition and labelling, and these institutional struggles ensure that boundaries are never stable or objects of study immutable. In fact, new fields emerge with surprising speed between and across disciplines in the modern university. Established disciplines such as biology, for example, seem to multiply rapidly, with bioinformatics, biomechanics and biotechnology gaining disciplinary status in the last few years. In fact, it can be hard to see what is actually delimited by a 'discipline' when comparing university structures. Instead of uniformity we find fluid and permeable entities impossible to pin down with precision. In other words, a discipline is as much determined by social power as epistemological categories and it might be prudent to distinguish between *forms of knowledge* and *knowledge communities*.

Discourse, however, can be a useful way of describing the literacies and practices of individual disciplines, providing insights into the ways academics understand their communities. Bazerman (1988), for example, reveals the different approaches to knowledge making in Watson and Crick's seminal DNA paper compared with essays from the sociology of science and literary studies. He shows how disciplines mediate reality through the distinct ways that writers draw on disciplinary literature, code knowledge in accepted modes of argument, and represent themselves in their texts. More specifically, the ways writers mark topic-relevance in their abstracts or introductions helps to strongly signal community co-participation. Constant progress is a central part of scientific cultures, for example, and so scientists tend to stress the novelty of their work while engineers emphasize its utility, mainly to the industrial world which relies on it (Hyland, 2004b).

ii. Specialist sub-fields

The fact that no single method of inquiry, definitive set of concepts, or agreed overarching theory uniquely characterizes each discipline has

led researchers to look to sub-fields as a way of understanding variations in academic discourse. Structures of work are fundamental to
academic practice and such specialisms are typically organized around
particular subject areas, theoretical positions or methodological
approaches which exist within and across broader disciplines. Some
domains of interest may not be sufficiently well established to have
developed a distinctive culture, but while they are less formally recognizable than disciplines and subject to greater flux, sub-fields represent
a more immediate and cohesive professional experiences for many academics. In fact, some observers see disciplines internally organized as
a honeycomb of overlapping specialist interest groups which spread
across adjoining disciplines (Crane, 1972).

Such groups are particularly important in the natural sciences where
the sheer volume of knowledge and its rapid expansion oblige individuals to establish their own niche of expertise. One reason for this is that
research in the natural sciences is typically characterized by linearity
and well-defined and agreed upon problems (Toulmin, 1972). New
knowledge is generated from what is known and each new finding
inexorably contributes to the eventual solution of the issue under study.
Specialism is encouraged by this as research often occupies considerable investments in money, training, equipment and expertise, and is
frequently concentrated at a few sites. Individuals are therefore often
committed to involvement in particular research areas for many years
and achieve status within their profession by an ability to make precise
contributions to a highly delimited field.

Such hard knowledge specialisms are also more likely to exhibit
what Becher and Trowler (2001) refer to as 'urban' features where a relatively small number of problems is pursued by a substantial number
of scientists, whether in response to fashion, funding, or paradigmatic
breakthrough. In contrast to more 'rural' specialisms where research is
spread out over a broad range of topics with long range solutions, urban
specialisms tend to cluster around a few salient topics and encourage
relatively quick, short range solutions to a series of questions. They
argue that in urban specialisms there is

> alongside a densely concentrated population, a generally busy –
> occasionally frenetic – pace of life, a high level of collective activity,
> close competition for space and resources, and a rapid and heavily
> used information network.
>
> (Becher and Trowler, 2001: 106)

These practices tend to be reflected in communication patterns with
fierce rivalry between labs and research teams to establish priority by

publishing first, greater secrecy and fear of plagiarism, and rapid dissemination of results with less reflection than in 'rural' environments.

These differences may even result in a preference for different discourse forms. Rural research specialisms, such as branches of history and education, for example, tend to employ books as their main vehicles for scholarship, while these are virtually unknown in the sciences. In fact, for the fastest moving urban specialisms in physics, chemistry and microbiology, concern with innovation and speed of dissemination has led to the publication of separate letters journals. These facilitate the rapid circulation of new and urgent findings by restricting length and streamlining the review process to accomplish publication within weeks.

Sub-fields can therefore be identified by the kinds of problems, or knowledge-making tasks, they are oriented to, and these may influence the ways members do research and disseminate results. Macdonald (1994), for instance, explored the discourse practices of three sub-fields in the humanities and social sciences: attachment research in psychology, colonial New England social history, and renaissance new historicism in literary studies. Analysing what writers draw attention to as grammatical subjects, MacDonald suggests that articles in the psychology sub-field tend to foreground research methods and warrants and give greater prominence to building an argument on previous literature. New historicists, in contrast, are constrained by a lack of generalizable patterns and so define more particular problems and give relatively little attention to explicating methods.

While such sentence-level differences help identify different practices and perceptions of writers working in sub-fields, other studies have explored the textual practices of local communities. One is Swales' (1998) site-study of three relatively self-contained units within a single building at the University of Michigan is mentioned in Chapter 2. His study reveals the lived experiences of individuals participating in communities which are local and immediately real to them. The study captures the different practices, genres and cultures of those working in the computer centre, the Herbarium and the university English Language Centre in a vivid way, showing how sub-disciplines are experienced in specific local contexts.

iii. Knowledge domains

An alternative conception of communities employs a wider frame than disciplines and looks for discourse affinities within *disciplinary domains*. For centuries the traditional dividing line in the history of science and scholarship has been between natural sciences and technology

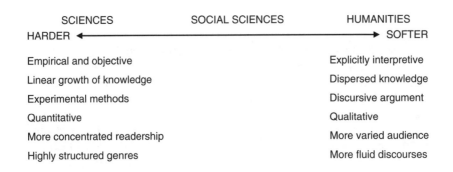

Figure 3.1   *Continuum of academic knowledge*

on one side and humanities and social sciences on the other. Here we find a more glacial pace of change than in disciplines and their various subdivisions, and it is here that we tend to see the clearest discoursal variation and rhetorical distinctiveness. Figure 3.1 offers a general schematic of these broad distinctions.

Essentially, the sciences see knowledge as a cumulative development from prior knowledge accepted on the basis of experimental proof. Science writing reinforces this empirical basis by highlighting a gap in knowledge, presenting a hypothesis related to this gap, and then experiments and findings to support this hypothesis. Disciplines in the humanities rely more on case studies, and introspection and claims are accepted or rejected on the strength of argument. Between these the social sciences have partly adopted methods of the sciences but in applying these to less predictable human data give greater importance to explicit interpretation.

The concept of hard and soft domains of knowledge is obviously not without problems. This is partly because it is an everyday distinction which carries connotations of clear-cut divisions and so runs the risk of reductionism, or even reification, by packing a multitude of complex abstractions into a few simple opposites. Moreover, for some the terms may seem ideologically loaded, privileging a particular mode of knowing based on the structural perspectives, symbolic representations and model-building methods of the natural sciences. There are also irregularities along the scale, as psychology, for instance, is hard in its experimental form and soft in psychoanalytical areas. However, the hard–soft scheme is more directly related to established disciplinary groupings than some more abstract categorizations (Becher and Trowler, 2001). Moreover, evidence from a questionnaire survey of academics

(Biglan, 1973) and from psychometric tests of students' learning strategy preferences (Kolb, 1981) suggest that it may actually represent actors' own perceptions of the areas in which they are engaged. By seeing the hard–soft distinction as a continuum, rather than as unidimensional scales, it can offer a useful way of examining contrasts while avoiding rigidly demarcated categories.

There are, in fact, considerable differences in the ways academics engage with their subject matter in these broad domains. In Kuhn's (1970) 'normal science' model, natural scientists produce public knowledge through relatively steady cumulative growth so that problems tend to emerge on the back of earlier problems as results throw up further questions to be followed up with further research. There are fairly clear-cut criteria of what constitutes a new contribution and how it builds on what has come before so there is greater scope for patterning and reproducibility than in the soft fields (Bazerman, 1993). This feature is widely recognized by practitioners themselves, as some of my own academic informants noted:

> *My personal view of science is that of a huge volcano and lava is flowing down and I'm at the end of one stream of lava.*
> (Physicist interview)

> *There are many groups making infinitely small steps forward on a particular problem, eventually someone may make a bigger step and get a Nobel Prize, but if not, the groups will get there anyway.*
> (Electronic Engineer interview)

This representation may, of course, merely reflect conventional epistemological ideologies which portray science as an objective, cooperative endeavour, but it nevertheless has practical and rhetorical effects. The empiricist viewpoint that truth is discovered by observing the world is reflected, for example, in the fact that over three-fourths of all features marking author visibility and explicit interaction with readers in research articles occur in the humanities and social sciences (Hyland, 2005a – see Chapter 4). Science, for example, avoids writer self-mention and explicit evaluation to represent real events without the mediation of actors or arguments: the authority of the individual must be subordinated to the authority of scientific procedure and appropriate practical reasoning.

There seem to be good reasons for taking domain as the point of departure for understanding discourse variation in the academy. In particular, this is because domains represent broad categorizations of knowledge which remain relatively untroubled by the vertical struggles over recognition and the horizontal struggles over resources which we find among disciplines and specialisms. Domains are relatively stable over time and exhibit considerable rhetorical consistency, remaining aloof from the arbitrary consequences of particular social tussles and institutional fiat to offer the most robust way of discussing communities. Academic communities can therefore be seen as being multilayered and overlapping, with domain, discipline and specialism constituting the principal manifestations. Academics simultaneously participate in more specialized, overlapping communities of disciplines and subfields as they go about their daily professional lives, but are likely to be oriented to the more general social and rhetorical practices of broader spheres.

3.4 Final thoughts

The kinds of critiques and discussion around the notion of community explored in this chapter have not only questioned the construct but sharpened some of its meaning. So we have moved beyond identifying sets of norms and orientations to see academic communities in terms of an individual's engagement in certain discourses and practices. We have learnt that academic cultures, disciplinary ideologies and academic discourses are inseparably entwined and so one can only be understood by reference to the others. This, in turn, means looking to the idea of community as a framework for conceptualizing the expectations, conventions and practises which influence academic communication.

Groupings like social class, gender and race are often brought forward to explain our social identities and cultural behaviours. But institutional, professional and workplace experiences, including those in the academy, all help to shape our values and ideas and how we express these and realize our social roles. Thus our membership of different groups offers us a multiplicity of identities that can be configured and balanced against each other in different ways, but we tend to draw on similar conventions and expectations to realize our participation in any one of them. Put simply, social forces structure the identity options available to individuals and disciplinary practices reduce them.

In the academy the authority exercised by peers, editors, reviewers and other community figures influence who gets heard, who gets accepted and whose arguments are seen as persuasive. Such contexts privilege certain ways of making meanings and so encourage the performance of certain kinds of professional identities. They place restrictions on the rhetorical resources participants can bring from their past experiences and influence what they are able to appropriate from those made available by the context. These constraints therefore contribute to the meanings that can be created and to judgements of persuasiveness by readers. While our social identities emerge from the values, beliefs and commitments we hold as members of different groups, the version of self that will be rewarded may be constrained in this way.

Uncertainties remain, of course, concerning how we pin down such communities. In the academy a discourse community is constituted largely by its sense of what still needs to be known and the questions that need to be asked around an area of inquiry. We might therefore see our memberships in specialisms, disciplines and domains, as simultaneous and overlapping, with one dominant at different times. At the level of domain we have relatively stable practices and ideologies, while at the level of specialism, held together by specific problems, issues and argument forms, may shift frequently. For now, however, perhaps the term *discipline* might be seen as a shorthand form for the various identities, roles, positions, relationships, reputations, reward systems and other dimensions of social practices constructed and expressed through language in the academy.

So, with the idea of *discourse community* we arrive at a more rounded and socially informed theory of texts and contexts. It provides a principled way of understanding how meaning is produced *in interaction* and proves useful in identifying how writers' rhetorical choices depend on purposes, setting and audience. We always have to remember, however, that an individual's participation in academic discourse communities does not occur in a vacuum, and that the language we draw on to communicate with our academic peers or assessors is likely to be influenced by a range of social and experiential factors. So while it remains a contested concept, the notion of community does foreground what is an important influence on social interaction. It draws attention to the fact that discourse is socially situated and helps illuminate something of what writers and readers bring to a text, emphasizing that both production and interpretation depends on assumptions about the other.

4 Research discourses

An important thread of the three previous chapters is that academic discourse is the basis of all university activity: the means by which institutions legitimate knowledge, reward success, regulate admission, control membership and induct novices. Only by writing and speaking can academics and students get feedback on their work, earn respect for their ideas and progress in their careers. The main business of the academy, however, is to produce knowledge, and the genres which contribute to this carry the greatest prestige and have received the greatest attention from scholars.

Research discourses have evolved for functional reasons and have accrued considerable status as a result (Halliday and Martin, 1993). They are, in addition, associated with power in Western cultures because of the control they provide over our physical and social environments. The success of academic, and particularly scientific, representations of reality dominates the ways we understand the world and underpins the technical and bureaucratic practices at the heart of modern capitalism. More immediately, they influence the lives of countless academics as universities around the world now require staff to present at international conferences and, more crucially, publish in major, high-impact, peer-reviewed Anglophone journals as a prerequisite for tenure, promotion and career advancement. This chapter explores key aspects of these discourses, focusing mainly on articles and conference presentations but concluding by briefly looking at a number of other genres.

4.1 The research article

Despite competition from electronic publishing alternatives such as e-journals and personal websites, the research article (RA) remains the pre-eminent genre of the academy. Beginning life in the form of the letters published in *The Philosophical Transactions of the Royal Society* in the mid-seventeenth century, the RA is now not only the principal site of disciplinary knowledge-making but, as Montgomery (1996) has it, 'the master narrative of our time'. One reason for this pre-eminence is the value attached by the scholarly establishment to the processes of peer review as a control mechanism for transforming beliefs into knowledge. Another is the prestige attached to a genre which restructures the processes of thought and research it describes to establish a discourse for scientific fact-creation. Language becomes a form of technology which attempts to present interpretations and position participants in particular ways as a means of establishing knowledge. Consequently, the RA is a genre which has generated such a volume of research that it defies easy summary. In this section, however, I will sketch an outline of what we know about this extraordinary genre.

i. Review and revision

One prominent feature of the RA is that it is the outcome of a prolonged, and often tortuous, writing and peer-review process. A manuscript develops slowly through several drafts with inputs from colleagues, language specialists, proofreaders, reviewers and editors, what Lillis and Curry (2006) call 'literacy brokers'. This often frustrates writers, but contributes to the final polished product shaped to the cognitive and rhetorical frameworks of a disciplinary community. The brokering of published research therefore mediates academic cultures as well as texts. The process not only manages the quality of published research, but also functions as an apparatus of community control by regulating appropriate topics, methodologies and the boundaries within which negotiation can occur. For newcomers to a discipline it is both a crucial situated learning experience and a rite de passage that marks the route to full membership.

Myers (1990) and Berkenkotter and Huckin (1995), following scientists through the review process, illustrate the importance of reviewers' comments in guiding writers to rhetorically accommodate their laboratory activity to the concerns of the discipline. Through reviewers' recommendations to modify the strength of their claims, provide propositional warrants, and establish a narrative context through citation, they found that writers gradually integrated their new claims into the weave of disciplinary relevance and prior work. This process indicates that new facts are not added piecemeal to the heap of existing knowledge, but are the extension of an ongoing conversation among members, conducted in a shared 'theory-laden' language and particular patterns of argumentation. Both Myers and Berkenkotter and Huckin therefore see academic writing as a tension between originality and deference to the community. So while Berkenkotter and Huckin's case study subject sought to gain acceptance for original, and therefore significant, work, for instance, the reviewers insisted 'that to be science her report had to include an intertextual framework for her local knowledge' (p. 59).

The challenges of writing for publication are daunting to all academics, particularly in today's competitive climate where journals in some fields have rejection rates of over 90 per cent. One of the most central causes of difficulty for novice writers, particularly those working outside the metropolitan centres of research, is their isolation from current literature and the demand that they situate their work in a rhetorical tradition. Non-Native English scholars themselves, however, often cite their lack of language abilities as a problem. About half of Flowerdew's (1999) 585 Hong Kong academics, for example, reported that they felt at a disadvantage compared with Native Scholars (NSs) in this area. This is clearly illustrated in the fact that many of while St John's (1987) sample of Spanish researchers often resorted to translation from Spanish when revising papers for publication.

Research into the writing processes adopted by novice Non-Native English Speaking academics also suggests what a laborious task writing for publication can be. Li (2006), for example, tracked a Chinese Doctoral student through six drafts and several painstaking resubmissions guided by supervisors, a journal editor and reviewers before her paper was finally accepted. Gosden (1996) also found considerable text revisions by seven Japanese postgraduate students. In response to reviewers' comments they made over 320 changes between the first draft and published paper, changes which Gosden sees as a movement towards more mature writing characterized by a greater range of cohesive devices, explicitness, hedging and subordination. Not is the process made easier by what Flowerdew and Dudley-Evans (2002) found in their study of editorial correspondence, which is often opaque to authors due to poor structuring and indirectness.

Essentially, revisions represent a reworking of the rhetorical goals of a paper to more clearly meet the perceived needs of readers, and this is tricky for all novice writers irrespective of their first language. Swales, in fact, takes the view that the most important distinction in publishing is not between Native and Non-Native English speakers, but

> between experienced or 'senior' researcher/scholars and less experienced or 'junior' ones – between those who know the academic ropes in their chosen specialisms and those who are learning them.
> (2004: 56)

Participation in the publication process, in fact, contributes to learning these academic ropes. Following situated learning and social constructionist theories, the redrafting process can be seen not just as the transformation of a text, but also the apprenticing of an individual writer into the knowledge constructing practices of a discipline.

The metaphor of 'apprenticeship' has been used to describe this process, although Lave and Wenger (1991) talk of 'legitimate peripheral participation' to conceptualize learning as engagement in the sociocultural activities of communities of practice. In other words novices learn by doing; gradually developing an academic identity as they come to write and think in the ways of their discipline under the guidance of more experienced peers, and the comments of editors and reviewers (Casanave and Vandrick, 2003). When considering writing for publication, this apprenticeship involves a careful negotiation with two principal audiences: the journal gatekeepers who will judge the paper as ready for publication and the community of scholars who will read the finished paper and hopefully cite it and use it in their own research.

ii. Novelty and relevance

As we have seen, a key part of the textual reshaping of an RA through peer review involves situating local research in the broader concerns of the discipline, managing innovation for a target community by establishing explicit intertextual links to existing knowledge. To be new, work must recognize the knowledge which has already gained consent and against which it makes a claim for change. Novelty thus acknowledges what has gone before and builds on the field's organizational structures, beliefs and current hot topics. Topics, in fact are more than a research focus: they represent resources of joint attention which coordinate activities and mark co-participation in communities. Selecting a topic and arguing for its novelty and relevance is thus critical in securing colleagues' interest and in displaying membership credentials. There is a certain marketization involved in this, a promotion of oneself and one's research which is analogous to the promotion of goods, thereby borrowing from the discursive practices of a wider promotional culture (e.g. Fairclough, 1995).

The marketing of an RA begins with the **abstract** where writers have to gain readers' attention and persuade them to read on by demonstrating that they have both something new and worthwhile to say. While often considered as merely a 'representation' (Bazerman, 1984: 58) or 'summary' (Kaplan *et al.*, 1994: 405) of the full paper, a study of 800 abstracts from journals in eight disciplines (Hyland, 2004b) shows things to be more complex. The abstract, in fact, selectively sets out the writer's stall to highlight importance and draw the reader into the paper. As we might expect, there are disciplinary differences in this process. The hard knowledge abstracts tend to stress novelty and benefit, while writers in the social sciences largely draw on the notion of importance to promote their work. Novelty is obviously a raison *d'être* of science fields where constant innovation and progress are expected and practitioners look for new results to develop their own research. Examples like these are common:

1. The assays presented herein illustrate two novel approaches to monitor the intracellular dynamics of nuclear proteins.
    (Biology).

    A new design for a minimum inductance, distributed current, longitudinal (z) gradient coil, fabricated on the surface of an elliptic cylinder is proposed.
    (Physics)

Engineers, on the other hand, underlined their practical, applied orientation by combining novelty with the utility of their research to the industrial world:

2. The new model gives significantly improved predictions for both liquid holdup and pressure drop during gas-liquid, stratified-wavy flow in horizontal pipelines.
    (Mechanical Engineering)

    This paper answers these questions by developing an integer nonlinear programming model and solving it using a very efficient dynamic programming approach.
    (Electrical Engineering)

A great deal of rhetorical effort also goes on in the **introduction** of an article where writers seek to create a research space to justify the importance of their work. This ecological metaphor owes its popularity to Swales who famously suggested a model of article introductions consisting of three sequential rhetorical moves in which writers

> need to re-establish in the eyes of the discourse community the significance of the research field itself; the need to 'situate' the actual research in terms of that significance; and the need to show how this niche in the wider ecosystem will be occupied and defended.
> (1990: 142)

Like plants competing for light and nutrients, the RA competes for a research niche and an audience. This is largely achieved in the introduction through a text which attracts readers by foregrounding what is already known, then establishing an opening for the current work by showing that this prior knowledge is somehow incomplete, as here:

3. Research into public drinking in natural settings has been conducted for many decades since the early observational

study of a public house in an English industrial town (Mass Observation: 1943). However, few studies have focused specifically on violence.

(Sociology RA)

Stiffened planes are commonly used in many engineering structures (e.g. bridge decks, ship superstructures, aerospace structures, etc). Despite their wide application, little is known about their behaviour.

(Mechanical Engineering RA)

The second sentence in each of these examples therefore sets up the basis from which the novelty of the writer's work can be understood.

Claims for novelty are thus assembled by reference to what social communities know and what they believe is worth knowing. This is more carefully elaborated in the **literature review**, which seeks to justify the value of the current research and show why it is distinct from what has gone before (Kwan, 2006). Here writers construct a story for their study, persuading the reader that some organizing principle links their work into a coherent chain of disciplinary activity. Similarly, the **results** of the study, often thought to be a bland list of findings, actually contribute to the persuasive unity of the paper. Rather than stepping back to allow results to neutrally speak for themselves, writers urge the value of their research onto the reader through a series of rhetorical moves designed to justify the methodology and evaluate results (e.g. Ruiying and Allison, 2003).

In many science papers a **methods** section is often inserted between the introduction and results and this can be more or less succinct or elaborate, depending on readers' assumed familiarity with the procedures and the extent to which they are likely to accept them. While data collection is rarely straightforward, reports typically omit reference to unreliable equipment, sub-standard materials, uncooperative participants, and false turns to present a smooth and unproblematic process which is simply labelled rather than explained. Methods are often taken on trust in a way that can defy obvious replication, as in this example:

Each FID was baseline corrected and apodized with a 750-Hz exponential before being Fourier transformed. In order to perform the curve fitting, the spectra were fitted with a Caussian lineshape, and the peak intensity was recorded. The spectral processing and analysis were performed with the routines of NMRI. The curve fitting was performed using the Levenberg-Marquardt method.

(Physics RA)

Indeed, the methodology section is increasingly downplayed in science RAs, frequently printed at the end of the article in a smaller font to save space.

The current work is most vigorously 'sold' in the **Discussion** section. Here previous research is treated as background and introduced to compare, support or invigorate the new claim with opposition, as the writer fends off counterclaims to celebrate the new (Lewin, *et al.*, 2001). Berkenkotter and Huckin (1995) also argue that there is an active promotion of news value in the discussion, a finding confirmed by Swales and Luebs (2002) in psychology articles and apparently common in other disciplines, as we can see in these examples:

4. These results are important with respect to the physiological roles of the different proteins studied here.

(Biology RA)

Ours is the first research that offers evidence that word-of-mouth about forgone alternatives can affect satisfaction with the chosen alternative.

(Marketing RA)

We offer a new way of theorising ageism itself, as a contingent and negotiated interactional practice.

(Lingusitics RA)

Less obviously, perhaps, something of this promotionalism is captured in the increased use of argumentation, personal involvement and evaluative commentary that we tend to find in discussions. One example of this is authors' preferred theme choices, or what serves as the starting point of the message. Compared to other parts of the article, themes in discussion sections have been found to express the author's efforts to persuade readers by having a high proportion of interpersonal themes realized by mood and comment adjuncts (Gosden, 1993):

5. <u>Interestingly</u>, a decrease of the a, values was observed again at higher light intensifies (about 1200 pmol $m^{-2} S^{-1}$).

(Electrical Engineering RA)

<u>It is possible that</u> a large number of the barristers who said that they did not think computers were relevant to their work, actually did not know how to use them either.

(Sociology RA)

<u>It is thus clear that</u> the formation of central bursting in the extrusion process is controlled by the growth of voids.

(Mechanical Engineering RA)

These structures allow writers to highlight warrants and evaluations in support of their arguments as they move from a relatively low-interpersonal intervention in earlier stages of the text to a more prominent writer engagement in discussions.

iii.   Stance and engagement

Academic persuasion is only partly accomplished by establishing claims for novelty and relevance: Writers must also seek to offer a credible representation of themselves and their work by claiming solidarity with readers, evaluating their material and acknowledging alternative views in appropriate ways. These interactions are accomplished in academic writing through the systems of stance and engagement (Hyland, 2005a) and I will elaborate these in this section.

I will use the term *stance* to refer to the writer's textual 'voice' or community recognized personality. This is an attitudinal, writer-oriented function which concerns the ways writers present themselves and convey their judgements, opinions and commitments. *Engagement*, on the other hand, is more of an alignment function. It concerns the ways that writers rhetorically recognize the presence of their readers to actively pull them along with the argument, include them as discourse participants, and guide them to interpretations (Hyland, 2005a). In other words, statements must incorporate an appropriate awareness of self and audience by presenting a credible writer persona and anticipating readers' possible objections and alternative positions. The rhetorical resources which realize these interactional functions are summarized in Figure 4.1.

Together these resources have a dialogic purpose in that they refer to, anticipate or otherwise take up the actual or anticipated voices and positions of potential readers (Bakhtin, 1986). I will briefly elaborate on each of these resources below, although it should be remembered that

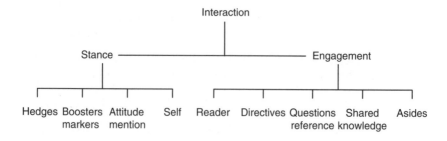

Figure 4.1   *Key resources of academic interaction*

these features have different salience across fields, with some 75 per cent of explicit stance and engagement features occurring in the humanities and social sciences.

a.   Stance features

Hedges are devices which withhold complete commitment to a proposition, allowing information to be presented as an opinion rather than fact (Hyland, 1998). They imply that a claim is based on plausible reasoning rather than certain knowledge and so both indicate the degree of confidence it might be wise to attribute to a claim while allowing writers to open a discursive space for readers to dispute interpretations. This is an example from biology:

> 6.   We propose several <u>possible</u> reasons for this: (1) pressures increase upon freezing and thus <u>may</u> force bubbles back into solution at the time of thaw; (2) since xylem water is degassed by freezing there is <u>a strong tendency</u> for bubbles to redissolve at the time of thaw; and (3) xylem water <u>may</u> flow in advance of ice formation and <u>could</u> refill some of the previously embolized vessels.
>
> (Biology RA)

Boosters, on the other hand, allow writers to express their certainty in what they say and to mark involvement with the topic and solidarity with their audience (Hyland, 2005a). While they restrict opportunities for alternative voices, boosters also often stress shared information and group membership as we tend to get behind those ideas which have a good chance of being accepted. Like hedges, they often occur in clusters, underlining the writer's conviction in an argument:

> 7.   <u>Of course</u>, I do not contend that there are no historical contingencies. On the contrary, the role of contingencies <u>should be</u> stressed. If there were no contingencies, there would be no innovations, whether scientific or moral. On this point, we must <u>definitely</u> stop following Hegel's intuitions. <u>Nobody</u> can foretell that tomorrow totalitarian regimes will not reappear and eventually spread over the planet.
>
> (Sociology RA)

Both boosters and hedges represent a writer's response to the potential viewpoints of readers and an acknowledgement of disciplinary norms of appropriate argument. Both strategies emphasize that statements don't just communicate ideas, but also the writer's attitude to them and to readers.

75

Attitude markers indicate the writer's affective, rather than epistemic, attitude to propositions, conveying surprise, agreement, importance, frustration, and so on, rather than commitment. Attitude can be expressed in a wide range of ways, as Martin (2000) and Martin and White (2005) have attempted to show by mapping the options available to speakers in conveying *affect* in their model of *appraisal*. Attitude is most explicitly signalled by attitude verbs, sentence adverbs and adjectives, and this marking of attitude in academic writing allows writers both take a stand and align themselves with disciplinary-oriented value positions.

8. No doubt there are a number of criticisms that adherents to the justice-based paradigm might make of the moral model Dworkin proposes. Still, <u>I believe that</u> Dworkin's investment model has <u>remarkable</u> resonance and <u>extraordinary</u> potential power. <u>The worry I have</u> about Dworkin's proposal arises from inside his model. It is <u>interesting</u> right off the bat to notice that . . .

(Philosophy RA)

Self-mention refers to the use of first person pronouns and possessive adjectives to present information (Hyland, 2001). Presenting a discoursal self is central to the writing process (Ivanic, 1998), and we cannot avoid projecting an impression of ourselves and how we stand in relation to our arguments, discipline and readers. The presence or absence of explicit author reference is therefore a conscious choice by writers to adopt a particular stance and disciplinary-situated authorial identity. The soft fields are particularly 'author-saturated' in this way:

9. <u>Our</u> investigation of writing at the local government office comprised an analysis of the norms and attitudes of each individual. <u>We</u> asked the different employees about their norms concerning a good text and a good writer. <u>We</u> also asked them about their attitudes toward writing at work. What <u>we</u> found interesting about this context, however, is the degree of uniformity of their norms and attitudes.

(Sociology RA)

b. Engagement features

Reader pronouns offer the most explicit ways of bringing readers into a discourse but *you* and *your* are rare in research articles, perhaps because they imply a separation between participants, rather than seek connections, and this helps to account for the high use of the inclusive *we*. There are several motivations for using this form, but most centrally it identifies the reader as someone who shares similar understandings to the writer as a member of the same discipline. At the same time as expressing peer solidarity, however, *we* also anticipates reader objections, presuming mutual understandings while weaving the potential point of view of the reader into the argument.

Directives are mainly expressed through *imperatives* and *obligation modals* and they direct readers to engage in three main kinds of activity:

- **textual acts** direct readers to another part of the text or to another text (e.g. *see Smith 1999, refer to table 2*, etc.)
- **physical acts** direct readers how to carry out some action in the real-world (e.g. *open the valve, heat the mixture*).
- **cognitive acts** instruct readers how to interpret an argument, explicitly positioning readers by encouraging them to *note, concede* or *consider* some argument or claim in the text.

Personal asides allow writers to address readers directly by briefly interrupting the argument to offer a comment on what has been said. By turning to the reader in mid-flow, the writer acknowledges and responds to an active audience, often to initiate a brief dialogue that is largely interpersonal, adding more to the writer-reader relationship than to propositional development:

10. And – as I believe many TESOL professionals will readily acknowledge – critical thinking has now begun to make its mark, particularly in the area of L2 composition.

(Applied Linguistics)

He above all provoked the mistrust of academics, both because of his trenchant opinions (often, it is true, insufficiently thought out) and his political opinions.

(Sociology)

Appeals to shared knowledge are marked by explicit signals asking readers to recognize something as familiar or accepted, irrespective of whether this is the actual case or not. These constructions of solidarity ask readers to identify with particular views and in so doing construct readers by assigning to them a role in creating the argument, acknowledging their contribution while moving the focus of the discourse away from the writer to shape the role of the reader:

11. It is, <u>of course</u>, possible to realize capacitors using the inter-metal, linearmetal-poly, metal-diffusion, or poly diffusion (with an SiO_2 dielectric) capacitances.

(Electrical Engineering)

This tendency <u>obviously</u> reflects the preponderance of brand-image advertising in fashion merchandizing.

(Marketing)

Finally, ***questions***. These are the strategy of dialogic involvement par excellence, inviting engagement, encouraging curiosity and bringing interlocutors into an arena where they can be led to the writer's viewpoint (Hyland, 2002a). Over 80 per cent of questions in my corpus of 240 research articles, however, were rhetorical, presenting an opinion as an interrogative so the reader appears to be the judge, but actually expecting no response. This is most apparent when writers answer their question immediately:

> 12. Is it, in fact, necessary to choose between nurture and nature? My contention is that it is not.
>
> (Sociology)
>
> What do these two have in common, one might ask? The answer is that they share the same politics.
>
> (Applied Linguistics)

The expression of stance and engagement is an important feature of academic writing, with frequencies actually greater than those for passives and past tense verbs (Hyland, 2005a). Overall, stance markers are about five times more common than engagement features and hedges dominate the frequencies, underlining the importance of distinguishing fact from opinion and the need for writers to present their claims with appropriate caution. Perhaps more importantly, these features represent choices based on a process of audience evaluation assisting writers to construct an effective argument and revealing how language is related to specific institutional contexts.

Despite the brevity of this sketch, we begin to get an idea of the rhetorical complexity of the RA genre as a textual weave of interpersonal and ideational resources which brings together novelty, affiliation, interpersonality and intertextuality in support of the writer's claims. Constantly evolving, and as we shall see at the end of this chapter, perhaps giving way as the principle genre of knowledge construction in some fields, the RA remains a defining feature of different disciplines and the jewel in the crown of academic communication.

4.2 The conference presentation

Despite receiving little of the attention lavished on the research article, a key means by which academic research is disseminated is through papers at academic conferences. One reason for this neglect is doubtless the problems of collecting and transcribing spoken data and of coding for intonation, gesture, visuals and other non-verbal contextual information. Another difficulty, however, is that it is a genre of uncertain boundaries, covering contexts which range from an invited one hour plenary to a short parallel paper. It may present research at various levels of completion, from work in progress to post-publication overview, and be delivered to an audience of various sizes, homogeneity and expertise. At this stage of our understanding, however, there are good reasons for regarding the conference presentation (CP) as a distinct genre. In most cases, for example, it is likely to be written to be spoken, at least in note form, and so contain features of both modes; it also tends to be closely related to the emergence of a published written text; and to contain claims which have an as yet uncertain future. For these reasons the CP will be discussed as a single discourse in this section, acknowledging differences where the literature allows it.

i. The presentation context

One thing that is certain about the CP is that, from the participants' perspective, it is inextricably embedded in the wider conference experience. Attending sessions and giving a paper are inseparable from meeting old friends, making new contacts, the buzz at coffee breaks, the book fair, the posters, the gossip, the academic celebrities, and the general intellectual charge of the event (Shalom, 2002). This mixing of social and research-process genres is a somewhat ephemeral, almost self-contained universe of discourse with its interpersonal encounters, brief excitements and occasional disappointments. The conference is thus a key event which offers members a momentary sense of belonging and community – often in stark contrast to their workaday university lives. Ventola (2002) uses the term 'semiotic spanning' to capture something of the intermeshing of the CP in this sequence of events, and how the conference itself seems to be marked off from the more enduring discourse worlds which conferees bring to the event and to which they return.

This is not to say that the CP, or a conference itself, is a stand-alone event, divorced from the community structures that support it. While commentators have noted the increasing dominance of English as the lingua franca of international conferences in many fields (e.g. Ventola, 2002), CPs remain very much a product of their specialisms that are organized, promoted and attended by members themselves. Conferences are important forums for enacting genre knowledge and affirming community affiliations through close encounters with colleagues and competitors. In this sense they are what Porter (1992: 107) refers to as 'a concrete, local manifestation of the operation of a discourse community'. The relationship between community and conference is therefore mutually dependent, or symbiotic. As a result, the conference reflects the particular norms and patterns which communities have evolved for what goes on in such forums and the particular genres that adorn it.

More than this, through its embedding in a chain of community genres, a conference paper is very much part of the weave of working, talking and writing which characterizes the emergence of research in a discipline. Räisänen (2002), for example, shows the potential complexity of this embedding at a crash-safety conference where the CP is the end point of a sequence of genres. This begins with a conference announcement and a call for abstracts and is followed by submission, reviews and redrafting as the paper is published in conference proceedings and made available to participants before it is finally read and discussed at the conference. Awareness of a chain of events and genres like these can help participants to plan ahead and consider the reactions of different audiences to a series of abstracts, written drafts and orally delivered paper.

While some CPs are delivered following their written publication in this way, this sequence actually seems to be more common in the social sciences where funding bodies often require grant recipients to disseminate their research results in a variety of oral and written forums. The plenary talk also often tends to present already published work; being less an exposition of cutting edge research than a post-hoc celebratory overview of the field by an invited luminary. Perhaps more typically, however, the CP occupies an intermediate status between data and science (Ziman, 1974) or the actual research work and a published journal article. The CP thus provides an opportunity for testing the waters with a new idea and getting feedback on a current project as it moves from embryonic hypothesis to published paper.

As a result, it can often reveal something of the contingency of research, so that 'one glimpses research as it is actually conducted, before it is sanitized to present a picture of straight-line progress towards public knowledge' (Dubois, 1980: 143). This example from Rowley-Jolivet (2002: 104), for instance, shows how the challenges of real-world experiments are frankly acknowledged in the face-to-face presentation at a physics conference (13) while omitted from the final published paper (14):

> 13. With antenna in air we have the diamond data points where we were really getting killed by corona losses (. . .) I'll call your attention to this little gas bag at the feed section. Actually this turned out to be too small, we had to put a gas bag all the way up to about this area to protect the feed section which has very high electric fields from corona losses.

14. When very high voltage is applied to the antenna, losses to corona loading can be surprisingly severe. (. . .) One means of reducing corona losses is to enclose the high field portions of the antenna in an insulating gas.

The sense of physical constraints, the confusions and tinkering of practical activity, are absent in the written version while the oral presented CP enables us to recover something of the actual, concrete work invested in the research itself.

ii. The conference abstract

An early link in the chain of conference genres is the submission of an abstract. While regulated for text length and topic breadth by a public announcement, this is essentially a stand-alone genre which enters competition for available conference slots. While the abstract might point towards another, as yet probably unwritten, text it has a different and more urgent purpose than the paper itself. Typically submitted months ahead of the conference and blind reviewed, the abstract may be as far as the incipient CP actually gets, as rejection ends the chain for the submitting author and often means that he or she is unable to get funding to attend the conference. The abstract, then, is the point where the reader must be hooked. With rejection rates as high as 75 per cent in some fields, the CP abstract is necessarily a highly promotional genre which is more like a grant proposal or job application letter than an RA abstract (Hallack and Connor, 2006).

Both the research and the writer are therefore under close scrutiny in conference abstracts and because of this, writers tend to foreground their main claims and to carefully present themselves as competent community members. While Swales and Feak (2000: 42) point out the dangers of promising too much in an abstract, gaining acceptance means that writers need to demonstrate that they have something new and worthwhile to say. Because this is an 'occluded genre', largely hidden from public view, what we know of abstracts tends to come from fields most easily accessible to discourse analysts, such as rhetoric (Berkenkotter and Huckin, 1995; Faber, 1996), applied linguistics (Kaplan *et al.*, 1994; Yakhontova, 2002), and TESOL (Hallack and Connor, 2006). These point to a number of core rhetorical moves in the genre, with texts typically having a structure of *problem or purpose* ⇨ *method* ⇨ *results* ⇨ *conclusion*, although a general finding is that the presence of these moves does not seem to differ significantly between accepted and rejected proposals.

Despite the inability of a generic text model to explain the quality of an abstract, review committees appear to be impressed by texts which can sell their originality and interestingness to an insider audience. Berkenkotter and Huckin's (1995) study of abstracts sent to the *Conference on College Composition and Communication* over three years, for example, shows that successful proposals were judged interesting in terms of topic selection, problem definition, and novelty. Writers of accepted abstracts were thus able to package their research in ways that highlighted its relevance and their own insider credibility to experienced members of the discourse community. Novelty and the projection of 'an insider ethos through the use of terminology, special topoi, and/ or explicit or implicit references to the scholarly literature' (ibid.: 102) was what counted in judging successful abstracts.

Clearly, what is considered interesting and novel will vary across fields, but these studies suggest that it has much to do with how an issue is framed and problematized in an abstract. Successful writers use eye-catching titles and currently popular approaches. All this implies an insider status and an ability to persuade the programme panel that the writer is able, eventually, to deliver a high-quality paper at the convention. Successful writers thus establish a valued disciplinary context and situate themselves within it, defining their work as interesting and themselves as competent professionals.

iii.   The presentation

In the conference presentation itself we find a range of presentation styles. In his celebrated '*The presentation of self in everyday life*', Ervin Goffman (1981) identified three types of presentation: 'memorization', 'reading aloud' and 'fresh talk'. Dudley-Evans (1994) distinguishes 'reading style', where the speaker reads from notes, 'conversation style', which is more informal, and a more expansive, performer-oriented 'rhetorical style'. These characterizations capture the tension noted above between what is a highly reflective text, with many features that correspond to written research writing, and the immediacy of audience in time and in place which pushes a presentation towards a more interactive text. But while conference participants may encounter a range of different styles at an event, there appears to be a trend towards a more interactive pattern as the speaker shapes the message to connect with the immediate context.

The importance of interpersonal management and real-time text organization in conference presentations can be seen in a range of linguistics features which distinguish them from published papers. Compared with research articles, then, research into science presentations suggest that presentations contain:

- greater use of subject + active verb rather than passive forms (Rowley-Jolivet, 2002);
- more discussion of research failures (Thompson, 2002);
- more informal boundary markers such as *OK, right, now* (Webber, 2005);
- far greater use of self-mention (Luukka, 1996);
- greater imprecision in describing results (e.g. *roughly 0.3 in most cases*) (Dubois, 1987);
- more humour and self-irony (Frobert-Adamo, 2002);
- less use of extraposition ('*it is clear that*', '*it is possible that*' . . .);
- far more use of *existential there* ('*there are several reasons for this*') (Carter-Thomas and Rowley-Jolivet, 2001).

Interestingly, many of the features marking greater informality are particularly common in plenary presentations rather than CPs, perhaps because of the greater time available to create rapport with an audience (Webber, 2005). Overall, however, we can see the presence of these features as indicating a more interactive, spoken genre which involves real-time information management and engagement with a live audience. Additionally, however, they also point to the provisional and emergent nature of what is presented.

Something of the interpersonal effort invested in a CP is illustrated in this example from the opening of an applied linguistics presentation taken from Shalom (2002: 63):

15. Yes I'm sorry um this is the last talk right before tea and I've given you a rather dense handout there with lots of numbers on it. I will try to keep you awake throughout the session in spite of that um I actually won't be going through every single one of those numbers much to everyone's relief but I thought you might be interested in having them. Yeh I'm doing my PhD research with (name) at (institution) um sorry to mention your name like that I take all the blame for everything okay in (topic) and the focus on the talk is . . .

While such interactional work is also typical of experienced presenters, here we see a novice community member contextualizing her paper by orienting to the audience. As Shalom points out, this involves the use of considerable mitigation, humour and forewarning to bring listeners onside and perhaps offset criticism of the paper. At the same time, the speaker positions herself in relation to the community as a PhD student and therefore a 'modest knower' but with the protection of a well-known supervisor.

But while presenters may use more informal, explicitly interactive features than writers to protect themselves from criticism and win over a potentially sceptical audience, this does not release them from the obligation of novelty (Rowley-Jolivet, 2002). In fact, because the CP is closer to the original research than what is likely to appear only very much later in a published paper, this expectation is even greater. Participants are often looking for the latest developments in the field at conferences and speakers usually oblige them. These extracts from Rowley-Jolivet's (2002: 99–100) data from medicine and geology conferences suggest how speakers stress the news value and preliminary nature of their work in CP introductions:

16. I don't think that you'll find anything more up to date than some of these data that I'd like to show you now.

   What I would like to present now is preliminary results of a small Mesozoic alkaline . . .

   I suppose this is the key diagram in this talk, the full implications of which we probably haven't fully worked through.

The CP therefore offers opportunities to refine interpretations from feedback and to steal a march on others by presenting cutting edge results. Less welcome, however, is that it also opens the door to criticism and attack, particularly in the question stage which follows it. The ability to manage both textual organization and social relations becomes even more important in the Q and A session following many talks. Webber's (2002) data from medical conferences show, for instance, that while only 30 per cent of the 130 questions recorded were explicitly critical of some aspect of the CP, she notes that 'even neutral request for clarification may be perceived as a challenge by the presenter if it is difficult to answer' (Webber, 2002: 229). But although the presenter has the advantage of having rights to more speaking time and the option to judge a question as irrelevant, the Q and A can be difficult to negotiate, particularly as most of the information questions in Webber's study addressed issues outside the scope of the preceding paper. Presenters may be reluctant to be sidetracked or give away too much, but they are also interested in promoting and getting reactions to develop their work, and this represents an interactional challenge to all but the most accomplished speakers.

iv. Visuals and handouts

An important feature of CPs is their increasingly multimodal nature as talk is supported and organized by visual channels of communications such as PowerPoint, projected slides, overheads and handouts. The non-verbal dimension of presentations is particularly important in scientific, medical and technical fields where they not only carry the main information load of the presentation but also help to structure the discourse through phrases like 'the last slide please' (Swales, 2004: 198). In fact, speakers often extemporize around their slides or video clips which serve to prompt their presentations with minimal use of notes.

This example from Räisänen (2002: 83) gives a sense of this 'on the hoof' visual-dependence:

> 17. I would now like to show a video of ah some of the cadaver sled tests. OK. First I'm showing a 3-point-belt restraint cadaver sled test. [Pause to let audience watch] I would like you to notice how the shoulder belt is positioned in all these cadaver sled tests. [Pause] This is a 2-point-belt restraint knee-bolster. [Pause] You can see the knee impacting the knee bolster. [Pause] This is another 2-point-belt restraint knee-bolster test. OK that's it.

This presenter at an automotive crash-safety conference uses the video as a means to organize his talk around experimental results from cadaver tests and to highlight particular aspects of these, mixing visual and oral discourses for persuasive purposes. As Räisänen points out, the visual mode here allows the audience to 'virtually witness' the results in the same way as the researchers did, adding persuasive force to the presentation.

Although presenters in mathematics may still use a blackboard, visuals appear to be replacing more elaborate verbal expositions in many fields as photographic and PowerPoint slides become ubiquitous in medicine, science and technology. Rowley-Jolivet (1999), for instance, found an average of one slide every 50 seconds in her corpus of 90 CPs in oncology, petrology and physics, with graphical representations exceeding textual and numerical slides in each of these disciplines. This perhaps reinforces the ideational, textual and interpersonal roles that visuals play in CPs, so that we can see visuals not only as providing information and structuring the development of the talk, but also as contributing to its interactive dimension by capturing the imagination of the audience through immediate access to data. This can be seen in Example 17 above, for example, and in the frequent use of photographs in some fields. Because photographs give direct access to raw data, as compared with the abstractions of graphs and tables, they function to reinforce the newness and immediacy of what is being presented (Rowley-Jolivet, 2002).

85

In some humanities fields such as history and linguistics, however, the role of visuals tends to be less apparent as papers are often read with no visual support at all. Handouts tend to be common in the soft fields, however, with exemplar sentences accompanied by a reference list being the preferred format in applied linguistics (Belles and Fortanet, 2004). There is, moreover, perhaps a certain scepticism among academics about the value which technology adds to presentations in the soft fields. Myers, for example, not only complains of the ways PowerPoint has introduced commercial styles into academic presentations, but notes its powerful impact on the relationship between the discourse and the presenter:

> [T]he written text, produced by the machine, has become the star; I am reduced to an unseen voiceover of my own lectures . . . it marks a shift in what Goffman (1981) called footing; that is, I am seen as the animator rather than the source of the utterance. Instead of my speaking with the aid of some visual device, the text is speaking with my aid.
>
> (Myers 2000: 184)

In sum, the conference presentation is a key research genre. Not only does it situate knowledge claims closer to their source than a published article, but it is also central to both the knowledge-making practices of academic communities and its members sense of participation and belonging. It appears, moreover, that the CP is a complex, multi-semiotic event in which oral and visual, formal and informal, prepared and impromptu discourses all co-occur. It is a genre where co-presence, interaction and risk reside so that the whole becomes an expert rhetorical accomplishment where the speaker projects a competent, accessible persona while relating cutting edge information to meet the real-time processing and interactional needs of a live audience.

4.3 Other research genres

While research articles and conference presentations have the greatest visibility and frequency in the disciplines, they do not exhaust the genres which populate the research landscape. Reports, manuals and proposals dominate in technical fields (Killingsworth and Gilbertson, 1992); reviews and essays in literature; and book reviews in history (Becher and Trowler, 2001).

The journal article, as Griffith and Small (1983) point out, 'is a poor vehicle of communication' for many areas of the social sciences, 'ill-suited to discuss extremely complex issues'. The detailed discursive attention and elaborate justification of interpretation which the monograph offers writers make it a more effective medium for disseminating and evaluating research in fields such as sociology and history, for example. Despite increasing pressures from Research Assessment panels towards the uniform production of peer-reviewed articles, it is still the case that single authored, leisurely gestated books still sell and accumulate esteem for their writers in many soft fields. There also appears to be space for even more esoteric and glacially developed research genres such as the *flora* and the *treatment* which classify plant species in Systematic Botany (Swales, 1998). In this section I look briefly at some of the more common and well-studied research genres: science letters, book reviews and e-journals.

i. Scientific letters

The emergence and rapid growth of the scientific letter genre is a discoursal response to social and academic changes in academic research. In the fast-paced world of modern science, increasing specialization and rapid knowledge growth have led to intense competition. Many hard knowledge fields are characterized by fierce rivalry as the rewards of reputation, including the funding to continue one's research, are often tied to establishing priority through first announcement. One outcome has been the emergence of the scientific letter, 'squib', or 'quick report' which facilitate the rapid circulation of new and urgent findings by restricting length and streamlining the review process.

Typically less than six pages long, letters are often published online within days of acceptance and in print within five to seven weeks of submission, assisting both writers with quick publication and information saturated scientists with succinct access to new research. This description from the webpage of one such journal summarizes the advantages for authors:

> *Statistics & Probability Letters* is an international journal covering all fields of statistics and probability, and providing an outlet for rapid publication of short communications in the field. Many statisticians today are concerned by the labyrinth of research to be conquered in order to reach the specific information they require. To combat this tendency, *Statistics & Probability Letters* has been designed outside the realm of the traditional statistics journal. The concise article format (limited to six journal pages including references and figures) permits the editorial board to process papers rapidly and enables the reader to learn about new results and developments efficiently. Letters allow readers to quickly and easily digest large amounts of material and to stay up-to-date with developments in all areas of statistics and probability.

This is an objective more succinctly captured in the breathless prose of another letters journal as: '*Finance Research Letters* offers an exciting publication outlet for novel and frontier finance'.

87

Letters journals have largely evolved from short communications reporting work in progress in parent journals to become the primary forum for the dissemination of innovative work in the natural sciences. *Physical Review Letters, Chemistry Letters,* and *FEBS letters* are now among the leading journals in their fields, accounting for a massive output of work, often publishing monthly, or even weekly, and containing over 40 papers in each issue. The letter now rivals its established uncle the research article, in institutional respectability and is the preferred forum for announcing new breakthroughs. As a result, letters tend to focus on what is currently fashionable and exciting in science while research articles have taken on a more archival function, containing detailed elaborations and proofs, as a previous editor of *Physics Review Letters* observes:

> Letters journals swing back and forth from one field to another while the archival journals plod resolutely along, collecting and cataloging the accumulating wisdom of the scientific community.
> (Passell, 1988: 37)

Letters are pre-eminently declarations of findings and in keeping with this goal foreground novel claims and newsworthy information. They are 'characterized by a sense of urgency and importance, and they have a style and structure which allows authors to display key ideas prominently' (Blakeslee, 1994: 91). Titles and abstracts are written to announce findings and interpretations and to foreground what is innovative in the work, while methods are typically cursory. Background is generally scanty and the literature largely assumed, while introductions are used to foreground importance and originality. One example of the promotionalism in the genre is the greater use of boosters compared with research articles (Hyland, 2004b), allowing writers to present their work with assurance while strategically engaging with colleagues:

18. <u>This unambiguously shows</u> that the picture of antiferromagnetically coupled pairs is not adequate to describe the thermodynamics of local moments in the metallic phase.
    (Physics)

    <u>The results demonstrate a striking effect</u> of INH and <u>establish</u> a basis for further investigation of growth cycle-related phenomena in mycobacteria by flow cytometry.
    (Biology)

It is noteworthy that boosters often occurred in introductions and conclusions as these are the sections that Bazerman (1988: 243) identified as being those first read by physicists when scanning a paper to judge its relevance to their own work.

But while letters often lack the closely argued detail and elaboration typically associated with scientific writing, they appear to be evolving to ever more closely resemble research articles. A scan of 30 such letters journals shows a number of these short communications to be taking on some of the more obvious characteristics of the standard RA. Perhaps this is because innovative experimental methods require greater elaboration, or maybe there is an irresistible pull for scientists towards the 'empiricist repertoire' of the IMRD format?

ii. Book reviews

While often neglected as a research genre, the book review plays an important role in disciplinary communication as the public evaluation of research. Normally editorially commissioned, reviews occur in many academic journals and most disciplines, although they are more common in the soft knowledge fields where books are more prominent forms of scholarship. Highly visible, often read and carefully considered, book reviews provide both junior and established academics with a platform to proclaim a public position without detailed argument, empirical data, or a protracted review process. As this informant stressed:

> In philosophy a book review can go down as a serious contribution to research in the field and it will be cited because in that review it may be the first time a person has articulated an argument which other people have found persuasive. Philosophers really take book reviews seriously. They try very hard to say sometimes very smart. It's also contributing to the knowledge in the field.
>
> (Philosophy interview)

The review functions as 'a change agent, creating a critical climate of opinion' (Orteza y Miranda, 1996: 191), and is considered to be 'a crucial site of disciplinary engagement' (Hyland, 2004b: 41), allowing community members to debate each other's ideas and analyses in a public forum (Hyland, 2004b; Tse and Hyland, 2008). Unlike research articles, book reviews do not simply respond to a general body of impersonal literature but offer a direct, and often critical, encounter with a particular text and its author. Interactions here are a key element of the discourse, balancing critique and collegiality to send clear signals of how writers wish to position themselves in relation to their readers, target author and disciplinary community. While all academic writing is evaluative in some way, book reviews are explicitly so (Hyland, 2004b), as in these examples:

19. This is an excellent and timely book that should be in the library of every self-respecting Department of Biochemistry or Plant Science.

(Biology)

> The authors' treatment of psychometric issues is spotty and disorganized.
>
> (Marketing)

> This promise is not wholly fulfilled and the chapter disappointingly concludes . . .
>
> (Sociology)

Here, then, we see the workings of the peer group in perhaps its most nakedly normative role, publicly setting out standards, assessing merit and, indirectly, evaluating reputations.

For these reasons, researchers have seen reviews as an ideal place to explore disciplinary values and rhetorical strategies. In a study of evaluation in 160 reviews, for example, I found a balance of praise and criticism overall, but a marked tendency for praise to be given to global aspects of the book (20) and criticism to be directed to specific issues (21) (Hyland, 2004b):

> 20. Would that this excellent paperback had been available 20 years ago!
>
> (Mechanical Engineering)

> *Challenging Codes* is certainly the best introduction to the study of . . .
>
> (Sociology)

> Simpson's book is an excellent guide.
>
> (Physics)

> 21. On p. 195 it is not made clear why SO_4^{2-} competitive inhibition of . . .
>
> (Biology)

> But this claim turns out to be misleading.
>
> (Philosophy)

> It does not give much of an explanation why neural networks are useful, and does not derive any of the equations.
>
> (Electrical Engineering)

This pattern reflects editors' admonishments for reviewers to provide an overview of the text for prospective readers while raising particular problematic issues for the field, but it also limits the scope of negative comment. Global criticism condemns the entire work, a particularly threatening act, and this seems to have been avoided as far as possible in these reviews and, where it occurred, was often mitigated, either by diffusing the criticism in some way or by restricting it to an individual opinion (Hyland, 2004b).

There was also considerable disciplinary differences in the *balance* of evaluation with substantially more criticism in the soft disciplines. Praise tended to be more fulsome and criticism more acerbic in the soft knowledge papers, with the latter actually exceeding the former in philosophy and sociology reviews. Because the issues in the social sciences and humanities are fairly loosely defined and inquiry tends to be treated as a reiterative process involving repeated close scrutiny of earlier problems, the appraisal of an individual's work can be a significant means of getting to grips with important questions. Writers therefore sought to use this discursive space to explore issues in some depth, anchoring the text in the concerns of the wider discipline and often expounding their own views at length. Reviews in science and engineering, on the other hand, were much shorter and dominated by praise, which was almost twice as frequent per 1000 words as in the soft domains.

There also appear to be gender differences in the rhetorical practices of book reviewers. Among the findings of Tse and Hyland's (2008) study of metadiscourse in 56 reviews in biology and philosophy was that male writers tended to make bolder statements, boost their arguments more, and generally take a more confident and uncompromising line. A practice perhaps afforded them by seniority in the field, as these informants noted:

> Yes scientists are mainly male . . . the imbalance is even greater when you go up the ladder. . . . It's hard because part of being confident depends on how you're perceived. You know, many people think women are not as good in writing that kind of 'factual' report. I know this perception is wrong but it affects how you see and present yourself.
>
> (Female Biology interview)

> Unfortunately there is a huge gender imbalance in professional philosophy. The observation that men use more 'I' and are more assertive may be due to the hierarchical thing that the women feel that they have to be more careful or less assertive and this has to do with masculine aggressivity.
>
> (Male Philosophy interview)

It may be, however, that status, rather than gender is the key influence here, and overall our data tend to support Francis *et al.*'s (2001) contention that the academic writing of men and women exhibits far more similarities than differences. There were, in fact, greater variations between *disciplines* than between *genders*, with the philosophy reviews containing far more metadiscourse than the biology texts. Essentially metadiscourse is a collective term for various interpersonal features of discourse (Hyland, 2005b) and so it is not surprising to find it more frequently used in the more discursive, explicitly interpretive

91

soft fields. But we also need to recognize that the reviews were responding to very different kinds of books. As I noted earlier, while books written in philosophy are regarded as important vehicles for advancing scholarship and presenting original research, those in biology often assemble already codified knowledge for students. As a result, philosophers wrote their reviews to engage, critique and expound upon fine points of argument, while this was not usually the case in biology.

Interestingly, however, while disciplinary activity encourages the performance of certain kinds of professional identities, there seem to be gender differences in the enactment of these identities. Female philosophers tended to use more *interactive* metadiscourse, or features which manage information flow and signal the arrangement of texts with regard to readers' likely understandings. Males, in contrast, used far more *interactional* features such as engagement markers and boosters which express greater attitude, commitment, and reader involvement. While both sets of options are available to both men and women, there is a clear gender-preferred argument repertoire, which several informants recognized:

> Argument is central in our field, but there are different ways to do it [. . .] clarity and logic is most valued in the field and it is relatively easy to learn how to write clearly and logically than to forcefully express something, because it only takes more practice to write clearly, but it may involve changing your own personality if you want a battle.
>
> (Female Philosophy interview)

> I won't say men pay less attention to organizing their arguments. But I do want to do more than simply set out my views. I also want to convince people and present different views in a way such that some would carry greater force, . . . this is about the philosophical spirit of questioning and arguing.
>
> (Male Philosophy interview)

The directly challenging style of philosophical debate described by Bloor (1996) as 'mind-to-mind combat', is therefore largely rejected by the female reviews in favour of the construction of a persona which respects philosophical values of rationality and careful exemplification.

In sum, while this is a potentially threatening genre, both for the author of the text reviewed and the community more generally, the review works because both writer and reader approach the text with 'mutual co-awareness' of the other (Nystrand, 1987). Its meaning draws on both readers' familiarity with research networks and disciplinary knowledge, and also of an interpretive framework which includes an understanding of appropriate social interactions.

iii. Electronic journals

While there are other research genres worthy of discussion, I will con-
clude this already long chapter by looking at recent changes and future
directions of published research. Scholarly publication is changing
radically as a result of the internet, with submission practices, peer-
review, publication methods, and access to the literature all undergoing
development and change, especially as research funding agencies often
require authors to submit their articles for inclusion on internet plat-
forms such as *PubMedCentral* or subject repositories. It is electronic
journals, however, which have perhaps had the greatest impact on academic communication practices to date. The number of academic
e-journals has increased from about 25 in 1991 to over 5,000 in 2001
(Hovav and Gray, 2002). Today almost all academic journals have digital versions, with several moving entirely to electronic publication, and
as libraries increasingly purchase subscriptions to the electronic
versions this has become the principal source of access for academics.

The explosion of the digital dissemination of research has come
about due to the same pressures for rapid publication and wider access
which has propelled the growth of scientific letter journals. Clearly the
typical publication delays of several months makes print journals a
cumbersome format for disseminating the latest scientific research. An
editorial in the *Journal of Health Communication*, for example, argues
that the terrorist release of anthrax spores into the US postal system in
2001 underlined a need for a 48 hour publishing deadline to alert clini-
cians and other healthcare specialists to new agents in order to avert
epidemics and save lives (Ratzan, 2003). While such speeds involve
radical new review procedures, many journals now publish electronic
versions of papers as soon as they are peer-reviewed and ready, without
waiting for proofreading by production staff or the assembly of a complete issue, cutting production times by months.

Such rapid publication times, however, are not rapid enough for all
fast moving sciences and the exchange and sharing of information now
often occurs well in advance of the final publication. New web-based
tools enable academics to share their findings and so potentially remove
the need to consult formal journal articles. In some fields such as
astronomy and high-energy physics, for instance, the role of print journals in disseminating research has largely been replaced by preprint
databases such as *arXiv.org*. While preprints have long been circulated
among academics to communicate current results and get immediate
feedback prior to publication, the posting of preprints on arXiv is now
commonplace. It is true that material uploaded to such preprint databases is eventually published in peer-reviewed journals, but this is

largely for purposes of quality control, archiving and establishing scientific credit rather than communicating findings.

In addition to publication speed, e-journals potentially transform the way research is done by enabling more targeted and immediate literature searches. It is clear that the volume of scientific literature now greatly exceeds the ability of academics to identify all information germane to their research. Sophisticated search facilities are therefore now essential to allow convenient access to relevant e-published literature. The *Scopus* database, for instance, gives users fully searchable access to 40 million abstracts and 18,000 journal titles from 4,000 publishers, making it faster and more convenient to search and retrieve literature from the user's office computer. These research opportunities are also extended to previously disenfranchised users around the world through the articles which are freely available online through Open Access channels of various kinds, most notably the UN sponsored *HINARI, AGORA* and *OARE* initiatives (see Chapter 8).

While the full discoursal and rhetorical impacts of electronic publishing on research reporting have yet to be described, or even realized (Hovav and Gray, 2002), the hypertextual character of the web allows more than improved access to text, figures, and high-resolution images. It is, in fact, a medium which actualizes intertextuality, transforming the potential connections between texts into real ones by giving readers immediate access to associated texts. The fact that e-journals allow writers to provide links to digitized graphics, video, sounds, animation, and equations through resources such as the *ARTstor Digital Library* or the *NIST Digital Library* of Mathematical Functions, for example, provides a very different reading experience by mixing the visual and the verbal in new ways. Kress (1998) characterizes this as a 'tectonic shift' in semiotic practices which requires new competencies to understand and use. This is because the meanings represented in these different ways cannot simply be translated across modes, but 'offer fundamentally distinct possibilities for engagement with the world' (Kress, 1998: 67).

In addition, the ability to link immediately from a reference to the content of a source text through digital switchboards such as *Cross-Ref* not only enhances the efficiency of browsing the academic literature, but also enables readers to construct pathways through the text which better reflect their own specific research interests. This web of interconnected textual elements has important implications, as it transforms the familiar linear space of print and gives the reader greater freedom in how he or she can approach the text. As, Douglas noted a decade ago:

> The beauty of hypertext is (. . .) that it propels us from the straightened 'either/or' world that print has come to represent and into a universe where the 'and/and/and' is always possible. It is an

environment more conducive to relativistic philosophy and analysis, where no single account is privileged over any others, yet, because it is written in code, writers can ensure that readers traverse some bits of the argumentative landscape more easily and more frequently than others, or that readers are left to make their own connections between one bit of text and another.

(1998: 155)

Finally, the reference links that readers choose to follow are also likely to be of interest to bibliometricians and others who seek to track the ways which cognitive influence is exercised and social research networks operate (e.g. Cronin, 2001). Not only does this carry the potential to gain a greater understanding of how academic research is conducted and the extent of cross-disciplinary activity, but it may also mean that the principles of citation indexing can be applied more widely that at present. Currently the ISI, which measures the impact factor of articles and journals, has a coverage limited to a relatively small set of (overwhelmingly English language) periodicals, but the extension of citation indexing tools to open electronic publishing contexts means more accurate counting of a wider constituency. This means that work in currently non-indexed journals will be more visible and that citations to an individuals work, or perhaps even to an individual's contribution noted in acknowledgements, can be measured. Such practices are likely increase an academic's standing and perhaps even impact on university promotion and tenure decisions.

Such possibilities, together with other radical proposals such as those for self-publishing and open peer review lie in the future, but they suggest that electronic publishing has only just begun to have an effect on both research practices and discourses.

4.4 Conclusions

In this chapter I have provided something of an overview of the key discourses which communicate research and so carry the prestige of the academy. While it is only possible to scratch the surface of such a complex area in a single chapter, I have sketched central features of the main research genres and sought to show the connections between research products and processes. The chapter has also highlighted issues raised in earlier chapters, such as the promotionalism of academic communication, its disciplinary character, and the fact that academics do not only produce texts that plausibly represent an external reality, but use language to acknowledge, construct and negotiate social relations. In the next chapter I turn to instructional discourses and, in particular, to the importance of talk in academic communication.

5 Instructional discourses

While research discourses have gathered considerable celebrity and attention, genres concerned with the more work-a-day functions of teaching and learning have, until quite recently, been of less interest to researchers. Lectures, classroom teaching and textbooks, however, are the bread and butter of university life. Not only are they the genres which students are most likely to encounter, but they occupy much of the working lives of academics in preparation and delivery. Concerned with disseminating knowledge rather than constructing it, these genres function to establish both the content and the discourse of a discipline for students, acculturating newcomers into the schema of their fields.

When students enter university they are faced with a range of adjustments to the ways they are expected to learn, behave and understand the world. Among the most challenging of these is the need to extend their linguistic competence to deal with new demands of reading, listening, interpreting, recording and understanding required by university study. As I have discussed in previous chapters, this not only involves the ability to work in a general academic register, but to cope with the demands of individual disciplines. Ballard and Clanchy made this clear many years ago:

> Just as modes of analysis vary with disciplines and with the groups that practise them (physicists, psychologists, and literary critics), so too does language. For the student new to a discipline, the task of learning the distinctive mode of analysis . . . is indivisible from the task of learning the language of the discipline . . . One area of development cannot proceed without the other.
>
> (1988: 17)

Competence in a discipline means understanding its concepts, its ways of working and its language, and this is largely achieved through the instructional discourses of the academy, particularly lectures, seminars and textbooks.

5.1 University lectures

The large formal lecture is perhaps *the* prototypical genre of information-transfer. Emphasizing transmission over negotiation and monologue rather than dialogue, it is seen by universities as the most practical and cost-effective way of imparting subject content *en masse* to growing intakes of undergraduate students. Critics point out that lecturing is mainly a one-way form of communication, an institutionalized extended holding-of-the-floor that does not involve significant audience participation. But while teacher-led monologic sessions may be the traditional form of lecture, it is just one type of class session which can include small lectures, seminars, tutorials, 'labinars' and discussion sessions. A survey of 900 lecturers in four US universities by Ferris and Tagg (1996), for example, found a range of practices across different disciplines and graduate/undergraduate levels, with lecturing styles apparently evolving towards less formal, more conversational interactive styles.

Academic speech genres have been largely neglected by discourse analysts until recently, however, and we know very little of how they vary within or between each other. This is, at least in part, because university lectures have not traditionally been available to outsiders. It was only a few years ago, for example, that Flowerdew (2002: 110) complained about the lack of spoken corpora for academic purposes, a situation Nesi (2003) blames for discouraging research into spoken texts and for hindering the development of authentic lecturing materials for EAP students. This situation is now beginning to change, however, and this section highlights what we know of academic lectures. I restrict the term 'lecture' here to a classroom learning event of 40 students or more primarily led by a lecturer, although it may well involve contributions from students.[1] I begin with a brief consideration of students' perceptions and experiences of the genre.

i. Comprehension and perceptions

The centrality of lectures to undergraduate teaching and learning has long been recognized. It is also widely acknowledged, however, that listening to lectures can present a considerable processing burden to students, especially those working in a foreign language (e.g. Flowerdew, 1994). Comprehending lectures is challenging for students as it requires two main cognitive operations: First, academic listening involves 'bottom-up' processing of language input in real time, requiring students to attend to data in the incoming stream of speech signals. Second, it also draws on 'top-down' analysis of what is being said by utilizing prior knowledge and expectations to create meaning (Rost, 1990).

Research shows that among the most significant demands affecting students' effective comprehension of lectures are:

- The speed of the lecturer's delivery
- The failure of humour to cross cultural boundaries

97

- A lack of understanding of phonological structuring of discourse organization
- Difficulties of engaging in the participatory style of lecture preferred by western lecturers
- The lecturer's use of unknown vocabulary and specialist terminology
- Maintaining concentration for 50 minutes or longer
- Identifying the topic, main themes and ideas of a lecture and how these are connected
- Taking effective notes of the main points
- Coping with the demands of simultaneous visual and verbal inputs

(List compiled from Flowerdew, 1994; Flowerdew and Miller, 1996; Thompson, 2003). Lectures are therefore both linguistically and cognitively demanding, and L2 students are likely to experience greater difficulty with each of these skills.

One reason for these difficulties is that students often have little idea of what to expect when their studies begin, typically anticipating a dry, monologic delivery of core material and basic facts, where the tutor is 'the main giver of information' (Furneaux, *et al.*, 1991: 80). Such expectations can be a major obstacle to comprehension for learners, as 'not only the language forms (vocabulary, syntax, etc.) but also the underlying cultural grammar and interpretive strategies my be initially unknown' (Benson, 1994: 181).

Flowerdew and Miller (1996), for example, found this was particularly problematic for undergraduates in Hong Kong, where there was a serious mismatch in both perceptions and behaviours between the students and their British lecturers. While most lecturers talked about using lectures to help develop students' judgements and thinking skills, the students simply saw them as a way of getting the core facts from the course. They regarded the lecturer as an uncontested authority and lectures as a means of effecting a one-way transfer of information. The authors attribute this to a clash of academic cultures, forcefully expressed by one of their lecturers in this way:

> They [the students] sit there like goldfish with their mouths open waiting for me to pour information into them. . . . They only experience a system which requires them to learn the 'right' answer and to regurgitate it. The concept of evaluation, analysis etc. appears to be totally lacking.
>
> (Flowerdew and Miller, 1996: 125)

98

Other studies have focused on particular features of lectures and students' responses to these. Simpson (2004), for instance, points to the potential difficulties for students caused by high-frequency multi-word clusters such as *the thing is, you could say* and *look at it like*, which can be used to focus the discussion, negate a point or introduce complexities. Similarly, discourse markers such as *right, well* and *OK*, which indicate shifts in the exposition (Swales and Malczewski, 2001), and 'phonological paragraphing',[2] which chunks spoken discourse into paragraph planning units (Thompson, 2003), appear to be crucial to understanding lectures. Finally, research also shows how schematic knowledge of the different ways of structuring a lecture is vital to comprehension. Listeners must create a mental map of the organization of the lecture as a 'sequential-hierarchic network-structure' (Givon, 1995: 64) in which information is not only received linearly but where topics and sub-topics are structured and connections made. In other words, without a familiar framework for situating information, students find it extremely difficult to follow a lecturer's argument (Allison and Tauroza, 1995).

Lectures themselves, however, are often aware of students' difficulties and employ various strategies to assist comprehension. In their Hong Kong data, for instance, Flowerdew and Miller (1997) observed lecturers adopting these techniques:

- *Features of language*: attention to micro-structuring and verbal labelling of main points
- *Interpersonal*: attempting to make lectures less threatening, personalization, checking
- *Structuring*: use of narrative thread, macro-signals of organization, rhetorical questions
- *Other media*: use of visual aids, pre- and post-reading material and tutorial discussion

These strategies, however, are rarely found in materials designed to prepare students for university study. Textbooks typically depart from an authentic lecture experience, for example, by requiring students to listen and take notes from short extracts which contain no visual material and involve a speaker reading from a script (Tauroza, 2001; Thompson, 2003). The emphasis, in other words, is limited to practising discrete, bottom-up listening skills, while more global and interactive features are largely neglected. One reason for this is that textbooks are frequently informed by research conducted in controlled, non-naturalistic conditions which fail to capture either the spoken features of face-to-face monologic discourse or replicate the student lecture experience.

ii. Informality and information

The development of spoken academic corpora in the last few years has provided greater access to authentic academic speech[3] and begun to both increase our understanding of lecture discourse and inform EAP pedagogy.[4] Perhaps the most striking feature revealed by these analyses is that, at least at first glance, lectures appear to depart from our general impressions of academic discourse and contain many linguistic characteristics that seem closer to conversation. This example from the MICASE corpus gives some idea of this (dots denote micro pauses):

1. Darwin's not the only one who, notices that. lots of competing theorists are noticing the same thing, that in . . . that organisms seem to . . . match with . . . adapt to their environments. what Darwin does that's different, from the other theories of evolution, is propose that the mechanism by which that adaptation occurs and the mechanism that he proposes is natural selection. *<PAUSE: 05>* now I wanna spend a little bit of time talking about natural selection because, but f- first I'll just read this definition which is any inherited characteristics, that increase the likelihood of survival in reproduction are selected for, if it helps you it's gonna be selected for, and any that decrease the likelihood of survival, are selected against. now uh, one of the things that's . . . hard to get about natural selection is often . . . people think about natural selection as being this sentient knowledgeable all-knowing guided planful . . . thing out there . . . as though . . . nature natural selection has a grand plan for each of us . . . and it's gonna determine what things are good and what things are bad. um in fact last night I was watching with Michael we were flipping through the Discovery Channel and they had a program on, about. . . . these guys who were diving down to three hundred feet underneath the water trying to find a species of fish . . .

This extract from an *Introduction to Psychology* lecture given to 250 students illustrates the colloquial character of much impromptu lecturing. We see, for example, the hesitations, false starts, fragments and repetitions typical of online production, as well as filled pauses, contractions (*gonna* and *wanna*), vagueness (*thing, a little bit*) and informal constructions (*what Darwin does is, one of the things that's hard to get, these guys*) familiar from casual conversation. There is also considerable effort invested in directly acknowledging and engaging with a live audience, as the speaker takes care to set out what she will do, anticipates how the students might react to the idea of natural selection and provides a personal example involving watching TV with her partner. Finally, turning to grammar, we might note the clausal structure of the piece and see how the text is composed of a series of conversation-like short clauses rather than the phrasal syntax of text-books (e.g. Biber, 2006).

But while lectures tend to have many of the features of conversation, they also follow the conventions of an academic register. Research tells us, for instance, that lectures are heavily hedged, particularly in human-ities and social science disciplines, although this is not always for the traditional reasons of uncertainty or modesty. Poos and Simpson (2002) observe that the high frequency of '*sort of/sorta*' and '*kind of/kinda*' in arts and social science lectures often serve to socialize undergraduate students into the discipline by highlighting the negotiability of rela-tively vague terms such as *culture* and *communication*. Lectures also tend to be highly reflexive (Mauranen, 2001) with an abundance of metadiscursive expressions used to structure on-going speech. As we can see from the extract above, lecturers like to heavily signpost their presentations. Framing constructions (*now I wanna spend a little bit of time talking about natural selection*), and what Swales and Malczewski (2001) call 'new episode flags' (*OK, now, right*), which mark shifts in the discourse, can help enormously in guiding students through a lecture (Crawford Camiciottoli, 2004).

The extract also suggests the importance of definitions and examples in lectures. In a study of 16 lectures, for instance, Flowerdew (1992) found there was a definition about every 2 minutes as lecturers intro-duced terms on the fly, as in these examples from MICASE:

2. what is a false reference blank? okay <u>that is</u> any reference blank that <u>that is</u> incorrectly designed and it happens in research all the time

    if the cation is a hydrogen ion H-plus, then <u>we'll be calling it</u> an acid if it's got O-H-minus <u>we call it</u> a base, and if it's got oxygen O-two-minus, <u>we call</u> it an acid-anhydride.

Swales (2001) and Simpson (2004) also note the high frequency of formulaic expressions in lectures which function to manage the dis-course and highlight key information, much like in written academic genres (Hyland, 2008a):

3. Sun, just two years ago by default wouldn't compile ANSI-C you had to tell them specially, compile ANSI-C for me. so, <u>the point is</u> these, slight differences among versions of the lan-guage, do impact us in a practical way.

101

> but actually <u>it turns out that</u> the blood stream is not a particularly hospitable place, for cancer cells and in fact very few cancer cells, actually survive the trip.

> but <u>the thing is</u>, it's perfectly elastic, so it was it had become a correspondence that C-F could be anything, as long as, number one holds.

Such similarities with written academic texts are a consequence of the need to construe experience in ways which encourage learners to think about content not just as facts, but as complex systems. It is a language suited to talking about thinking itself and about sets of complex relationships. This involves presenting material in certain conventional ways which require, in part, speakers and writers to explicitly label their discourse structure and direction, highlight key points and rework utterances to offer a reformulation or concrete instance of what they have said.

iii. Interaction and evaluation

Perhaps counter intuitively, the most distinguishing feature of academic lectures is their relatively high levels of involvement and interactivity: the ways they bring the speaker and audience closer and so add a dimension that is absent from most textbooks. Interactive lecturing, where the lecturer speaks from notes or visuals, for example, seems to be growing in popularity in the UK (Flowerdew, 1994).

In part, interactivity is achieved by the kinds of explicit signalling of intent I mentioned above as speakers frame stretches of talk to actively engage listeners, but we can also see how other features contribute to learner involvement in this short extract from a MICASE biology lecture. Here, through the informal label 'folks', inclusive pronouns, questions and the adoption of a personal stance, the speaker takes the trouble to address his audience directly:

> 4. okay folks. I think I'm gonna, bring us back now. um, so I wanna talk now about micro-evolution, which is usually defined as the mechanism of evolution. um I first wanna make clear a couple of things. um first of all what is it exactly that evolves? I mean we've all talked about how our ideas are evolving or our, our um, our relationships evolve but as biological beings . . . individual organisms do not evolve.

Woven into the ideational content concerning how the concept of evolution should be understood are statements which call attention to the discourse itself and its possible reception. These statements provide information about how the lecture will be organized and about the relationship the speaker wants to establish with her audience.

One of the most obvious mechanisms a speaker can use to establish a relationship with an audience is pronominal reference. Walsh (2004) adopts Goffman's (1981) notion of 'footing' to make the point that while the relationship between lecture participants remains relatively fixed at the level of speech event, the speaker can vary this at utterance level by adopting different allegiances and projecting different roles onto students. This is most easily done in English by exploiting the vagueness of pronoun reference; shifting the scope of *you* and *we* to more directly engage students in both the material and the learning process. This is clear in the use of 'inclusive we' in acts of discourse framing to involve students in the unfolding speech event:

> 5. and yes this is up on the web <PAUSE : 15> are <u>we</u> okay? oh <u>we</u> have time to do this okay. now, <u>let's</u> do the Marxist over here first, because this is what <u>we've</u> just done and then I wanna contrast it with liberal pluralists.

We and *you* play a key role in creating an atmosphere of interaction and involvement in lectures and are often used to include students in the community of experts, drawing them into the processes of disciplinary research and the questions which motivate them:

> 6. what <u>we</u> want to know is which is the most parsimonious cladogram. that's what <u>you</u> would be, that's the question that <u>you're</u> asking, in doing a particular analysis. the first thing <u>you</u> wanna do is <u>you</u> have a bunch of traits that <u>you've</u> observed, on these organisms, then <u>you</u> want to know how to analyze these traits. the first thing <u>you</u> have to do since <u>you</u> only want to look at shared derived features, features that are not primitive, and features that are shared, is that <u>you</u> have to determine polarity. how do <u>you</u> know whether something's a primitive trait or a derived trait?

Second person pronouns also function to involve students when discussing the occurrence or existence of something. They can, for example, be used to replace more predictable passive or *there* structures (Example 7), or to assign students roles in hypothetical worlds of action to bring alive examples or cases (Example 8):

> 7. so just because <u>we</u> can't see bacteria, doesn't mean <u>we</u> can't study them scientifically, because <u>we</u> have microscopes and other machines that can help <u>us</u> see bacteria

103

8. if there was a wrongful death, so <u>you</u> could go to the government, and <u>you</u> could petition, the shogun, <u>you</u> could petition the government and say, I wish to have a license to go and kill somebody as a vendetta, and they would grant <u>you</u> that.

In addition to inclusive pronouns, evaluative language helps to create and negotiate interpersonal relations between the speaker and an audience. Bamford (2004), for instance, points to the importance of signalling nouns such as *problem* which is often used in lectures to prospectively or retrospectively frame a stretch of talk in the judgments of the discipline, alerting students to the shared norms and understandings of the field.

9. and, another <u>problem</u> is, that he's often misrepresented and simplified, by both folks who . . . are Marxist or claim to be Marxist and by folks who, oppose Marxism.

   so they therefore are not totally respectful of the idea of other people owning land. so that's another <u>problem</u>.

Perhaps more explicitly, evaluations function interactively in cases where the lecturer takes a clear stance towards the propositional content of his or her talk using modal verbs and stance adverbs (Biber, 2006). In Biber's data, modals frequently signalled upcoming information or future topics (*we will look at, I'd like you to*), but they are also widely used to express possibility in the MICASE lectures, particularly *would* and *might*. Lecturers also frequently use stance adverbs, sometimes to identify information as factual and beyond dispute (Example 10), but more generally to express likelihood and convey something of the tentativeness of academic discourse (Example 11):

10. . . . this high frequency is <u>definitely</u> not due to the fact that this allele confers any advantage.

    . . . and <u>in fact</u> if you look, one or two days after you've injected those cancer cells in the lungs, you will find lots of cancer cells, lodged in the lungs.

11. <u>presumably</u>, this is not a five-H-T-two-A receptor. but, some other one is. and it's, <u>probably</u> postsynaptic.

    . . . the blood vessel they're, li- most <u>likely to</u> invade into is gonna be a very tiny capillary cuz it's got the thinnest wall.

Finally, a word about questions. Successful interaction depends on a sense of co-occupation of the same social space and questions are a frequent means of making the shared here and now a salient feature of the discourse. In fact, questions in lectures play both textual and interpersonal roles, organizing the flow of information and indicating a desire for a more dialogic discourse. Not all questions expect a response however, and the majority of questions in lectures fail to open the floor to students at all. Instead, they tend to be either rhetorical, pulling students along with the monologue, or act as comprehension checks, ensuring that students are following the line of argument. This extract from a MICASE management lecture gives some flavour of these uses:

12. There are three questions you wanna ask, when you wanna know, if people are motivated or not. The first one is direction right? Where is their effort directed? What tasks are getting done? Right? This, basic thing, where is their effort directed? The second, is amplitude right? How much effort are they devoting, to a particular task? How much of a task is getting done? That's the second diagnostic question when we wanna figure out if people are motivated, or not, to do something that we want, that we want them to get done. Finally persistence, right? How long does their effort last? How long are they doing a particular task? Okay those are the three, questions for, detecting whether in fact, what we want to motivate, is being motivated right?

Overall, it is clear that not everything which occurs in a lecture works to convey information. Speakers not only seek to ensure that the information they present is intelligible, but also that it is understood, accepted and, hopefully, acted upon. Students must be drawn in, engaged, motivated to follow along, and perhaps be persuaded by the discourse and to do this speakers attempt to shape their texts to the anticipated expectations and requirements of receivers.

5.2 Seminars

Although lectures tend to predominate at lower levels of university instruction, classes often become smaller and the interaction in them more frequent as students progress. Seminars seek to further the disciplinary acculturation of graduate and advanced students and are often based around texts, groupwork activities (Northcott, 2001) or student presentations (Basturkmen, 2002; Weissberg, 1993). Essentially, however, they can be seen as relatively informal, small group, tutor-led events at which everyone present is asked to participate. This overt participation is highly regarded by students and appears to make instruction more effective (Morell, 2007). It can also encourage greater involvement by non-native English speaking students (Kang, 2005), although interaction may simply increase the cognitive demands of an already difficult listening task (Northcott, 2001). Once again, however, we know very little about how this genre works or its impact on learning, although research allows us to say something about its key features.

i. Interactivity and personalization

Clearly, explicit interactivity is a defining feature of seminars. The MICASE statistics, for example, show that students contributed 35 per cent of the total words in the seminar corpus compared with just 6 per cent in the large lectures. Class size and students' knowledge of the subject will obviously influence how far participation is possible, but equally important is the skill of the tutor in facilitating it. Interactivity in spoken discourse requires speakers to demonstrate their involvement in the flow of talk and engagement in a shared context. They do this largely by expressing a personal stance to the topic and by referring to themselves and addressees, which means that we find seminars contain more of the features identified by Morell (2004) as characteristic of interactive lectures: personal pronouns, discourse markers, elicitations, questions and negotiation.

One way we can see the distinctiveness of seminars is to make use of the Wordsmith KeyWords[5] tool, which highlights statistically significant differences between corpora. This shows us that the words which best distinguish seminars from large lectures in MICASE are those which also characterize the interactivity of informal conversation, that is *I, yeah, mhm, know, like, right, um*. More helpfully, we can see the distinctiveness of seminars by comparing the extensive use of personal pronouns in this genre. Table 5.1, for instance, shows that the MICASE seminars contain almost 50 per cent more cases than the large lecture corpus. While these findings may be skewed by low frequencies,[6] they indicate some key differences between the two genres and something of the interaction that occurs in them.

Table 5.1 *Personal reference in seminars and large lectures (per 1,000 words)*

	I	Me	You (Subject and object)	We	Us	Let's	Totals
Seminars	29.5	1.7	28.7	7.9	0.8	0.6	69.2
Large lectures	13.8	1.3	21.6	10.2	0.8	1.0	48.7

It is not surprising to find fewer cases of *we* in the seminars, for example. Audience inclusive *we* tends to be the predominant form in spoken academic discourse (Fortanet, 2004), and I noted above that in lectures it largely works to reduce the distance between speaker and audience to promote awareness of a common purpose. The greater social and physical proximity of the graduate seminar, however, perhaps makes such explicit structuring of involvement less urgent. In most seminars there tends to be greater overlap of knowledge and more opportunities provided by the context for participants to see how they might contribute to the discussion.

Something of the immediacy and interactivity of the seminar is also shown by the more frequent use of *I* and *you* in the seminars, and this also points to the different ways that speakers tend to engage with each other in these events. Table 5.2, for example shows that the pronoun *you* collocates principally with cognition verbs such as *think* and *know* in the seminars and with verbs of perception and ability like *look, see* and *can* in the lectures. At first glance, this might suggest that perhaps there is more emphasis on speaker stance and direct participant involvement in the seminars and more concern with the management of learning in lectures.

Essentially, as we noted above, *you* is often used by lecturers to orientate listeners to the discourse and focus students' attention on the topic. The clusters (or frequently occurring sequences) shown in Table 5.2 are common ways of doing this:

13. . . . <u>you have to</u> convert, to capital X and capital Y. okay?

. . . <u>you can see</u> you just get slightly different results.

. . . so <u>if you look</u> in your guide, you'll see that some plants, are rated, for their hardiness

Table 5.2 *Main collocates of 'you' in MICASE seminars and lectures*

Seminars						Lectures		
you know you	81	and you know	49	you have to	81	you have a	44
you know I	75	that you know	48	you can see	79	that you can	43
you know the	72	you know that	42	you look at	55	so if you	40
uh you know	65	do you know	40	if you look	48	and if you	38
um you know	52	you know uh	37	and you can	47	you know you	38

In the seminars, however, *you* occurs principally with the verb *know*, which on closer study is only partly due to the speaker attributing understanding to others. More often, it occurs in the unplanned speech of student contributors to buy time as they organize their thoughts:

14. Student: then like the other one is like, totally strong and you know but, Offred is like, she's more like what a Christian woman should be because she's not like, you know too extreme or too evil

     Student: uh well you know you can claim that the, overall picture you know could be, uh you know that it's correlated with many things and and that there's not necessarily a causal relationship

The frequency of this pattern as a floor holding strategy in the seminar discourse indicates the online planning and direct orientation to interlocutors typical of less formal oral genres and illustrates the very different patterns of a more egalitarian discourse than found in the lectures.

The most striking difference between the seminars and lectures, however, is in the use of the first person, with twice as many examples in the seminars (see Table 5.1 above). The pronoun I often occurs in cetain fixed patterns or clusters and helps confirm Biber *et al's.* (2004) observation that classroom teaching contains far more stance clusters than either conversation or written academic genres. In the seminar corpus where clusters with *I* overwhelmingly convey attitudes or assessments of relative certainty:

15. Student: mhm. Although I think that Benjamin himself doesn't, necessarily see all the advantages and disadvantages.

     Student: so, you know I think that that's, that's an incomplete solution, and I don't think it's, the cure all that you're, you're claiming it is.

In fact, by far the most frequent 3-word *I* cluster in the seminar data is *I don't know*. This is a collocation which can express the speaker's unfamiliarity or uncertainty with a topic, but which more often helps oil the interactional wheels. This is typically achieved either by interjecting a personal note into an academic comment, or by hedging a statement to tone down its impact on the hearer, as in this exchange:

16. Student: um, yeah, famille d'yeux I don't know, that's a good question. cuz I saw this being a, a poem very much between, the narrator and les yeux des pauvres, and not, the narrator and this woman

> Tutor: um, <u>I don't know</u>, I feel like it would, it would kinda cheat, the s- the strength of the satire. Okay? So unless you mean, something like, well actually within this novel, we see instances of, real service or you know, um, persecution that should be borne, right? Unless you mean that, uh <u>I don't know</u>, I don't quite, I don't quite follow why, you are, objecting the way you are.

Such strategies are useful to both lecturers attempting to maintain social cohesion by reducing the privileged status of their contributions and students wishing to avoid appearing too unfashionably swotish.

ii. Turns and exchanges

I have, until now, illustrated aspects of spoken discourse as isolated example utterances, but we have to remember that seminars are dialogic, or often multi-logic, in that the discourse is jointly constructed and multi-authored. While often including lengthy monologic episodes, they typically evolve through the taking of successive, relatively short, turns by different participants. These may be unsolicited questions and comments by students to the tutor or student presenters, but more often they are orchestrated by a tutor-led discussion following some initial presentation or group work.

Questions are important here. Unlike their role in managing the flow and understanding of information in lectures, questions in seminars are oriented to content and function to raise issues, introduce information and get responses. The hierarchical relationships of the lecture remain however, as most questions come from the seminar leader, either thrown out generally or through nomination:

> 17. Tutor: what do you think? [S4: um] things you would change? If any?
>
> Tutor: Jeremy, why don't you start and, tell us what your, thoughts were about this.
>
> Tutor: does anyone else wanna tease anything else out of that poem?
>
> Tutor: uh does the audience have any questions they want to ask either of the teams? Yeah, Harry?

While questions are typically designed to elicit the knowledge and experience of the students, they also serve to guide the interaction and structure the discourse.

In her study of student-to-student discussions following case-study presentations in MBA seminars, for example, Basturkmen (2002) found that the most frequent pattern of interaction was the simple Initiation–Response–Feedback sequence. This was originally identified by Sinclair and Coulthard (1991) as the basic exchange unit in school classrooms, as here:

Initiation	Teacher:	Where does he live?
Response	Student:	Rome
Follow-up	Teacher:	Rome, yes

The remaining interactions in the seminars involved an elaboration of this pattern, with the first speaker using the follow-up move to re-initiate another sequence. Basturkmen notes that this typically occurred when the speaker was dissatisfied with a response, with the exchange continuing until reaching an acceptable outcome. In the MICASE data however, such extended chains of utterances are the spine of the discourse. This is a key way in which this genre develops as the seminar leader works to draw more students into the discourse and create a discussion.

Ultimately, then, interlocutors work together to jointly construct and negotiate meaning through a dialogic process in which ideas and views emerge. This example is typical of this process:

18. Initiation: Tutor: what do you think?

    Response: S13: don't you need to you have to do undergrad before you do PhD.

    Follow up/initiation: Tutor: yeah, so?

    Response: S13: so if there's less people going to undergraduate school then there's less people available to go, get a PhD.

    Follow up/initiation: Tutor: absolutely there's a, uh you know that's right, fewer people and what what else might happen? why are these things like you didn't actually link it [S12: right] specifically in your paper but, they're they are linked, yeah.

    Response: S2: there'll be uh a skew in, in the type of information that is produced and in the type of research perhaps that is uh, that they partake in.

Follow up/initiation: Tutor: why would that be?

Response: S2: well if you, if there's a decrease in minorities for instance, in the undergraduate and then therefore there's a decrease in minorities then in the PhD program, there's less, research just by the the the trends, that have been taken. uh more people tend to do research that is pertinent to themselves.

While tutor questions help drive the discussions, not all contributions are explicitly solicited. Individuals respond to each other, or more usually the tutor, to express a view or comment on what has been said. Interestingly, these utterances rely heavily on concession and the interpersonal paraphernalia of spoken interaction, with due care given to the protection of personal face and the maintenance of group solidarity. Making a contribution to a seminar is an assertion of power and so calls for mitigation. Here, for example, we see some of the ways that students mark their interventions with appropriate tentativeness and humility:

19. He also <u>sort of</u> attributes that conformity to um, the fact that, like Haussmann and um, the emperor were <u>basically just, sort of</u> in bed with the same five, real estate companies <u>right</u>?

Another thing there is, <u>I don't know exactly how that works</u> but, but <u>I thought</u> it was interesting the way that all those, <u>um</u>, new apartments, had, <u>like</u> the, the side that faced the, the street was, the living room and the dining room and so, <u>in a sense like</u>, the, the everyday life is also uniformed in its relation of the public and private, areas.

. . . but, but <u>I don't think</u> she is though. <u>I think that</u> her, it could be interpreted that way but <u>I don't think</u> that's the way she <u>uh</u> . . .

Finally, seminar discourse is also fashioned through student questions. These are largely requests for clarification on certain points of content and, interestingly, they are often prefaced with an explicit labelling of the speech act, possibly to reduce the abruptness of an intervention or any suspicion that the contribution might be seeking to challenge what has gone before. These examples are typical:

19. S8: can I ask a quick <u>question</u>? um, are the percentages, what are can you just, explain the percentages again to me?

> S3: okay my <u>question</u> is, how do we know that the numina does not already have these, processes already involved?

> S3: I have a <u>question</u> [Tutor: yeah] so the main difference between the- this hypothesis and the other one is that the action of, the serotonin is either presynaptic or postsynaptic?

Such requests are common in the MICASE seminar data and once again underline the role that negotiation of meaning plays in this instructional discourse, allowing different participants to work together to arrive at a mutual understanding of their utterances and the topic.

This overview is clearly very preliminary and there are many other features of this genre worthy of study. We might, for example, profitably explore the role of humour and irony, rephrasing and elaboration, topic management, the expression of evaluation and the oral style of student presentations themselves. I hope to have shown, however, that the graduate seminar is a rich and interesting discourse which will amply reward further study.

5.3 Undergraduate textbooks

Textbooks are indispensable to academic life, facilitating the professional's role as a teacher and constituting one of the primary means by which the concepts and analytical methods of a discipline are acquired. They play a major role in the learners' experience and understanding of a subject by providing a coherently ordered epistemological map of the disciplinary landscape and, through their textual practices, can help convey the values and ideologies of a particular academic culture. This link to the discipline is crucial for novices seeking to extend their competence into new areas of knowledge and trying to cope with the specific demands of a new interpretive community. Thus students, particularly in the sciences, often see textbooks as concrete embodiments of the knowledge of their field.

University textbooks, however, are, once again, something of a neglected genre. Little is known about their rhetorical structure, their relationship to other genres, or the ways that they vary across disciplines. This section looks at this important genre to examine the ways that textbook authors speak to students, and indirectly to their peers, in constructing a plausible vision of their disciplines.

i. *Authority and intertextuality*

Textbooks are widely regarded, particularly by undergraduate students, as repositories of codified knowledge and disciplinary lore: places where the accepted theories of a discipline are defined and acknowledged fact represented. Brown refers to this as canonizing discourse:

> At any point in time, the canon is fixed in that it represents as conventional wisdom that any competent member of the discipline would except as uncontroversial. In this way the canon presents a view of the discipline that epitomizes and underscores the disciplines own sense of identity and intellectual tradition.
>
> (1993: 65)

The canon then, is a dominant perspective that helps construct a coherent conception of what the discipline is and what it stands for. It is an ideological representation of stability and authority. Bakhtin (1981: 427) refers to this as 'undialogized' discourse: privileged in its absolute definition of reality, thus the textbook represents an attempt to shape and order the disputes, controversies and variety of a field, reducing the mulitivocity of past texts to a single voice of authority.

So textbooks are both evidence of a paradigm (Kuhn, 1970) and examples of intertextuality. That is, the property that texts have of being comprised of 'snatches of other texts, which may be explicitly demarcated or merged in, and which the text may assimilate, contradict, ironically echo, and so forth' (Fairclough, 1992: 84). Textbooks are, by definition, composed of other texts. Their value depends on them representing the issues, ideas, current beliefs and chief findings of the discipline by borrowing and incorporating these from their original sources. Other texts are adopted for a new audience and developed through commentary, tasks, examples or analyses, with the original words of their authors being recast as bullet points, sidebars, flowcharts, paraphrases, summaries or otherwise worked into a new discourse and recoverable from it.

In addition to such explicit intertextuality, however, textbooks also borrow interdiscursively from the conventions, values and practices of their fields. Most obviously, there are differences in the form and presentation of textbooks. Those in business studies, for example, often resemble coffee-table books and display marketing norms in their use of colour and glossy presentation, while the taxonomies and electron micrographs common in biology textbooks help represent and construct a knowable, objective world. More importantly, writers draw on the genres, models and beliefs of their communities in constructing their material, representing their field in particular ways. They are not concerned only with presenting an accessible introduction to subject matter, but with providing students with a framework for understanding the field. In economics, for example, the repetition of patterns which move from general statements about economic processes to historical or hypothetical examples helps acculturate students into a disciplinary schema (Bondi, 1999). Similarly, the structure of geology textbooks, based on the cycle of past processes producing present geological features which in turn provide evidence for these processes, reflect the basic taxonomic principles of the discipline (Love, 1993).

Textbooks thus both contain evidence of other texts and of the 'ways of seeing' of their disciplines. They are also creatures of their communities in other ways, and in particular in the roles they play in different fields. In hard knowledge fields the discipline appears to be defined in its textbooks, embodying its truths and current areas of professional activity. So, in the sciences and hard social sciences, certitude, abstract nominalizations, thematic structure and style, seem to reinforce existing paradigms. In philosophy and composition, on the other hand, textbooks are altogether more circumspect and are often important vehicles for presenting original research (e.g. Gebhardt, 1993). The regular publication of new editions of textbooks in communication theory and marketing, for example, both updates fast changing information and disseminates new work.

ii. Audiences and literacies

For many students textbooks do not only represent the knowledge and methods of a discipline but also provide a model of literacy practices: how the discipline discusses what it knows. But while students attempt to acquire the specialized narratives of their community along with its subject knowledge, the language used in setting out a canon is very different from that of arguing for new claims (e.g. Hyland, 2004b). In concealing much of the argumentative nature of science, the textbook reshuffles its discourse to replace the novel and provisional with the familiar and accredited.

For one thing, authors feel less need to explicitly reference earlier work. Because they are attempting to weave currently accepted knowledge into a coherent whole rather than construct academic facts, tying ideas to their sources is less imperative. This absence of acknowledgment itself bestows an implicit acceptance on what is reported and establishes a very different representational context. While students in the soft fields are more likely to encounter argument structures which reach outside the text by citing the source of claims, evidence in the sciences is largely presented in terms of general experimental work or unassigned activity in the field:

> 20. Surface structures of the pathogenic Neisseria have been the
>   subject of intense microbiological investigations for some
>   time.

> (Biology)

A great amount of research has been carried out in the past years to improve the toughness of ceramic materials.

(Physics)

Experiments indicate that such behavior does indeed occur for impact velocities in excess of the critical impact velocity, and. . . .

(Mechanical Engineering)

It has also often been noted that textbooks contain far more unmodified assertions than other forms of academic writing, disdaining the caution of research genres to underscore the factual status of propositions (e.g. Latour and Woolgar, 1979). As in these examples:

21. It is a well-established fact that if the mechanical resonance frequency occurs inside or near the servo bandwidth, the loop's stability is degraded . . .

(Mechanical Engineering)

It is generally agreed that the stigma attached to divorce has been considerably reduced. This, in itself, will make divorce easier.

(Sociology)

Einstein suggested that this might be possible, and indeed this has been experimentally confirmed countless times and forms the basis for many important processes.

(Biology)

When qualifications are omitted the result is both greater certainty and less deference, reflecting a different attitude to both information and readers. Here is a pedagogic model where the expert is distinguished from the novice and the process of learning treated as a one-way transfer of knowledge. The student, in other words, is initiated through the text into a new world of cultural and social competence.

The textbook genre, however, is not simply a celebration of academic truths. While hedges are far more common in the soft knowledge fields (Hyland, 2004b), all writers pick their way through the information they present, sorting the taken-for-granted from the still uncertain. This is particularly the case where authors speculate about the future or distant past (Example 22), or when generalizations may attract challenges if presented baldly (Example 23):

22. . . . earliest cells could also have obtained energy by chemoorganotrophic mechanisms, most likely simple fermentations. Photosynthesis is also a possibility but seems less likely . . .

(Biology)

<u>We cannot say as yet</u> how far these extreme inequalities of gender are <u>likely to</u> become less acute in the near future. It is <u>possible</u> that there are . . .

(Sociology)

23. In such systems, use of an amplifier with a differential input together with the use of input guarding will <u>probably</u> be the answer to this ground-loop problem

(Electrical Engineering)

They <u>seem to be</u> very fundamental functions of language, <u>perhaps</u> because they derive from the basic components of any interaction . . .

(Applied Linguistics)

In contrast, boosters are often used to give readers a clear picture of scientific progress, distinguishing the false assumptions of the past from the assurances of the present. The manipulation of certainty can therefore help establish an ideological schema for students concerning the increasing ability of their discipline to describe the world:

24. <u>We now know that</u> the various components of the substrate are far from exhausted after the initial flushes of growth and sporulation. <u>What has really happened is</u> that Coprinus has seized control by suppressing most of the other fungi. Hyphae of Coprinus <u>are actually</u> . . .

(Biology)

This kind of authorial assuredness helps the writer gain scholastic influence among students. But it is, of course, addressed as much to colleagues as to learners, imprinting a personal stamp on what peers might otherwise see as a recounting of disciplinary orthodoxy. In fact, regarding textbooks as a purely instructional discourse simplifies a rhetorically more complex picture. While writers gain little institutional credit for producing textbooks, an activity often regarded as commercial and unscholarly by university promotion committees, they are aware that they are writing for a professional as well as student audience. It is disciplinary peers who recommend textbook adoptions and orchestrate their use in classes, and it is only with the peer audience that credibility is gained and copies sold (Swales, 1995).

Writers therefore tread a line between representing new material for learners and constructing an acceptable representation of the discipline for colleagues, and this helps to account for the intrusion of personal attitudes and evaluation in this genre. The explicit presence of the writer marks out an individual perspective on the discipline and announces a confident and expert guide in full control of the material, as these examples suggest:

25. <u>I am convinced, for my part, that</u> no ontology – that is to say, no apprehension of ontological mystery in whatever degree- is possible . . .

    (Philosophy)

    <u>My own view is that</u> Krashen's hypotheses do not, on closer inspection, conform to the three linguistic questions.
    (Applied Linguistics)

    <u>What is most interesting is that</u> we can also subtract n (or add -n) by moving the arrow 16 – it positions clockwise.
    (Electrical Engineering)

Textbook authors, then, appear to be very alive to both the role of textbooks in introducing neophytes to the practices of their disciplines and to the judgements of their fellow professionals.

iii. Arguments and asymmetries

While textbooks express something of the literacy practices of their disciplines and their writers' desire to gain professional credibility among their peers, they are principally instructional discourses. The use of both *interactive* resources, which help guide the reader through a text, and *interactional* features, designed to involve the reader in the discourse underline this goal (Hyland and Tse, 2004). We see in these choices a complex array of motives, but most centrally a didactic model concerned with laying out disciplinary content as clearly as possible and constructing the participant identities of professional and novice through the writer's assumptions about reader competence.

Looking at interactive items first, we can identify a range of features in textbooks which display writers' sensitivity to their readers' prior knowledge and processing needs. Perhaps the most obvious of these is the explicit signalling of logicality. Essentially, novices lack the domain knowledge of the expert to make connections between entities and to see the implicit cohesion of a text, and this means that writers must provide a framework which shows links between ideas more explicitly. The following two extracts dealing with lipids, the first from a research article and the second from a textbook, illustrate these different ways of structuring texts:

26. Steryl glucosides are characteristic lipids of plant membranes. The biosynthesis of these lipids is catalyzed by the membrane-bound UDP-glucose sterol glucosyltransferase.

The purified enzyme (Warnecke and Heinz, 1994) has been used for the cloning of a corresponding CDNA from oat (*Avena sativa L.*). Amino acid sequences derived from the amino terminus of the purified protein and from peptides of a trypsin digestion were used to construct oligonucleotide primers for polymerase chain reaction experiments.

(Biology)

27. Although the nature of the fatty acid can be highly variable, the key point is that the chemical linkage to glycerol is an ester link. By contrast, archaeal lipids consist of ether-linked molecules (see Figure 20.1). In ester-linked lipids, the fatty acids are straight chain (linear) molecules, whereas in ether-linked lipids, branched chained hydrocarbons are present. In Archaea, long chain branched hydrocarbons, either of the phytanyl or biphytanyl type, are bonded by ether linkage to glycerol molecules (see Figure 20.1).

(Biology)

While the reader needs domain knowledge to infer connections in the first example, this textbook author takes considerable trouble to spell these out. Using connectives, evaluative commentary, references to examples and code glosses giving on-the-fly definitions, he attempts to link readers' existing knowledge with the new specialized terms of the discipline.

This concern with what the audience can be expected to know and what needs to be spelt out, is also apparent in the copious use of examples and, in the sciences, the constant to-ing and fro-ing between text and visuals. Lemke (1998: 87) observes that scientific concepts are typically 'semiotic hybrids, simultaneously and essentially verbal, mathematical, visual-graphical, and action-operational' so that meanings are created through the rhetorical combination of images and text. Switching the reader between these modes therefore not only highlights particular features of content, but also exposes learners to the ways that the verbal and visual interact in the sciences and the different affordances of these modes. Thus constant exposure, to examples such as these, help induct learners into the discourses of their fields.

28. The radial-vane design shown in Figure 3.14 is just such a variation and does in fact have a nearly linear scale.

(Electrical Engineering)

Figure 10.49 compares the thermal conductivities of many ceramic materials as a function of temperature.

(Physics)

The use of visuals in textbooks, therefore, represents important conventions of field-specific argumentation. By requiring students to interpret and orient to this way of representing reality this contributes towards their acquisition of a new literacy.

Textbooks also take more care than research articles to keep readers informed about where they are in the unfolding text and where they are going. The use of frame markers (Hyland, 2004a and 2005b) to announce discourse goals, indicate topic shifts and label text stages, however, not only helps the reader to process information but can simultaneously construct the writer as an expert guide and the reader as a passive novice following the trail laid down:

29. <u>Finally, one must consider</u> the effects of the measurement methods used to obtain data for repeatability and accuracy.
(Mechanical Engineering)

<u>This chapter discusses </u>the characteristics of the different types of meter movements used to measure alternating current (ac).
(Electrical Engineering)

<u>We shall see in this section that</u> these differences in emphasis imply quite different analyses of the role and functions of the capitalist state.
(Sociology)

The writer speaks here as an authority, an expert knower possessing superior knowledge in an interaction which simultaneously constitutes the reader as less expert.

This differentiation of status is equally clear in the use of interactional features, and particularly in the heavy use of second person pronouns, which are rare in peer-to-peer genres such as research articles. By explicitly acknowledging the readers' presence, *you* is ostensibly the most interactive of pronouns. But as it clearly distinguishes writer and reader it also differentiates categories of knowledge and competence, allocating participants into different groups:

30. Perhaps now <u>you can understand</u> why <u>I and many other teaching mycologists</u> ask our classes to put their culturally determined attitudes on hold, . . .
(Biology)

<u>You should encourage your</u> local engineering chapters, such as Tau Beta Pi, to invite outside lecturers to discuss these topics with you. It is important that <u>you learn how to protect</u>

yourself from being found guilty by a judge or jury for a 'dangerous product design'.

(Mechanical Engineering)

Watch for the answers to the following questions <u>as you read</u> the chapter. They should <u>help you understand</u> the material presented.

(Electrical Engineering)

Once more, then, there is a clear implication that the writer is an expert in full command of the topic and the audience. The texts establish clear role relationships, with the writer acting as a primary-knower in assisting novice readers towards a range of values, facts and practices that will enable them to interpret and employ academic knowledge in institutionally approved ways.

Perhaps the most obvious manifestation of how writers negotiate an asymmetrical relationship of competence, however, is through the use of directives, which expressly emphasize correct courses of action or thought through imperatives and necessity modals:

31. <u>It must be noted that</u> sometimes the molecular weight distribution can be important in ways that are not obvious.

(Physics)

Here are the introduction and instructions <u>you should read</u> to respondents, <u>practice reading</u> them beforehand until they sound fairly conversational.

(Sociology)

As you read this excerpt, <u>pay particular attention to</u> how the teacher sets up the structure of the student–student interaction.

(Applied Linguistics)

While directives are also heavily used in research papers in the sciences (see Chapter 4), they are more common and often more personal in the textbooks, explicitly positioning readers through choices which assume an inequality that is closer to classroom than peer interaction.

Textbooks are therefore a distinctive form of academic discourse. In framing disciplinary knowledge through selecting and sequencing content, writers commit themselves to a perspective on their fields. At the same time, they build both an authoritative picture of their discipline for learners, and an uncontroversial depiction of its central features for peers. By asking (mainly rhetorical) questions, varying their certainty, evaluating ideas, issuing directives, providing definitions and leading readers to particular interpretations, writers massively intervene in

these texts to construct themselves as experts and establish a knowl-
edge-transfer perspective of teaching. At the same time, however,
textbooks are not blandly uniform and in various ways represent the
discourse of their parent cultures, helping students to gain some understanding of the ways that meanings are encoded in their disciplines.

5.4 Conclusions

Although collected here under the heading of 'instructional discourses',
it is clear that the three genres examined in this chapter vary considerably in the ways they map disciplinary knowledge, negotiate information
and establish participant relationships. It is also the case that contextual factors such as discipline, student level, mode of learning and so
on, will play a significant part in how students experience these genres
as part of their courses. Most obviously, however, it would be wrong
to understand any of these three genres in terms of straightforward
information-transfer, as participant relations and complex interactional
patterns lie at the heart of each of them.

Textbooks seem to have a very conservative role and are often
depicted as representations of disciplinary orthodoxy established
through writers' attempts to construct an expert–novice relationship,
while large lectures seem to offer few opportunities for interaction. Corpus data, however, suggests an increasing tendency for these genres to
recognize that students need to be actively involved in learning. We
have seen, in fact, that lecturers, seminar leaders and textbook writers
go to some lengths to establish connections with their students to
encourage engagement and facilitate learning. This is because it is by
no means certain that employing rhetorical choices which distance
one-who-knows and one-who-doesn't can be the basis for successful
learning (Bourdieu and Passeron, 1996). Vygotsky (1978), for example,
has stressed that learning is not simply a passive transference of knowledge from the more to the less competent but involves an interactive
process in which learners increasingly participate in a community of
social practice (Lave and Wenger, 1991). Explicit interaction and negotiation, long established in seminars, are therefore beginning to find
their way into lectures, with questions, discourse markers and personal
pronouns becoming particularly prominent.

Another feature of instructional genres, emphasized in my discussion of textbooks in particular, is that while they principally address
the informational needs of the uninitiated, they are also embedded
in the rhetorical and social conventions of their discipline. Learning a
disciplinary culture and learning its language are inseparable, as this is
the only context in which the language has meaning. Students, in other

words, do not learn disciplinary knowledge independently of language but become competent through an understanding of how language constitutes and is constituted by interaction within a discipline. Instructional discourses are a key way through which this is achieved.

Notes

1. This follows the MICASE classification of academic speech events at the University of Michigan.
2. There is some disagreement about which phonological features are important here, but most analysts accept that a basic requirement is that the speaker ends a phonological paragraph with low termination followed by a jump up to relatively high pitch on the onset syllable of the next unit, sometimes with a pause between them.
3. Both the MICASE and BASE corpora are publicly available and openly accessible through online software.
4. The main spoken academic corpora are:

   - TOEFL 2000 Spoken and Written Academic Language Corpus (T2K-SWAL)
   - Hong Kong Corpus of Spoken English (HKCSE) http://www.engl.polyu.edu.hk/department/academicstaff/Personal/ChengWinnie/HKCorpus_SpokenEnglish.htm
   - Michigan Corpus of Academic Spoken English (MICASE) http://quod.lib.umich.edu/m/micase/
   - British Academic Spoken English (BASE) corpus http://www2.warwick.ac.uk/fac/soc/celte/research/base/

5. This program identifies words and phrases that occur significantly more frequently in one corpus than another using a log-likelihood statistic. This offers a better characterization of the differences between two corpora than a simple comparison of individual words ranked for frequency as it identifies items which are 'key' differentiators across many files, rather than being dominated by the most common words in each corpus.
6. The version of MICASE used here contains 31 large lectures of 257,300 words and 8 seminars of 151,000 words.

6 Student discourses

As I discussed in Chapter 1, student discourse, and particularly writing, is at the heart of teaching and learning in Higher Education. For one thing, this is because knowledge is inseparable from discourse. The subject content that students must acquire is only accessible through specialist forms of language and, in turn, it is this content which gives meaning to those forms. More directly, the spoken and written genres students are asked to produce at university serve the institutional purposes of demonstrating learning and determining progress. They are used to reveal the nature and extent of students' understanding of subject content and control of disciplinary literacies; and this can mean success or failure for students. But while these genres are typically taken-for-granted as straightforward and unproblematic by tutors, they are often regarded with uncertainty and incomprehension by students. Student discourses make communicative demands on students which are very different from those of the home, school or workplace, and in this chapter I turn to look at some of these genres and the issues which surround them.

6.1 Literacy practices

In discussing student discourses it is worthwhile reviewing some of the recent work on the nature of these discourses and students' participation in them. As I noted earlier, dominant perspectives of literacy which regard it as a set of autonomous skills have been challenged in recent years by a view which see writing and speaking as part of peoples' active, material lives. This view takes into account the cultural and epistemological foundations of behaviour and reframes literacy as social practice; re-establishing the importance of context in meaning-making. It reminds us that the ways we use language become *routinized* with repetition and thus established, both in the lives of individuals, what Bourdieu (1991) calls 'habitus', and in the practices of institutions. Concrete instances of language use, such as specific essays, dissertations and presentations, involve drawing on these existing resources, as writers shape their texts according to their personal under-standings, proclivities and purposes.

It is through such views of literacy that we begin to see how actual acts of writing help construct, maintain and change particular social practices and the institutions in which they are embedded. They there-fore offer a more powerful way of understanding student writing than those expressed in terms of skills and deficit, and in this section I explore, very briefly, some implications of this.

i.   Engagement and alienation

The idea of literacy as a social practice provides a way of conceptualiz-ing the link between dominant institutional genres and the individual student's experience of them. It acknowledges that the literacy prac-tices of the academy invoke certain values, beliefs and identities which help support particular social structures and institutional arrangements (e.g. Ivanic, 1998; Lillis, 2001). Scollon and Scollon (1981) use the term 'essayist literacy' to refer to the specific literacy practices which are privileged in Higher Education, and I have discussed some of the features of these, such as incongruence, abstraction and technicality, in Chapter 1. The notion of *practices* therefore helps to locate language use in the activities of social communities, the particular ways they have evolved to engage with the world and construct meanings through discourse. In addition, it also suggests how an essayist literacy might contrast with other practices.

The forms of writing that have grown up around the disciplines are founded on participants suppressing their personal interests and dis-tinctive social and cultural identities to foreground disciplinary arguments and subject matter. Students are typically required to adopt a style of writing at university which involves anonymizing themselves and adopting the guise of a rational, disinterested, asocial seeker of truth. For Halliday and Martin (1993) the acquisition of an academic variety of language involves both significant losses and gains. By step-ping into an essayist literacy writers sacrifice concreteness, empathy with discussed entities and ways of representing change as a dynamic process. On the other hand, they gain the ability to discuss abstract things and relations, and to categorize, quantify and evaluate according to the perspectives of their discipline. Such gains, of course, are only perceived as such if students value what this literacy allows them to do, and the kinds of people it allows them to be.

These particular ways of understanding and discussing the world therefore mean that the acquisition of an essayist literacy not only pro-vides access to new communities and experiences, but is also closely linked to issues of identity. Specific forms and wordings are marked as

124

more or less institutionally appropriate so that authoring is a complex negotiation of a sense of identity and the institutional regulation of meaning-making. But students are not always willing to drop their everyday lives to take up this new identity. The requirement to do so, in fact, often creates conflicts with the experiences they bring from their home community and the habits of meaning they have learnt there. A Creole/English speaking student, for example, responded to Lillis' questions about the non-acceptability of contracted forms in this way:

> It makes me sick . . . I don't think it's important at all [laughs]. But you have to do it? It's like I'm imprisoned, honest to God [laughs]. . . . Everybody knows what 'I'm not' means. It's like trying to segregate, you know, you've got like a boundary that sets, you know, you apart from other people. Why? What difference does it make as long as you get your message across . . .?
>
> (2001: 85)

Adopting these grammatical and lexical choices position writers as sharing the interests, beliefs and practices of an academic community, and clearly this is not too everyone's liking.

This feeling of opposition between the new identity they are being asked to assume and those they are already comfortable with seems to be particularly strongly felt by minority students and by mature students returning to study after a long absence from education. Both Lin (2000), in the case of Hong Kong students, and Canagarajah (1999) in the case of Sri Lankan Tamils, show how students passively resist the assumptions and values which they are assumed to share by using the language. Ivanic (1998), discussing L1 students, argues that returning adults often find the literacy demands of the academy alienating and their practical knowledge undervalued:

> Their identities are threatened and they respond either by attempting to accommodate to the established values and practices of the context they are entering, or – more radically – by questioning and challenging the dominant values and practices, and recognising the possibility of change.
>
> (Ivanic, 1998: 9)

In other words, the identity which manifests itself in discourse is often one which is painfully and consciously constructed for writers and which can involve contesting the valued discourses of their fields.

ii. Culture and preference

While some learners resist the top–down structuring of knowledge as expertise and the imposition of disciplinary identities, many simply remain confused by these conventions. The different cultural *schema,* or system for storing and retrieving past knowledge, they are familiar with are difficult to mesh with those expected in their studies. Culture plays a key role here. Seen ethnolinguistically and institutionally, culture implies an historically transmitted and systematic network of meanings which allow us to develop and communicate our knowledge and beliefs about the world (Lantolf, 1999; Street, 1995). Language and learning are therefore closely bound up with culture and our lived experiences. The fact that cultural experiences help shape schemata means that the knowledge and expectations of minority students may be very different to academic practices and may disadvantage L2 students in particular.

These differences are partly a result of the fact that our cultural values are carried through language, but also because cultures make available certain taken-for-granted ways of organizing our understandings, including those we use to learn and communicate. In other words, they involve interpretation as well as performance, influencing our intuitions about language and expectations about appropriacy and correctness; our sense of audience and ourselves as text producers; our preferred ways of organizing ideas and structuring arguments; and our understandings of the social value of different text types (e.g. Connor, 2002; Hinkel, 2002).

One important element of all this is the potential for culturally divergent attitudes to knowledge to influence students' language use and to effect how their participation in academic discourses is understood. Ballard and Clanchy (1991) point out that these attitudes spread along a continuum from respecting knowledge to valuing its extension. Educational processes in western contexts reinforce an analytical, questioning, and evaluative stance to knowledge, encouraging students to criticise and recombine existing sources to dispute traditional wisdom and form their own points of view. Many Asian cultures, however, favour conserving and reproducing existing knowledge, establishing reverence for what is known through strategies such as memorization and imitation. While such strategies demonstrate respect for knowledge, they may look to Western teachers like reproducing others' ideas. So by ignoring cultural considerations, teachers may see this as plagiarism or repetition, and be mislead into recasting such respect for knowledge as either copying or as naïve and immature writing.

Another difficulty is that differences in rhetorical choices are not viewed as merely preferred alternative ways for expressing ideas, but have pragmatic consequences. A number of studies have commented on the difficulties L2 students can have in modifying the strength of their claims in academic writing, for example, so that their choices lend a direct and authoritative tone to their texts. In a study of hedges and boosters in 1800 GCE exam papers by Hong Kong (HK) and British school leavers, for example, Hyland and Milton (1997) found that the HK students used almost twice as many boosters and the UK students over a third as many hedges. While a small point, such marked choices can lead English speaking readers to make negative judgements about the writer.

We can see in this extract from a Hong Kong student's essay, for instance, that a generous peppering of boosters can make the writer appear rather assertive, over-confident and perhaps even dogmatic:

1. There is _strong_ evidence to _demonstrate_ the relationship between EQ and the academic performance. High EQ is _definitely_ an advantage in any domain of life and _we all know_ that a person with high EQ can _certainly_ manage their own feelings well and deal effectively with others. _The fact that_ the trend from overseas is _always_ affecting Hong Kong people means that schools _must_ now teach boys to be equal to female. They have their right to express emotion.

In contrast, the greater use of hedges in the Native English speaker sample below is perhaps more in line with what a tutor might expect and so attract positive qualities such as subtlety and circumspection to the writer:

2. Britain is _probably_ one of the few countries in the world where the constitution is not written down. This _might seem_ to be _somewhat_ disorganised and although it has worked _fairly_ well until now, I _suggest_ that this is _likely_ to be unrealistic for much longer and it is _possible_ we _may_ need a Bill of Rights as there is in the USA.

Clearly tutors need to be aware of the possible prejudicial effects of unconscious expectations, but it is equally unwise to attribute all aspects of L2 performance to L1 writing practices. Students have identities beyond the language and culture they were born into and we should avoid the tendency to stereotype them according to cultural dichotomies. Spack (1997), for instance, argues that invoking culture to explain writing differences prompts a normative, essentializing stance which leads to lumping students together on the basis of their first language. But while students are not merely cultural *types*, it is helpful to recognize that student difficulties in writing or speaking may be due to the disjunction of the writer's and reader's view of what is needed in a text and that different writing styles can be the result of culturally-learnt preferences. This encourages us to see the effects of different practices where we might otherwise only see individual inadequacies.

A major problem is that the rules of the game are often implicit and are treated as just 'common sense' by their subject tutors who misrepresent academic literacy as a naturalized, self-evident and non-contestable way of participating in academic communities. Simply, if literacy practices are not made explicit, then students failed attempts to produce them can be seen as examples of muddled thinking or illiteracy.

iii.   Situated literacies

While the term 'essayist literacy' is a useful way of characterizing the general register features and rhetorical practices of the academy, it actually conceals a wealth of discursive complexity. Academic language is not one single thing: there are as many literacies as there are socio-culturally distinctive practices (Barton, 1994; Street, 1995). Students entering university are expected to acquire a specialized literacy of discipline-specific rhetorical conventions, and the actual genres and conventions required will differ because each discipline's social practices and ways of thinking differ.

Surveys of tutors and students, for example, show that university writing tasks differ in terms of the type of sources used, prescribed length of texts, cognitive demands, patterns of exposition, and so on (e.g. Horowitz, 1986). More concretely, they are specific to discipline and related to educational level. In the humanities and social sciences, for example, analysing and synthesizing from multiple sources is important, while in science and technology, activity-based skills such as describing procedures, defining objects and planning solutions are required (Mateos *et al.*, 2007). In postgraduate programmes it seems that engineers give priority to describing charts while business studies students need to compare ideas and take a position (Bridgeman and Carlson, 1984). In undergraduate classes, questionnaire data suggests that lab reports are common in science (Jackson, *et al.*, 2006), program documentation in computer science, and article surveys in maths (Wallace, 1995). Collecting these impressions together, Coffin *et al.* (2003) argue that different kinds of writing assignments can be related to four main groupings of disciplines as shown in Figure 6.1.

Differences begin to multiply, moreover, when we move beyond these broad genre labels. When actual assignment handouts and essay scripts are considered, rather than questionnaire responses, it becomes clear that features of common genres can differ considerably across

Sciences	Social sciences	Humanities/Arts	Applied fields
Examples:			
Physics, Geology, Biology, Chemistry	Sociology, Politics, Economics, Media studies, Psychology	English, History, Languages, Classics, Fine arts, Religion	Business, Health and Social welfare, Music, Engineering
Typical genres:			
Lab reports, Project proposals and reports, Fieldwork notes, Essays, Theses	Essays, Project reports, Fieldwork notes, Theses	Essays, Projects, Critical analyses, Translations	Essays, Case studies, Theses, Project reports

Figure 6.1   *Disciplines and their typical written genres (Coffin et al., 2003: 46)*

disciplines. Braine (1995), for example, found that despite a common genre name, no two technical and engineering disciplines wrote experimental lab reports with the same generic structure. Ethnographic case studies of individual students working in particular courses reinforce this picture, revealing marked diversities of task and texts in different fields (e.g. Prior, 1998).

From the student point of view, then, a dominant feature of academic literacy is the need to switch their practices between one setting and another, to control a range of genres appropriate to each setting, and to handle the meanings and identities that each evokes. This is, needless to say, no easy task. It is especially difficult for students enrolled in interdisciplinary degrees such as business studies, for example, which may require students to produce texts in fields as diverse as accountancy and corporate planning. To illustrate this kind of genre juggling, Baynham asks us to think of

> The harassed first-year nursing student, hurrying from lecture to tutorial, backpack full of photocopied journal articles, notes and guidelines for an essay on the sociology of nursing, a clinical report, a case study, a reflective journal.
>
> (2000: 17)

Such balancing acts underline for students that writing and reading are not homogeneous and transferable skills which they can take with them as they move across different courses and assignments.

As we shall see in the following sections, the fact of multiple literacies is reinforced by a growing body of text analysis research which underlines the diversity of genre expectations. In addition, it shows once again that while academic genres are often identified by their conventional surface features, they are not just forms of language, but forms of social action.

129

6.2 Undergraduate genres

I want to distinguish undergraduate and postgraduate discourses in organizing the remainder of this chapter. This is because students at different levels undertake tasks that differ in length, complexity and resources, and because students themselves are engaged in rather different political, social and institutional contexts. In undergraduate environments argumentative genres play a major role in developing students' academic knowledge and socializing them into legitimized, and therefore powerful, social practices. Writing tasks in particular help provide students with the means to engage with 'the social and cognitive practices of evidence formation' (Kelly and Bazerman, 2003: 31) through the use of the disciplinary resources of a literature, theory, data and rhetorical tools. But as we have seen, this acculturation is challenging as the conventions which govern competent practice often remain opaque. In this section I briefly consider three key undergraduate genres: the essay, the project report and the oral presentation.

i. The essay

The 'essay' or 'library research paper' is perhaps the most common undergraduate genre and is found across the disciplinary spectrum from history and English to biology, computing and medicine (e.g. Hale *et al.*, 1996; Moore and Morton, 2005). In an historical survey, in fact, Russell (1991: 78) argues that the essay has 'defined extended student writing in mass Secondary and Higher Education'. Essentially, the 'essay' involves the presentation of a written argument to defend or explain a position, typically drawing on library sources rather than research that the student himself or herself has conducted. While some researchers have sought to describe its genre structure (e.g. Henry and Roseberry, 1997; Hyland, 1990), Larson (1982: 813) points out that the 'research paper as a generic, cross-disciplinary term, has no conceptual or substantive identity' while Johns (1997) observes that students themselves are often unsure what this genre label stands for.

Lillis (2001: 58), in fact, refers to the essay as 'an enactment of the institutional practice of mystery' where students struggle to work out what the tutor requires. In one study, for example, Nelson (1993) found that students different task interpretations influenced their strategies for completing the assignment, with one student relying on the unexamined assumption that the task was simply to assemble and reproduce material, leading to the last minute creation of a pastiche of a few sources. Non-native English speaking students appear to find essay demands particularly daunting, and in a large scale study of 1,457 essays written by speakers of seven languages, Hinkel found that

> 'NNS' academic essays displayed many features of personal narratives (e.g. first person pronouns and a preponderance of the past tense). . . . Even though NS and NNS texts alike exhibited many features of informal speech, the rates of their uses in NNS texts greatly exceed those found in NS academic essays (e.g. vague nouns, coordinating pronouns and predictive adjectives).
>
> (2002: 74)

In a questionnaire and interview study, Krause (2001) found that first-year undergraduates believed that their difficulties with writing assignments could potentially undermine their integration into the university community. They ranked locating relevant sources, working out which points to include and synthesizing ideas from a range of sources as the most difficult aspects of their first essay assignments. The demands of essay writing, in fact, often encapsulate the difficulties of making the transition from school to university, as this quote from one of Plum and Candlin's (2001) psychology first-year participants implies:

> At high school, writing is more straightforward − satisfy requirements and do the right steps: if fulfilled, you get a really good mark. At uni, fulfil requirements and you get an average mark; you have to go beyond requirements to get a good mark.

This lack of unfamiliarity with institutional practices means that students are often bewildered with the responses they get to their essays and often attribute grades to luck or the quirks of individual tutors. It is difficult to understand what counts as 'good writing' as they are given no way of unpacking the epistemological basis of writing and its connections to their disciplines.

In terms of its specialist purpose for undergraduates, the essay is often framed by course guidelines and tutors as a way of helping students to engage with primary research and with disciplinary knowledge building practices. Research suggests, in fact, that students do actually develop the ways of writing valued by the discipline over time. Hewings (2004), for example, found that third year geography students used far more interpersonal themes in their essays than first-years so that they were not simply recounting facts but taking a stance on topics. Similarly, Wu (2007) found that later essays displayed more evaluative stance in their writers' arguments.

In particular, essay writing is said to assist students with the ability to marshal evidence, evaluate it and mount a sustained argument. This is often characterized as moving learners beyond description, a form of 'knowledge telling' (Bereiter and Scardamalia, 1987) or textbook transferral, towards analysis. Most centrally it helps learners to develop a critical approach to texts. One of Woodward-Kron's (2002) teacher trainer interviewees put it like this:

> [I]f they don't have an understanding of how research is conducted, and have some kind of critical understanding of the limitations of research, they can be too easily buffeted by the winds of change. So I want them to be able to, to be actually in their teaching practice to be critical consumers of research that comes out. To question how, where this finding came from, how credible it is, and so on. How it compares.

The essay is therefore regarded as a key acculturation practice, encouraging a critical and questioning attitude and approach to writing which involves making connections between theory and practice, drawing links between theories, evaluating research, and arguing and reasoning.

Central to this enculturation into the literacy and epistemologies of their disciplines is the responses students receive on their essays. Written feedback by literacy tutors is generally welcomed and highly valued by students (Hyland, F., 1998) and seems to lead to improvements in writing (Ferris, 2003). Feedback from subject tutors also has considerable potential to develop an understanding of the cultural context students find themselves in by providing a sense of audience and the expectations of their new community. In addition, content tutors' comments can convey implicit messages about the values and beliefs of the academic community, about tutor and student roles, and about the nature of knowledge itself (Ivanic *et al.*, 2000). Ivanic *et al.* suggest, however, that subject tutors often feel uncertain and insecure about these messages. This is partly because grading not only underlines a power relationship but can, in some cases, conflict with disciplinary epistemologies by suggesting that writing is an object to be measured, that standards are absolute, and that there are right and wrong perspectives on an issue.

In addition to getting mixed messages from feedback, students often feel uncertain about the conventions of this new literacy and sometimes take refuge in borrowing extracts from other texts to express themselves in a suitably 'academic' way. Imitation is necessary in all learning as novices work towards transforming their practices by 'trying on' the discourses of a new community. But this often comes to replace the writer's individual creativity and critical thinking which represent 'good writing' in western contexts. It is true that textual borrowing and intertextuality are now widely seen as implicated in all writing, particularly in electronic contexts where any text becomes a temporary structure in a fluid maze of other texts from other times and contexts (e.g. Kress, 2003). Nevertheless, tutors still expect writers to voice their judgements, display their knowledge and critically evaluate theories, data and claims in their essays. Consequently the ability to display an authorial individuality within the textual practices of a discourse community is a tall order for almost all undergraduates.

ii.   Undergraduate dissertations

At the other end of the undergraduate experience is the *dissertation* or *final-year project report*. This is a major assessment genre in many universities and is the product of a directed research project, often spanning an entire year with credit for two courses. Students are typically assisted by a supervisor who, through regular consultations, approves their proposals, guides their research and monitors their progress.

The purposes of the genre are to assess students' ability to apply theories and methods learned in their courses, to display initiative and to effectively review literature, conduct research, analyse results and present findings. One university course handbook sets the aims out in this way:

> Students will be expected to investigate an area of their own choice to substantial depth, in a way that encourages application and integration of the knowledge gained through the course. The dissertation will allows the student to build self-confidence, demonstrate independence, and develop a professional approach to real-world problem-solving.
> (Materials Technology handbook, City University of Hong Kong)

Reports are typically between 8,000 and 12,000 words long, follow guidelines based on the research paper formats of the discipline, and are assessed partly in terms of meeting genre requirements.

This, then, is a high stakes genre for students and is by far the most substantial and sustained piece of writing that they will do in their undergraduate careers. For some students the demands of independence and systematicity this requires are too great and they drop out (Ho, 2003). Between the first-year essay and the final-year project report, however, most students' writing styles mature tremendously, and for Bloor (1996) this is most evident in their use of lexical metaphor. Her study of final-year project reports in computer science, for example, found considerable use of established metaphorical terminology such as *run, dump, store, housekeeping*, and so on. She argues that computer science undergraduates often have difficulty with such terms but must acquire an easy familiarity with thousands of them, for it is

> the very stuff of which Computer Science language is made, and hardly a sentence can be written in the field without the use of multiple examples of lexis derived by metaphorical extension.
>
> (ibid. p. 68)

More than this, however, she found considerable use of innovative metaphor in these reports as students coined new names for new processes and concepts they developed in their research, demonstrating an expertise with language that is highly regarded in the field.

The undergraduate dissertation is also a challenging interpersonal genre, with fairly unambiguous writer–reader relations. All writers need to consider who they are writing for and adjust their prose to meet the needs of readers. Anticipating readers' expectations and responses to what they write, however, can be very difficult for novice writers. Simply, they are not used to seeing writing as interactive or to imagining the perceptions, interests and requirements of a potential audience. In fact, the idea of audience itself is elusive. Should students be writing for their teachers, their peers or their examiners? What do these readers already know and what do they need to know? Should they be addressed as equals or as expert others? These awkward questions are rarely addressed by teachers or resolved by students and this can often make their writing seem gauche, informal, diffident or over-assertive.

Essentially writers must both present themselves as competent individuals by expressing a disciplinary persona and engaging with readers in accepted ways. The main rhetorical problem facing dissertation writers is to demonstrate an appropriate degree of intellectual autonomy while recognizing their readers' greater experience and knowledge of the field. In other words, they need to position themselves both in relation to their research and their readers, and this is particularly problematic for students from cultures which traditionally value respect for authority (Scollon and Scollon, 1995). As I have noted above, culture intrudes into our communicative practices in significant ways, and undergraduates familiar with different writing traditions and conceptions of teacher status have little incentive to challenge the authority of reader/examiners, particularly as the judgments of these readers have material consequences.

While writers can always resist the relationships implied in a genre, awareness of audience in this context is typically manifested in rhetorical choices which recognize the reader's authority. In Chapter 4, I used the term *engagement* to refer to the bundle of rhetorical strategies writers used to recognize the presence of their readers, and comparisons of student and expert uses are revealing. Table 6.1 contrasts the use of

Table 6.1 *Frequency of engagement features in articles and student reports (per 10,000 words)*

Discipline	Questions	Reader references	Directives	Shared knowledge	Asides	Totals
Student reports	3.8	5.5	11.6	2.6	0.3	23.9
Published articles	4.0	24.8	18.4	3.4	1.1	51.7

engagement features in 64 project reports written by Hong Kong students from 5 universities in 8 disciplines (630,000 words), with the 240 research articles in related disciplines discussed earlier.

As we can see, the research articles contained just over twice as many items and while reader pronouns and directives predominate the ways writers of both genres appealed directly to readers, the frequencies in the two corpora differed considerably.

On the face of it, *you* is the most interactive device in the writer's repertoire as it explicitly acknowledges the reader's presence, but this is rare in these reports. A study by Chang and Swales (1999) suggests that advanced writers often feel uncomfortable about using such informal features in their writing, and I found similar views in my focus group discussions. Students, in fact, often have firm views about what is actually appropriate:

> *Science writing is neutral. I know my supervisor will read my project but I cannot talk to him like in the tutorial. I must just put down the facts without personal idea, just show that I understand the books and that I follow the method.*
>
> (Biology student)

> *In school we learn not to say 'I' or 'you' in our essays. I can use these when I write to my friend, but you don't see them in the formal essays I think.*
>
> (Economics student)

Perhaps as a consequence of the personal implications of these forms, students mainly used *you* with a wider semantic reference, referring to people in general, similar to the indefinite pronoun *one*, rather than with specific participant reference:

3. Whenever you run Windows or any Windows application, you see the API in action.

> (Mechanical Engineering)

135

> Thanks for the advancement in information technology, today, you can get online and find the information you want and communicate with friends who live in foreign countries.
>
> (Information Science)

Here, *you* carries a more encompassing meaning than rhetorically focusing on an individual, seeking instead to engage with readers by recruiting them into a world of shared experiences.

Like academics, students had fewer misgivings about *inclusive we,* which were particularly common in the social science and business reports. The student texts, however, contained just 20 per cent of the inclusive pronouns of the articles, perhaps reflecting students' reluctance to explicitly mark a shared disciplinary membership with the reader. The fact that *we* places the student writer and expert teacher on an equal footing, moreover, can suggest an equivalent level of knowledge. As some students noted, this might be regarded as a shade risky:

> *I cannot tell my supervisor to that he must think this or that. My idea may be wrong and not what my supervisor believes. He might have a different idea.*
>
> (IT student)

> *I must be careful when I write. I don't want to make myself important. Of course it is my project and my result, but I am just ordinary student. Not an academic scholar with lots of knowledge and confident for myself.*
>
> (TESOL student)

As a result, the most common use of *we* was to include a wider audience altogether, making statements which claimed a universal acceptance.

> 4. So, we can not only find Playstation in those big chain stores and those individual game stores, but also in supermarkets as well.
>
> (Business Studies)

> Many people think that we should control scientific progress and prohibit its application to new human problems. But if we do that, we are choosing to have all the misery and suffering that we could prevent by further scientific progress.
>
> (Public Administration)

The most frequent devices used to initiate reader participation, comprising almost half of all engagement features, were directives. As I said in Chapter 4, these devices explicitly recognize the dialogic aspect of argument by instructing the reader to perform an action or to see things in a way determined by the writer (Hyland, 2002b). The fact that there were considerably fewer directives in the reports than the articles once again suggests the rhetorical sensitivity of writers to their readers and their awareness that directives represent something of a perilous strategy. Directives convey a very definite attitude, establishing control both over one's material and one's reader, and can therefore claim an authority which these L2 students did not wish to display, as two of my informants noted:

> *No, they are only for the method section. It is too strong to use them in the discussion.*
>
> (Mechanical Engineering student)

> *I never use 'must' or tell to 'notice' or 'consider'. These words are too strong. It is like a demand and I cannot demand my supervisor to agree with me.*
>
> (IT student)

But directives are complex rhetorical strategies rather than simply autocratic commands. Clearly, telling readers how to perform an experimental procedure is less likely to challenge readers' authority than telling them how to follow a line of argument or how they should understand a particular point. The students saw this use as a conventional means of describing procedures with no face-threatening implications:

> *In engineering we must be clear in describing our method so it can be easily followed. If we are direct then it can be done by another person without problems. I am only reporting what I did and how the method needs to be. It is a general procedure.*
>
> (Mechanical Engineering student)

As a result, students largely avoided the more imposing forms and largely employed directives to steer readers through research procedures. This use overwhelmingly occurred in the hard sciences, perhaps influenced by the traditions of precision and highly formalized argument structures in these fields:

5. Then a criterion function for comparing wear resistance performance <u>must be taken into account</u>.

(Biology)

Test results <u>should be recorded</u> and reported using the standard test report format.

(Information Science)

In sum, the reports contained far fewer of the explicitly interactive features and far fewer of the more imposing forms available to them, students thus preferred to adopt a more circumspect and respectful stance in their reports.

iii. Oral presentations

The type of oral discourses expected in university classes varies considerably, but student presentations, where one or more students speak formally to a class on a term project, lab work, or library research, seem ubiquitous in undergraduate courses across a range of disciplines (e.g. Ferris and Tagg, 1996). There has, however, been relatively little research into this area, despite the fact that ESL students in particular often report feeling intimidated by presenting a monologue to a class (Ferris, 1998; Morita, 2004). While L2 students routinely overcome their fears by reading aloud from a prepared paper or PowerPoint slides, this is generally frowned upon by tutors who regard the presentation as an opportunity for students to communicate directly with an audience (Weissberg, 1993).

One potential problem for speakers is the adoption of an appropriate tenor, or interpersonal attitude to the audience. This is because undergraduate speakers both seek to display knowledge and a presentational competence to the tutor for a class grade and also speak directly to a group of classmates. This peer audience, however, is likely to have broadly similar topic knowledge and perhaps be critical of the academic literacy conventions the genre requires. Speakers may therefore often face a dilemma: they need to convey an effective understanding of propositional matter while simultaneously avoiding the kinds of ideologically inscribed identities the discourse makes available. As a result, tutors tend to find their students choosing to position themselves as student presenters rather than as potential members of an academic community.

This instability of social footing (Goffman, 1981) can be seen in this extract from a MICASE undergraduate presentation:

> 6. Okay we just went through that. Alright so basically how is this all found out? They um, did a lot of work on mice and rats obviously and they're they have O-B O-B mice which um are lacking the O-B gene and these mi- so these mice they don't produce um, a lot of leptin and they were found to be obese as um, was hypothesized by the researchers. So then they went and they took out the gene that makes neuropeptide Y as well as the gene that makes leptin. And these mice so they thought okay since we're taking out both these genes there's not gonna be any leptin, but there's not gonna be any neuropeptide Y to stimulate feeding. So they thought that these mice um, should show decreased um decreased weight like, lower than normal or like about normal. But what actually ended up happening

was these mice were, heavier than the normal mice, but they were, lighter than the mice that were lacked in leptin altogether.

This is a successful presentation of facts, but we can see that the speaker is drawing selectively on the rhetorical resources of academic literacy. While accurately conveying information about the methodology of obesity experiments, he does this within a step-by-step narrative which foregrounds the decisions and actions of scientists rather than the findings or the wider concerns which drive the work. Specialized lexis and passives are mixed with run-on sentences and the conversational features of anecdote, while hesitations, repetitions, fillers, quotative thoughts and vagueness pepper the extract.

So while oral presentations are, like lectures, a monologic discourse concerned with information transfer, they are characterized by the informal, conversational expressions of seminars. A keywords comparison of the 11 presentations in MICASE with the full corpus of 62 lectures, for example, shows that *Um, I, like* and *yeah* are the most distinctive non-content words in the student presentations. A comparison of lexical clusters shows the same top ten most frequent 3-grams in these two genres, although the presence of *I think that* in the student list indicates a more personal and evaluative stance than found in the lectures. This extract gives a taste of this:

7. so I <u>I think that</u> really until you could get a little bit of information, from an oral r- some real data, it's gonna be hard to do to imagine what it is and I and <u>I think that</u> there's a lot of interference in terms of using a written task for some of these things then.

(Linguistics)

This kind of highly informal, 'audience friendly' presentation is often unexpected and extremely challenging for non-native English speakers, but more research is needed to understand the roles, purposes and contexts which inform language choices in these texts.

6.3 Postgraduate genres

The key feature of postgraduate education is the expectation of independence in research. While library research papers and project reports are again the most commonly assigned tasks across the curriculum (Cooper and Bikowski, 2007), this independence is largely demonstrated by conducting a project and presenting the results in written and oral form. Masters and Doctoral pathways clearly differ in this regard, particularly in the length of the examined text, how much credit is gained from coursework, the emphasis given to real world or theoretical topics, the amount of time and effort expended in the process, and the purposes behind it all. While Doctoral work is often a long, lonely apprenticeship for entry into an academic community and career, Masters' students are typically looking forward to returning to their professional workplaces with an additional qualification. Until fairly recently it was widely assumed that students would be able to manage all this without outside help. Current institutional trends, however, are redefining the postgraduate experience as 'training' by supporting students with a raft of writing and research courses. In this section I will focus on the texts produced at the highest level of academic literacy: PhD theses, vivas and acknowledgements.

i. Theses and dissertations[1]

The thesis is the defining element of postgraduate education, yet writing it is often a disheartening experience for students and a challenging one for supervisors. As one supervisor put things:

> PhDs are terrible things, and I don't yet know a PhD student who didn't go through a financial crisis, a mental crisis, a supervisor crisis or an emotional crisis, and that's why it's such an appalling system.
>
> (Delamont *et al.*, 2004: 12)

While this perhaps overstates matters a tad, a growing 'self-help' literature testifies to the challenges writers face, while research and writing courses for students and training for supervisors are now increasingly common in Doctoral programmes (Pearson and Brew, 2002).

The supervisory relationship, in fact, can be extremely fraught. While now a standard part of most academics' workloads, supervision remains something of a private matter and is certainly far less visible than undergraduate teaching. Supervisors, however, are under constant pressure to improve their practice, particularly as its complexities multiply with growing numbers of L2 students in Anglophone Doctoral programmes. One new area of supervisor expertise is advising students on their writing, or at least on where they can get such help. Shaw (1991) found a strong connection between effective writing and supportive supervision, but some thesis writers struggle because they are working without needed literacy support from outside the advisor-advisee relationship (Dong, 1998). Supervisors may not be skilled in recognizing the writing difficulties of their students while an institutional 'deficit discourse' can create an embarrassment which inhibits them from directly referring to a students' proficiency problems (Turner, 2003).

140

Beyond this, students themselves may not have the communication skills to access the information they need from their supervisors, especially if both are L2 speakers of English (Allison, *et al.*, 1998).

Until recently most of the literature on theses writing tended to be heavy on advice and light on analysis. This is largely because the intimidating length of these texts and their considerable variability in presentation limits what can be generalized about them. Thompson (2005), in fact, suggests that it may be impossible to define exactly what constitutes a PhD thesis genre given the wide variety of theses both within and across disciplines.

One of the most researched areas of the PhD thesis has focused on its macro-structure (Bunton, 1999; Ridley, 2000; Thompson, 1999). In a review, Paltridge (2002) identifies four basic types: traditional simple, complex, topic-based and compilation, as shown in Table 6.2.

Many style guides hold the view that there is a traditional thesis which is essentially a longer version of the IMRD format of the science research article. But while this comprised just over half the 30 texts in Paltridge's sample, many of these were Masters' dissertations, and it made up just three of Bunton's 21 PhD theses, one of Thompson's 14 and six of Ridley's 50. More frequent, particularly in the sciences, is what Thompson (1999) refers to as the 'complex traditional' type, which reports more than one study through a series of IMRD chapters following an optional chapter on core materials and methods. A third type Dudley-Evans (1999) calls a 'topic-based' thesis which typically opens

Table 6.2 *Four basic thesis types (based on Paltridge, 2002, pp. 131–132)*

Type	Function	Typical macro-structure
Simple traditional	Reports on a single study	Introduction→Review of the Literature → Materials and Methods → Results → Discussion→Conclusion
Complex traditional	Reports on more than one study	Introduction→Review of the Literature→ General Methods (optional)→Individual Studies^{1-n}→General Conclusions
Topic-based	Uses topics or themes to structure chapters	Introduction→Review of the Literature (optional)→Theory (optional)→ Sub-topic^{1-n}→Conclusions
Anthology	Series of research articles	Introduction→Review of the Literature→General Methods (optional)→Individual Studies^{1-n}→General Conclusions

with an introductory chapter followed by a series of chapters which have titles based on sub-topics of the area under investigation. Finally, Dong (1998) describes Doctoral theses which are based on a compilation of publishable research articles. Essentially this has a similar structure to the complex traditional thesis, but each research article chapter is more concise than the typical thesis chapter and is written more as 'experts writing for experts', than novices 'writing for admission to the academy'.

Swales (2004) summarizes these studies as showing an overall preference for the 'complex' structure which avoids a disproportionately bulky 'results' chapter in the middle of the thesis. He also observes that the Doctoral thesis 'is in a state of considerable flux' (p. 110) which technological change and the opportunities for multimedia dissertations can only hasten.

Another change has been the emergence of professional doctorate degrees, distinguished by the goal of producing 'researching professionals', rather than 'professional researchers' (Bourner, *et al.*, 2001). These doctorates are designed for mid-career professionals who undertake research that emerges from, and will be useful to, their own workplaces and professions, dealing with 'real-world' problems. The textual expectations of these new degrees, however, remain vague as some programmes require a thesis, others a series of publications, and yet others a portfolio of work. Supervisors themselves are often uncertain about requirements as some consider a portfolio to be quite similar to a thesis, 'whereas others see it as also possibly quite distinctive from the PhD and including a range of documents produced during workplace practice with an overarching critiquing document' (Malfroy and Yates, 2003: 127).

More fundamentally, different experiences and world views between practitioners and academics may result in divergent understandings as to what counts as legitimate knowledge and argument. San Miguel and Nelson's (2007) case study of two healthcare workers, for example, found that the key challenges for writers of practice-based research involved:

> framing a real-world issue as a research problem that can be investigated; structuring the text so that the literature contextualises and illuminates that problem; referring to one's own (and one's colleagues') work practices and perspectives without confusing or alienating academic readers; and linking action-knowledge with theory-knowledge – in other words, reflexively documenting professional expertise so that this can be 'counted' as knowledge in an academic sense and integrated effectively with published literature.

142

Another reason why it is difficult to pin down the features of Doctoral theses is because the genre has changed dramatically in some fields as a result of post-modernism and qualitative research methods which question traditional ideas of knowledge and the possibility of an 'objective researcher'. Belcher and Hirvela (2005: 189), for instance, identify the qualitative genre as 'ill defined' and 'fuzzy', while Flowerdew (1999) suggests that L2 writers may consciously avoid adopting qualitative research methods because of the challenges that a self-reflexive and rhetorically complex thesis poses. Richardson (2000) conceptualizes writing as a *method of inquiry* and argues that post-modernism has affected all disciplines by making the boundaries between them more fluid and knowledge more partial and locally situated. Writers therefore have the difficulty of positioning themselves textually in relation to subjectivity, authority, authorship and reflexivity. In a study of 20 recent history and sociology theses from an Australian university, for example, Starfield and Ravelli (2006) present a case for the emergence of a *New Humanities* doctorate marked by writers' construction of a 'reflexive self, unable to write with the classic detachment of positivism'.

Despite the kinds of innovation and change in the dissertation format I have mentioned here, this is essentially a conservative genre which fulfils a rhetorical ritual for institutions as much as it realizes the epistemological values of its writer. Turner (2003), for instance, refers to two unsuccessful submissions in Art History: a CD ROM with various hyperlink pathways and a thesis partly written as a play, partly as a narrative and partly as therapy. They both failed by not providing and defending an argument. As one supervisor noted:

> A doctorate is a public activity. There is no such thing as a private doctorate, and if you cannot communicate your ideas to others and convince others in a public space, it's no good saying 'I'm an unrecognised genius'. It's your responsibility to make yourself intelligible.
>
> (Turner, 2003: 49–50)

The risks of failure, for both student and supervisor, are too great under the present system to permit too much innovation. Change, then, at least for the present, is most likely at points where commitment, subjectivity and the recognition of personal experience come into play rather than at the level of genre experimentation.

ii. The viva

The *viva voce,* oral examination or dissertation defence, varies even more across geographical contexts than the thesis itself, with different ceremonial procedures, numbers of participants, levels of formality and length of meeting. In the UK and Hong Kong, for instance, it is conducted in rather informal fashion, in a closed room with an external and internal examiner and perhaps a chairperson. In Scandinavia, in contrast

> the examination is conducted in a large room, with as many as 50 people present, with a senior university official such as a dean presiding, everybody decidedly dressed up, the examiners in full academic regalia, the chair, examiners and candidate proceeding in and out of the room in a fixed order, and some of the ceremonial in Latin. The seating arrangements may resemble that of a court, and the external examiner is often called 'the opponent'.
>
> (Swales, 2004: 146)

In many European countries, then, the oral examination is a ceremonial event designed to display formal language, elegant debate and intellectual agility.

The US defence, as described by Grimshaw (1989) and Swales (2004), and broadly similar to the practice in many UK universities, is shown in Figure 6.2 (elements in parenthesis are optional).

This description is largely based on just four Michigan defences and Swales (2004: 159) admits that this broad outline is perhaps as specific as we can get given variations in individual cases. It is this structure, however, which gives the event its ritual character, proceeding as it does through a series of questions and responses punctuated by announcements of segment boundaries. The language itself turns out to be fairly relaxed and informal within certain constraints. As Swales points out, participants do not want to 'talk like books' yet they need to employ and display their expertise: they 'wear their scholarship sufficiently lightly so as not to alienate the other participants, whose reactions to their own utterances they (usually) closely monitor' (p. 149).

As evidence of this informality, Swales comments on the laconic way that chairpersons signal the main administrative moves of the event such as opening and closing the session, calling for questions and announcing the recess. He also notes the role of humour in oiling the wheels of the genre, with laughter occurring about once every three and a half minutes on average.

Often humor occurs near the beginning of the event as a way of defusing the tension and alleviating the ceremonial, as here when the chair opens the round of questions following a 1300 word opening presentation by the candidate:

8. Chair: okay, alright well now we'll get down to the hard part. *<SS: LAUGH>*

Chair: okay we'll go around the table and we'll uh uh, ask questions make comments, whatever, so Bob, you wanna start, with you?

(Music defence)

Or here, where the chair actually tells a joke to open proceedings:

9. Chair: I'm committee chair for Elizabeth Behenski, and I'm here to announce the, defense of um Beth's, thesis. and um I'd like to share with you something that um Josh Allens said and I think this had to do with completion of dissertations although the exact citation was not, clear. What he said was, consider the postage stamp. its usefulness lies in the fact that it sticks to one thing until it gets there. <SS: LAUGH>

(Fossil Plants Defence)

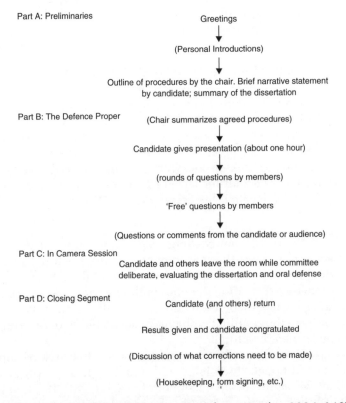

Part A: Preliminaries

Greetings
↓
(Personal Introductions)
↓
Outline of procedures by the chair. Brief narrative statement by candidate; summary of the dissertation

Part B: The Defence Proper

(Chair summarizes agreed procedures)
↓
Candidate gives presentation (about one hour)
↓
(rounds of questions by members)
↓
'Free' questions by members
↓
(Questions or comments from the candidate or audience)

Part C: In Camera Session

Candidate and others leave the room while committee deliberate, evaluating the dissertation and oral defense

Part D: Closing Segment

Candidate (and others) return
↓
Results given and candidate congratulated
↓
(Discussion of what corrections need to be made)
↓
(Housekeeping, form signing, etc.)

Figure 6.2 *Structure of the US dissertation defence (Swales, 2004: 160)*

Another salient feature of the genre is the politeness, concern, and general sense of unremitting goodwill which permeates the MICASE transcripts. While the candidate is often required to defend his or her research against some thoughtful and dogged questioning, there is little of the formal disputation found in some European traditions (e.g. Burling, 1997). One example of this is the apparent reluctance of examiners to engage in direct, no-holds-barred criticism of the candidate's research, as here:

> 10.   S4: uh I . . . uh um I can't really articulate, quite well what I'm, you know what I'm after but there seems something, when I ask myself, well I mean, what do we know about surprise and when would you be surprised and I mean the way, it sounds, in your piece is, that I need an explicit theory, uh that has spelled out, predictions and links between variables to be surprised. uh, I'm not sure I really believe that it seems to me, that, I often find things surprising even though I couldn't surprising or not surprising, even though I couldn't have, you know probably, got the predictions right or, wrong.
>
> (Social Psychology examiner)

> S4: well in his case it's sort of slightly uh colored by a kind of bitterness of lack of recognition mhm rather than overexposure but yeah um, but y- y- you might want to, expand that a little bit because I think you you lean towards it but you don't, re- de- dig, deep into it. the other thing I, would suggest um, remember I mentioned to you that uh, when you talk about, Braxton solo work, I- I I'm, a- a- as the background for for for for for for Jarrett I I wonder if you wouldn't want to um, s- locate it historically just a little.
>
> (Music examiner)

The hesitations, self-deprecations, repetitions and hedges in these extracts serve to suggest that participants see the event not just as an examination, but as an academic conversation. In the US, as in Britain, there is a general expectation that the candidate will pass, perhaps after some required changes or corrections; it is therefore both a rite of passage marking the candidates change of academic status and an intellectual engagement in a topic.

This regard for candidates by examiners seems to be reciprocated by the students, although there is an additional motivation provided by the evaluative nature of the encounter. Engaging with the examiners, and not just their questions, is perhaps a useful strategic option in these circumstances:

11. Candidate: mhm . . . wow, that's an interesting question um, y- you know I me- I mean of- th- the first thing that comes to my mind is . . .

(Music defence)

Candidate: alright, um . . . first of all I'd like to thank all of you, for agreeing to be on the committee, reading the draft, and coming to the defense, being, with me at, my last moment of, graduate school

(Social Psychology defence)

Overall then, discussion is characterized by cooperation and a carefully contrived sense of solidarity where the examiners' right to ask questions and the candidate's obligation to answer are embedded within an academic dialogue. Clearly the four MICASE defences may not be representative of practices in other countries where formality, hierarchy and ceremony play greater roles. They do, however, offer fascinating insights into a neglected student discourse and offer a source of comparison for further research.

iii. Acknowledgements

Finally, I turn to a relatively unsung and disregarded genre which occupies a-taken-for-granted part of the background of scholarly communication: acknowledgements. They are, however, central to the academic practice of reciprocal gift giving and, for students, offer an opportunity to give credit to institutions and individuals who have contributed to the thesis in some way and to make a favourable impression on readers. So while acknowledgements can act as a means of recognizing debts and achieving a sense of closure at the end of a long and demanding research process, they also reveal the writer as someone with a life beyond the page.

Acknowledgements are common in published articles, particularly in the sciences where their high frequency reflects the engagement of scientists in highly developed webs of mutual pre-print circulation, materials exchange and financial dependency (Cronin, *et al.*, 1993). But they are more than a simple catalogue of indebtedness and indication of scholarly interdependence. Ben-Ari (1987), for instance, also comments on their strategic role in 'careering', achieved through the author's management of his or her relations to the disciplinary community and affiliation to particular research groups, leading figures or academic orientations. The acknowledgement is a similarly multiple purposed genre for students, as I found in a corpus of 240 acknowledgements accompanying Masters' dissertations and PhD theses written by Hong Kong students in six disciplines (Hyland, 2003; 2004d).

Students use this public forum to simultaneously recognize academic assistance, research resources and moral support while constructing a particular persona (Hyland, 2004d). I found, for instance, that supervisors were mentioned in every acknowledgement and almost always before anyone else, revealing the intellectual, and often emotional, obligation writers feel towards them. As one student put it:

> *My supervisors really helped a lot in my project, I think it's not just*
> *a formality or politeness. It is like we went through all the difficul-*
> *ties together in these so many years and it is not an easy task.*
>
> (Public Administration PhD interview)

While ranging from the blandly formal to the near reverent, the thanks offered to supervisors is important beyond simple gratitude. Here is both recognition of the supervisors' contribution and perhaps an intimation of a future relationship of mutual indebtedness. For graduates, this can offer the guidance and professional contacts of an established academic, and for the supervisor the esteem and loyalty of a grateful mentee. This, then, as these examples suggest, may not be the end of a relationship but the beginnings of an even more fruitful one.

12. The author would like to express his thanks to his supervisor Dr. Wing Suen of School of Economic and Finance, the University of Hong Kong for his continuous guidance and giving the author a long lasting supervision, support and advice to do this research.

(Business PhD)

I would like to express my utmost gratitude to my research supervisor, Dr. Sze-Fong Mark Yau, for his sincere and selfless support, prompt and useful advice during my research. He gives me a lifetime unforgettable memory of his benevolence, patience, intelligence, diligence and erudition.

(Electrical Engineering PhD)

This strategic dimension of thanking for academic assistance has a more immediate focus in the recognition given to other academics, some only peripheral to the research. This is most pronounced in PhD acknowledgements in the sciences and engineering, where winning the protection and goodwill of established figures is often vital for gaining post-doctoral grants, a lab to work in, or a teaching position. Less obviously, perhaps, we can also see a promotional element where writers acknowledge help with resources such as access to data, clerical assistance, technical help and financial support. While research often crucially depends on this kind on support, we can also see the textual construction of an academic self in the detailing of thanks for prizes, prestigious scholarships, company sponsorships or travel grants.

> 13. The research for this thesis was financially supported by a postgraduate studentship from the University of Hong Kong, The Hong Kong and China Gas Company Postgraduate Scholarship, Epson Foundation Scholarship, two University of Hong Kong CRCG grants and an RCG grant.
>
> (Computer Science PhD)

These help mark the writer out as an individual whose academic talents have already been recognized and who may therefore be a deserving candidate for further honours, or at least a pass in the viva.

The assistance provided in gaining access to data can be no less tactical. In the sciences this tends to address other academics for furnishing preliminary findings, supplying pre-prints, making materials available, and so on. In the human sciences, however, it is largely given to subjects, and while they are unlikely to read the text, this can suggest a professional commitment and academic competence to professional readers. This example is perhaps more effusive than most, but underlines the point:

> 14. I hope this work has given justice to the voices from the margins. For reasons that they would understand, they would remain anonymous in this work. However, if someday they get the chance to read this work, I have no doubt that they will readily recognize their voices that have enlivened the many Sunday afternoons shared together in the parks, under the bridges and under the trees; in the sun and rain; enduring the heat and cold of the changing seasons. I also include those whose search for life's better promises have led them to the classrooms of the YMCA where I have had the opportunities to share moments, outside and inside classroom sessions, that have been made unforgettable by their laughter and tears. And the many nameless others whom I have met in countless encounters whose lives have touched and enriched mine in ways that I would find hard to articulate.
>
> (Applied Linguistics PhD)

Doubtless such expressions of gratitude are sincerely meant, but detailing the rapport established between researcher and subjects hints at the authority and involvement of the writer and of trials overcome. It is making a claim for status as an academic insider.

The fact that almost 40 per cent of the thanks in the corpus went to friends and family for companionship, encouragement and sympathy suggests that the genre is not simply an opportunity for strategizing. Acknowledgements also provided these students with the chance to mention what they considered to be decisive affective influences in completing their research.

15.   I should thank my dear parents and husband. Though they are thousands of miles away from me, their continuous encouragement, silent concern and endless love converge to my momentum to work hard and achieve the best I can.

(Business PhD)

Last, but definitely not the least, I am greatly indebted to my family. It was my parents' unconditional love, care, and tolerance which made the hardship of writing the thesis worthwhile.

(Public Administration PhD)

Such allusions to the tensions and difficulties of graduate study are common, and in thanks to family and friends we see the writer's expression of a personal self with a life and relationships outside the academic. Here writers become more human, individual and sympathetic to readers.

This, then, is perhaps the most explicitly interactional genre of the academy whose communicative purpose virtually obliges writers to represent themselves more openly. Here the writer can present a self disentangled from the conventions of powerful academic discourse types and reveal a real individual coping with the perplexing demands of research and overcoming its challenges. Yet the choices available are not entirely arbitrary. Acknowledgements are not random lists of thanks but a demonstration of competent participation in a disciplinary community. This, then, is a site where writers can textualize themselves as autonomous intellectuals worthy of respect, familiar with the norms and practices of their discipline, and deserving of the qualification sought.

6.4 Conclusions

The growing numbers of students in Higher Education, both graduate and undergraduate, international and domestic, has helped drive a belated interest in student discourses in recent years. As a result of this attention we now recognize far more clearly the kinds of language that are involved in both speaking and writing and the demands these place on students. Most importantly, it is now apparent that acquisition of disciplinary knowledge involves students encountering a new and dominant literacy, which often differs considerably from their previous experience. While disciplines rely on different genres, and to some extent on different strengths in communication, academic ability is frequently evaluated in terms of competence in this 'essayist literacy' so that students often find their own literacy practices to be marginalized and regarded as failed attempts to approximate standard forms.

Supervisors and teachers appear to be uncertain of their responsibilities in terms of literacy support and their responses vary widely. Many subscribe to an autonomous view of academic literacy, taking academic conventions to be unproblematic and seeing essayist literacy as a self-evident way of participating in university tasks. They simply assign a grade to a finished product and shunt students off to the Writing Centre or EAP Unit to fix-up their problems. Others are more sympathetic, but do not feel competent to assist their students with language issues, while yet others rewrite huge swathes of poorly written theses themselves. Each of these reactions assumes a single literacy which students have unsuccessfully mastered: communication difficulties are therefore seen as learners' own weaknesses and support as an exercise in language repair.

The kinds of descriptions of student discourses discussed in this chapter are beginning, together with social constructionist and new literacy perspectives on language in education, to inform our understanding of academic literacy practices. They reveal the fact that students inhabit complex academic and social worlds: taking elective courses outside their disciplines, delivering oral presentations and writing dissertations and engaging in a disparate range of spoken and written genres. Such epistemological, ontological, social and discoursal border-crossings pose enormous challenges for students and teachers alike, but we now recognize the literacy practices that help mark off these borders and begun to describe the genres which will assist students to manage these crossings while maintaining a sense of their own identities as writers.

Notes

1. The term *thesis* is used here, following UK-influenced educational settings, to refer to doctoral research and *dissertation* to Masters level work. I am aware that the terms are reversed in US-influenced contexts, but hope this choice won't cause too much confusion.

7 Popular discourses

A book about the ways of thinking and using language in the academy might seem to leave this chapter out on a limb. After all, popular texts rarely find their way into universities and seldom carry the same prestige as the research, instructional and student discourses we have explored in previous chapters. There is, however, as Cloitre and Shinn (1985) suggest, a continuum of genres used in academic communication and popularizations are part of this wider scientific discourse.

Over the last few chapters I have stressed how the social practices of the academy are interpreted through language for different audiences: for experts, for students, for industry, and for practitioners, and in each case, how this recontextualization offers different ways of understanding academic practices. Extending our interest beyond the mainstream, canonical discourses of the academy gives access to very different scientific practices; offering insights into how relations between science and society are mediated and how the cultural authority of science is promoted. In fact, popular science discourses play an enormous role in shaping most people's views of academic work: informing lay understandings of the interests, methods, discourses, and knowledge that it produces. Such differences suggest that 'science' is not a 'given' in the sense of a monolithic entity always understood in the same way, but a social construct created by different groups with different interests and that these draw upon and sometimes distort what others see as reality. In this sense, then, the books, articles and documentary broadcasts which seek to meet an apparently insatiable demand for the findings of academic research merit attention in this book.

7.1 What is popular science?

The term 'popular science' refers to articles, books, journals, and television programmes produced for audiences without a professional need for information about science. There is nothing new in this. Over a century ago scientists such as Michael Faraday and Thomas Huxley often sought to popularize their work through easily understood public lectures while popular journals regularly circulated research to a Victorian audience. Today popular science comprises an array of formats and a diverse assortment of topics. While dominated by technology, life sciences, and physics, we can see it as embracing all areas of academic popularization including history and linguistics, both of which have gained considerable mass appeal in recent years. Popular science also disseminates work to a range of different audiences. While magazines like *New Scientist* and *Scientific American* may be read by scientists as a way of keeping track of developments outside their own fields, the public gets most of its information about science from the popular media. Science journalism, in fact, has informed public debate and helped to establish research and policy agendas on issues as diverse as stem cell research and energy generation.

The emergence of such popular discourses is, at least in part, a response to the growing impact of science on public life and the maturation of a generation which grew up with 'Sputnik, the environmental movement, the war on cancer, the Space Program and the energy crisis' (Lewenstein, 1987). Some 40 per cent of American adults report having an interest in science and its popularity is born out by the shelf space devoted to it in bookshops, the number of documentaries in TV listings, and the success of specialist journals such as *Popular Science, New Scientist* and *History Today*. Most daily newspapers now have specialized science sections and the number of science articles in the press has been increasing (Pellechia, 1997). TV documentaries such as *Nova* in the USA and *Horizon* in Britain continue to win awards for their dissemination of science and this interest has even seeped into prime-time TV dramas. *CSI, Silent Witness* and *House*, for example, are all immersed in science and technology and have scientists as heroes. In this section I briefly define this area and identify some of its distinguishing features.

i. Celebrated and mass sciences

What unites the diverse genres of popular science is that they all have some personal relevance or entertainment value for a general audience. So, for example, the 2007 shortlist for the prestigious *Royal Society Prize for Science Books* included books on climate science, psychology, human evolution, biodiversity and medicine. The prize was won by Daniel Gilbert, a Harvard University psychology professor, for *Stumbling on Happiness* and some idea of the appeal of this type of discourse can be gained from the remarks by the chair of the judges who commented:

> *Daniel Gilbert's voice provides a witty companion throughout this exploration of the science behind the pursuit of happiness an issue*

153

> which fascinates us all. He uses cognitive science and psychology
> to provide intriguing insights into human nature, helping us to
> understand why we make the decisions we do.

These then are interpretations of academic activity recast with an eye
for the interests, beliefs and preoccupations of a new readership.

But while entertainment is certainly a key aspect of popular science,
it would be a great oversimplification to dismiss it as merely *infotain-
ment*. The author Bill Bryson captures something of this in discussing
his motivation for writing *A Short History of Nearly Everything*:

> The idea was to see if it isn't possible to understand and appreci-
> ate – marvel at, enjoy even – the wonder and accomplishments of
> science at a level that isn't too technical or demanding, but isn't
> entirely superficial either.
>
> (Bryson, 2003: 24)

Here then, is a discourse related to the academy, its work, and its forms
of communication conveying the complexity of scientific content but
stripped of its more forbidding rhetorical features and technical lexis.

Not all popularizations are alike, however, and here we might crudely
distinguish two ends of a cline: *celebrated science* and *mass science*.
Both are concerned with dissemination rather than discovery, but one
embraces the models, theories and events which contextualize discoveries and developments, and the other focuses on novelty and journalistic immediacy. The former celebrates the existence of science and its
professional traditions in a scholarly, essayist fashion concerned, essentially, with making scientific understandings available to an educated
elite eager for prestige knowledge. It is often written by scientists, some
of the stature of Richard Lewontin and Stephen Hawking, rather than
journalists, and deals with broad-ranging and challenging topics like
visual agnosia, black holes and the language instinct. Mass science, on
the other hand, is addressed to a wider audience concerned with science news, focusing on recent scientific developments, such as stem
cell research, space exploration and nanotechnology. It is the very
accessibility of such mass popularizations which permit many science-
related controversies, such as the long-running debates over biological
determinism and genetically modified foodstuffs, to play out in the
public realm where political, philosophical and ideological beliefs mix
freely with scientific evidence.

It is these mass discourses of science which have attracted the greatest research interest. Communications researchers and social scientists
have been particularly concerned with the ways scientific information is
presented to the general public and what impact this has upon social

practices, public policies and political affairs (e.g. Bates, 2005). This opinion-forming role is somewhat uncertain however, as it involves complex interactions between a text and readers' background beliefs. We always have the option to reject the information we encounter and adopt a stance ranging anywhere between the critical and the deferential (Phillips and Norris, 1999). It is interesting, for example, that despite the widespread dissemination of science in the most scientifically advanced country the world has ever seen, creationists can still persuade politicians, judges and ordinary citizens that evolution is a flawed, poorly supported fantasy and ensure that 'intelligent design' is taught as an alternative to evolution in US science classrooms. It is this uncertainty of response which means that popular science may also blur the boundaries between formal science and pseudoscience.

ii. Popular and professional sciences

As a bridge between the professional scientific literature and the realm of popular political and cultural discourse, popular science shares some of the purposes of both but is distinct from each. It generally attempts to wield the authority of science, sometimes even on social and political issues, but both scientific facts and the argument forms of professional science change considerably in translation. This has produced a rather disdainful attitude to popularizations by many who see the scientific elite as producing accurate, privileged knowledge for discerning experts and popularizers disseminating simplified accounts to a passive mass readership. But while some analysts condemn popular treatments for their inaccuracy and sensationalism, others criticize the impenetrability of professional academic writing as a means of enhancing the mystique of science.

Media research, in fact, is often damning of popular science. In a study of 42 science articles in different news genres, for example, Singer (1990) found 93 per cent contained errors of omission, emphasis and overstatement. In fact, scientists themselves are often critical of popular journalism as the stress on novelty in these accounts means that they often lack important information which allows readers to make informed judgements. Nor are such criticisms confined to journalists. Even the celebrated scientist Stephen Jay Gould has been taken to task by those whose research he popularizes as having trivialized their work (Goodell, 1985). But while coverage of specific topics, such as the alleged finding of the 'gay gene', have been sensationalized, others argue that popular science portrays a message created by the scientific community itself so that 'the hyping of research results might be part of a more systemic problem associated with the increasingly commercial nature of the research environment' (Caulfield, 2004).

Importantly, however, the discourse of popular science is not simply the reporting of scientific facts for a less specialist audience, merely eliminating mathematical formulae or complicating details and explaining concepts more thoroughly. Instead, it represents phenomena in different ways to achieve different purposes. Most simply, while scientists are interested in explaining natural and social events by producing evidence for claims, popular science writers are most concerned with establishing the novelty of their topic to attract a lay audience, particularly in the mass media where advertisers pay to access this audience.

Popularizers, then, actually transform the products of elite culture in the process of appropriating them and so influence the nature of elite science itself. Popular science constructs a dialogue across discursive domains by exploiting both science and popular understandings and this involves a very different kind of rhetoric to professional science. Fahnestock (1986), using an Aristotelian classification, identifies the rhetorical mode of these 'scientific accommodations' as 'epideictic' rather than 'forensic' in that their aim is to celebrate rather than validate findings. In other words, the purpose of the scientific literature is to persuade other specialists of the validity of conclusions and the effectiveness of methods. To do this they draw on a standard format and give prominence to results and to tables, figures and diagrams as representations of physical evidence. Popular science, in contrast, attempts to convince scientific outsiders (including scientists in other fields) of the significance of data and conclusions and to celebrate the results, with their validity largely taken for granted.

In speaking to a general audience, however, these texts cannot assume that their readers will always recognize the significance of information in the same way as experts, and so relevance has to be supplied in the text itself rather than presupposed in the context. This means that the original scientific claims are often 'boosted' in popularizations and supplemented with additional appeals which adjust new information to readers' assumptions and values. Myers (1994), for example, shows how facts in popular science are endowed with an authority they do not have in the specialist texts from which they originated. The qualified and tentative statements emphasizing that new observations are consistent with established knowledge are largely replaced by a discourse which emphasizes uniqueness, importance and generality. In terms of additional appeals, Fahnestock (1986) points out that these texts are usually explicit in their claims about the value of the scientific work they report, drawing on either 'wonder' or 'application' appeals by either praising its value or its potential for future benefits. Most simply: questions of utility replace questions of fact.

Such appeals are perhaps most obvious in the tones of breathless enthusiasm for the apparently endless breakthroughs reported in science journalism, reinforcing a technocratic ideology that our lives are constantly improved through scientific development. They are less obvious, however, in the 'broadsheet' end of the popular spectrum. In the books and quality documentaries of celebrated science the wonder and application appeals are more subtle, but ultimately remain supportive of scientific models and world views.

iii.   Popular with whom?

A central question of these discourses is who are popular science texts actually produced for and consumed by? Clearly the existence of both celebrated and mass science formats suggests diverse audiences. In fact, there is no 'public' for science but many publics: the specialist and the lay, the enthusiast and the dabbler, the powerful and the powerless.

Predominantly, however, this is a mass audience for newsworthy science; a group whose interests in current affairs extends beyond the social and political to developments in scientific and technological issues. It is, for example, the audience of the long-running US science documentary series *Nova* which offers 'science adventures for curious grownups', or of the *Scientific American* magazine, whose Homepage promises subscribers:

- 120 plus updates on the latest groundbreaking events in science and technology
- Nearly 60 important reports by leading experts on medicine, space, the environment, archaeology, weaponry and much more
- Intriguing facts, statistics and their implications

But this is just one audience, and very different one to those who enjoy the sophisticated, literary treatments of celebrated science in the books of Gould, Gribbin and Gleick, for instance. Here the term 'popular audience' takes on an altogether more restricted sense as science is recontextualized for an elite educated minority.

Perhaps these audiences might best be understood by looking at how they are constructed through the aims of the discourse producers themselves. Rowan (1989: 165) argues that the goals of popular science writing involve 'making a profit or educating the masses'. The advertisements for home-renewable energy, techno gizmos, and diet plans

157

which typically accompany TV and print mass science reminds us that these media provide manufacturers with access to a particular demographic. But while we can see the audience as consumers of products, the ideology of popular science, and celebrated science in particular, is strongly informational, or even educational. Discussing a radio phone-in programme he did following publication of his best-selling *The Blind Watchmaker*, for example, Richard Dawkins comments:

> The listeners who telephoned were genuinely interested in the subject of evolution. They were not hostile to it, they simply did not know anything about it. Instead of destroying arguments, I had the more constructive task of educating the innocent. . . . Aside from some vague nonsense about 'monkeys', they simply did not know what Darwinism was.
>
> (2006: xv)

Here is a clear educational purpose as writers themselves, whether scientists or journalists, often present popular science in terms of a democratic agenda to bring science to a wider audience.

We tend, therefore, to find a liberal anti-elitism in the justifications of many popular science writers which emphasizes demystification and the translation of the abstract and technical into the everyday and familiar. But while claims of egalitarianism and empowerment are common, some writers go further in regarding it as an improving discourse which can expand the horizons of the masses. In a recent Guardian podcast (Guardian 30 July 2007), for example, the critically acclaimed British novelist Ian McEwan referred to science as a 'marvellous form of engagement with the world', which was too important to be the property of scientists alone. Even more explicitly the palaeontologist Stephen Jay Gould arguably the most esteemed popularizer of them all, talks of academics 'sharing the power and beauty of their field with people in other professions' and reaching 'millions of Americans eager for intellectual stimulation without patronization' (Gould, 1992: 11).

For Fuller (1998), the faith in human intelligence, equality and universal reason which underlies these democratic views carries strong traces of Enlightenment thinking and Victorian philanthropic values. But she also points out that far from being a democratizing and inclusive discourse, 'much popular science has been foremost an attempt to construct dialogue between discursive elites, who for the main share cultural values' (Fuller, 1998: 39). Gould's writing in particular shows how this discourse 'cultivates' readers through a rhetorical flattery which draws on a 'high culture' of literary and classical allusions. More generally, however, the discourses of science, including the humanities, technology and social sciences, carry enormous prestige and

158

cultural authority in the West due to their apparent ability to answer our questions about the world, to explain its intricacies, satisfy our curiosities, and improve our futures. For this audience, then, popular science gives access to the dominant modes for interpreting reality and our own existence. It also accrues status to those who possess such prestige knowledge.

7.2   Two popular science genres

The distinctive language forms and audiences of these different popular science formats might best be illustrated by consideration of two very different genres. TV documentaries and the books of celebrated science written by eminent scientists and science writers offer contrasts not only in medium but also in the ways they represent their subjects. As we have seen in the last section, while celebrated science 'cultivates' it's readers by rhetorical practices which insinuate prestigious reader positions, documentaries are altogether more accessible and adopt different rhetorical practices.

i.   TV documentaries

Documentary films represent a broad category of visual expression that seek to 'document' reality in various ways, either by simple observational methods, or more often through a narrative format. The genre has a distinguished history and a new appetite among cinema-goers for 'long-form' documentaries, such as *Super Size Me*, *March of the Penguins* and *An Inconvenient Truth* together with a new 'short form' appearing on the web is breathing new life into the genre. On television, the popularity of documentaries has made the *Discovery Channel* the most widely distributed cable network in the US, reaching more than 92 million households, and giving it a global audience of 431 million homes in 170 countries.

A considerable amount of documentary output addresses scientific topics, particularly relating to history, natural history, health and medicine, physics, social geography, and technology. Perhaps the two main exponents of this genre are the long-running and popular series *Nova* and *Horizon*. *Nova* is a popular science series broadcast on PBS in the US and in more than 100 other countries. Using a format which often includes interviews with scientists directly involved in the subject, and occasionally footage from the actual moment of a particular discovery, it has covered topics such as global warming, elementary particles and string theory. In the UK, the BBC2 flagship programme *Horizon* enjoys similar prestige and longevity, still attracting large audiences after

159

45 years of broadcasting. During that time, however, both presentation styles, and audience expectations of documentaries have changed dramatically. In the 1960s the celebrated historian AJP Taylor could speak live directly to camera without notes, autocue or visual aids in his series of lectures on the *First World War*. In the last few years, in contrast, Peter and Dan Snow are supported in their *Battlefield Britain* by sophisticated computer graphics, re-enactments of the battles, and 'interviews' with soldiers from both sides.

One key feature of the science documentary genre is the use of strongly narrative storylines. Onega and Landa (1996: 6) observe that 'narrative creates its meaning by noting the contributions that actions and events make to a particular outcome and then configures these parts into a whole episode'. Since real events do not offer themselves to us as stories, this means shaping them from a particular point of view, generally by focusing on actors and their behaviour and by emphasizing the relationships between things rather than the things themselves. In popular science documentaries this reshaping often takes the form of a detective story: an interpretive repertoire in which only one theory of science is readily expressed and endorsed (Curtis, 1994).

The 'detective' metaphor is apparent in many episodes of *Horizon*, for example. An episode often begins with a 'taster' laying out the key issues as a problem, followed by a focus on an individual scientist's human and intellectual journey of discovery gathering facts and eliminating alternatives, usually with a 'plot twist' or breakthrough about midway just as defeat seems inevitable. It typically ends with commentary from a sequence of experts and people affected by the discovery edited together to create a sense of summary.

This format has been criticized as 'dumbing down' science and chasing ratings at the expense of content (Orlowski, 2006). One former *Horizon* editor, for instance, expressed concern about this narrative emphasis on human stories at the expense of science and its effect on the series:

> When the balance between science and human drama was right, then the results were exceptional. Lynch's prize-winning film, Fermat's Last Theorem, described as a love story between a man and his equation, achieved that balance. And mixed in a series with other approaches, it is a valid format. But the extent to which it came to be used and to which the science often took a secondary role began to change the feel of Horizon, compounded by its weakness in describing the big ideas.
>
> (Goodchild, 2004)

By arbitrarily adopting one position on an issue rather than presenting a variety of positions, the format suggests that the average viewer can only cope with one clear 'narrative', no matter how deceptive such a view of the world might be.

Curtis (1994) argues that this approach not only emphasizes the human over the scientific, but promotes a particular normative view of science. While appearing to simply describe events, detective narratives conform to particular Baconian values about the proper conduct of scientific research. In contrast to the individualistically cut-throat and competitive depiction of research in Watson's (1980) account of the discovery of the structure of DNA, for example, the good detective avoids preconceptions, carefully gathers facts to test hypotheses, employs induction to eliminate alternatives, and eventually arrives at certainties. As Curtis (1994: 444) observes:

> It is not the vain, arrogant, disputatious cosmologist who succeeds in science, but rather the humble, plodding scientific gumshoe.

In the narrative of induction by elimination the choices open to the hero become increasingly limited and the final outcome is almost an inevitability. A good narrative, then, has a beginning, a middle and an end, moving from doubt to certainty and arriving at a resolution. Scientific investigations, in the narrative telling, always reach closure and the patient scientist is ultimately vindicated.

ii.   Popular science books

The Popular science book, as I have discussed earlier, is a very different creature to the documentary. More wide-ranging in subject matter, more discursive in presentation, and more meticulous in contextualization, these books represent an expression of an expert view on large topics like evolution, language, and the origins of the universe. They take the form of an argument rather than a narrative and move analysis to an altogether different level. This is not the plodding detective inductively sorting through clues, but the wide sweep of a confident assimilator weaving a detailed understanding of a topic while manoeuvring us towards a particular view of it.

In these texts a commonsense world of the everyday is gradually reconstrued into a technical one through the use of familiar landmarks and recognizable cultural allusions. The reader is not simply titillated by science as in popular documentaries, persuaded to accept a novel claim as in professional texts, or apprenticed into the semantic configurations of science as in instructional discourses. Instead, the science model is celebrated and an educated audience offered the writer's learned perspective. At the same time, however, the reader is being led to a schemata of what is known and how it can be known and while

161

encoded in different ways, these schemata draw on a similar explanatory repertoire to reinforce a strongly materialist vision.

Celebrated science very clearly rejects the positivist and technicist orientation which often characterizes popular science journalism by setting work more clearly in historical contexts. But while emphasizing humanist and social elements, it nevertheless offers an ideological interpretation of the world by endowing social relations with nature's authority. Essentially, this is a discourse of universal laws, analytical procedures, and controlled experiments in which organisms are removed from the systems in which they exist and represented as incapable of flexible responses to their environment (Lewontin, 1998: 117). All phenomena, from the molecular to the social, are seen as special cases of overarching laws where individuals are passively subject to forces which they confront but cannot influence. In their different ways, three of the most well known, and best-selling, poplar science books underpin this view: Richard Dawkins' *The Blind Watchmaker* (1986), Stephen Hawking's *A Brief History of Time* (1988), and Stephen Pinker's *The Language Instinct* (1995). Each attempts to explain its subject to a non-specialist audience in terms of a relatively unified theory of underlying order with which human subjects have little option but to comply.

Interestingly, although these arguments deal with widely different topics, they are characterized by considerable similarities in lexical choice. When common function words (pronouns, articles, conjunctions, etc.) and topic-specific terms (such as *species, cells, quarks, mass, grammatical*) are stripped out, then over half of all words in the most frequent 100 in each text are found in all three books. These fall roughly into four broad functional areas, shown here with a few examples:

Hedging:	*may, might, must, seems, should*
Vagueness:	*something, thing, people*
Argument:	*point, fact, know, means, example, case, meaning*
Description:	*difference, different, first, called, new, number*

While some of these words are also relatively common in research writing, only *different, may, number* and *example* occur in the top 150 words of my 1.5 million word research article corpus. These similarities across the three books compared with research papers point to the very different ways that this genre presents information and seeks to engage readers.

One distinctive feature is the ways celebratory science deploys the familiar academic signals of tentativeness and circumspection. Hedges are used extensively in professional texts to withhold commitment to a statement for personal protection against the possibility of being proved wrong or to open a space for readers' alternative views. A common use of hedging in this genre, however, is to present a mistaken belief which is then contradicted by the facts. Sometimes such beliefs are seen to be held by past generations of scientists as yet unenlightened by modern discoveries, but more often, these false assumptions are attributed to an unspecified general audience of the book (1):

1. Therefore they must be classified together with mammals. This may seem strange, but personally I can treat it with equanimity.
    (Dawkins, p. 279)

    Here, one would think, linguistics runs into the problem of any historical science: no one recorded the crucial events at the time they happened . . .
    (Pinker, p. 20)

    Imaginary time may sound like science fiction, but it is in fact a well defined mathematical concept . . .
    (Hawking, p. 139)

In fact, arguing with the reader by disabusing him or her of the incorrect beliefs which have been ascribed to them is a common rhetorical practice in these texts. The vague notion of *people*, for example, is often invoked to represent such straw-readers (Example 2) and the expression *in fact* frequently employed to contradict our complacent understandings of how things are (Example 3):

2. Many people do not like the idea that time has a beginning, probably because it smacks of divine intervention.
    (Hawking, p. 49)

    There are people for whom 'random' would have the following meaning, in my opinion a rather bizarre meaning.
    (Dawkins, p. 307)

3. The proposal was quickly withdrawn. There is a good reason why so-called laziness in pronunciation is in fact tightly regulated by phonological rules.
    (Pinker, p. 177)

    All very neat and orderly it seems. But in fact, on the disc itself the arrangement of the text is anything but neat and orderly.
    (Dawkins, p. 173)

Ultimately, however, following this oppositional expert–novice discourse, the reader is brought onside by a rhetoric of inclusion. The audience is inducted into the current consensus of science, or at least the writer's version of it, by establishing a platform of what we might all readily assent to. Reference to what we all know heralds that reader and scientist alike have triumphed over the limitations of common sense to achieve a more enlightened understanding:

4. We now know that neither the atoms nor the protons and neutrons that are within them are indivisible.

(Hawking, p. 68)

We know this because we find, scattered around the chromosomes, long strings of DNA text that are identical.

(Dawkin, p. 119)

We know fallible memory is the cause of these errors because the irregular verbs that are used the least often by parents. . . .

(Pinker, p. 178)

Reference to such relatively esoteric scientific knowledge as the common property of writer and audience therefore intimates a transfer of expertise to the reader as an honorary holder of the prestige understandings which they seek. The discourse of celebratory science therefore not only offers a persuasive and academically endorsed representation of the world, but also admits an educated elite into its mysteries. The conventions of academic argument, the ways that research is discursively reconstructed for social agreement, thus extend beyond the claims presented to peers or teachers to draw on values influenced by more everyday concerns and ideologies. For science's publics, as for scientists, what is accepted depends on the conceptual frameworks they employ – and these are social, not abstract intellectual constructs.

7.3 Science journalism

While documentaries and books are significant carriers of popular science discourses, the field is actually dominated by mass science journalism, which has grown considerably in recent years. Not only are bookstalls full of journals such as *New Scientist, History Today* and *National Geographic*, but science-related articles make a regular appearance in weekly international news journals such as *Time, Newsweek* and *The Economist*, as well as in daily papers. This then, is how most people encounter science. With an emphasis on uniqueness and generality expressed in a tone of factual authority, these texts present research as news and create a context for scientific information very different to that found in the research literature. In this section I discuss this rhetorical context of science journalism in more detail, focusing in particular on its organizational patterns, accommodation of readers, and expression of stance.

i. Narrative and novelty

The first thing that strikes a reader familiar with research reporting when browsing a mass science article is the way that it is organized. Instead of finding the main claim towards the end of the paper as in a research article, it is typically foregrounded at the beginning. Nwogu (1991), for instance, found that journalistic accounts typically open with a background move which contextualizes the research issue as a problem for readers and then follows this with the main outcome of the research, often including reference to the scientists themselves. These examples are typical:

> 5. A simple spit test could soon help police officers keep tired drivers off the road. Sleep researcher Paul Shaw and his team at the Washington University School of Medicine have discovered that amylase, an enzyme in saliva, correlates to sleepiness.
>
> (*Popular Science*, Nov 2007)
>
> New moms beware: If you want to shed those extra pounds you packed on while pregnant, you better get your sleep. A new study shows that women are more likely to lose baby fat if they get over five hours of shut-eye a night.
>
> (*Scientific American*, Nov 2007)

This deductive rhetorical pattern highlights the novelty and importance of the topic rather than the steps taken to get there and this can be confusing for scientists. Myers (1990: 141), for example, reports how the editor of the *New England Journal of Medicine* published both an original immunology article and a version rewritten by a *Science* journalist who gave greater attention to organization, explication and clarity. General physicians subsequently wrote applauding the fact that even difficult topics could be made accessible to non-specialists while immunologists complained that the revised version was harder to read because information wasn't where they expected to find it. Both groups therefore had different views about the best way to write immunology based on their own needs, background knowledge, discourse expectations, and reading purposes.

Myers (1990) goes on to argue that, like the documentary genre discussed earlier, science journalism focuses on the *objects* of study rather than the disciplinary *procedures* by which they are studied. Professional papers construct what he calls a '*narrative of science*' which follows the argument of the scientist, arranging time into a parallel series of events and emphasizing the conceptual structure of the discipline in their syntax and vocabulary. The discourse embodies assumptions of impersonality, cumulative knowledge construction, and empiricism. The popular articles, on the other hand, present a '*narrative of nature*', focusing on the topic itself rather than the scientific activity of studying it. The presentation is chronological, and the syntax and vocabulary create a picture of nature which is external to scientific practices: the scientist acts alone and simply observes nature.

These different language choices convey different meanings of both research and science. This is most obvious at the opening of papers. Myers, for example, compares the titles and opening paragraphs from two articles reporting the same research: the first, in the scientific journal *Evolution* (Example 6) and the second in the popular *New Scientist* (Example 7):

6. **The reproductive behaviour and the nature of sexual selection in *Scato phaga stercoraria L.* (Diptera: Scatophagidae). IX. Spatial distribution of fertilization rates and evolution of male search strategy within the reproductive area.**

   The present series of papers is aimed towards constructing a comprehensive model of sexual selection and its influence on reproductive strategy in the dungfly, *Scatophaga stercoraria*. The technique used links ecological and behavioural data obtained in the field with laboratory data on sperm competition, for which a model has already been developed.

7. **Sex and the cow pats**

   Why do peacocks sport outrageously resplendent plumage compared with their more conservative mates? Why do majestic red deer stags engage in ferocious combat with each other for possession of harems, risking severe injury from their spear-point antlers?

The extract in (Example 6) has an extremely precise title and an opening paragraph which emphases a link between research methods and the promise of an explanatory model while (Example 7) has a title which highlights what is most interesting to lay readers and then hooks them by anthropomorphizing animal behaviour.

Another obvious way that popular journalism claims attention and establishes novelty is through the use of visuals. Figures, diagrams, photographs, and so on are a key means of conveying meaning in science research articles where they are manipulated and assembled to enhance the visibility of desired information and make the message more convincing (Knorr Cetina and Amann, 1990). But striking visual images have been used to attract readers and illustrate the wonders of nature in popular science journals since the mid-nineteenth century, although the messages they convey are very different. Miller (1998), for example, shows that while visual elements in academic texts are mainly arguments, following formal conventions organized for maximum persuasion and access to new information, in the popular press they function largely to attract the reader to the article and to explain rather than prove.

Visuals in popularizations often distort the argument through oversimplification or depict the implications of research without containing the original proofs. In the biological reports studied by Miller, for example, visuals transferred from research journals lost their comparative elements which showed cause and effect to depict the event as a narrative which separated steps in a story. The visuals in *Newsweek* served to pull the reader in with colour and anthropomorphism, summarizing the findings while losing the detailed argument. Thus, together with a narrative structure and a focus on the objects of study, visuals in popular science journalism work to grab the reader's attention and highlight innovation.

ii. Accommodating readers

In addition to structuring articles to stress novelty and present a story of research relevant to a mass audience, popularizations also differ from professional discourses in the ways they frame information for a non-science audience. This involves constantly defining new concepts, making explicit links between entities and personalizing research practices.

One obvious way in which this is done is to avoid jargon or offer an immediate gloss where this is not possible. Specialist terms and mathematical expressions are largely absent from popularizations and code glosses are inserted to clarify what the writer assumes may be an unfamiliar usage, as here:

> 8. Prozac, the popular antidepressant, blocks the action of a pump that sucks serotonin, a key mood-regulating chemical, out of the gaps between two neurons.
>
> (*Popular Science*, Nov, 2007)

> Chess's team took advantage of DNA microarray technology to survey the activity of certain gene variants in the genome of human B lymphocytes (white blood cells that, like T cells, help fight infection). By cataloguing point mutations in the genetic code, they could decipher when two different alleles were being transcribed from DNA into RNA (the template that provides the recipes to build specific proteins).
>
> (*Scientific American*, Nov 2007)

167

The unfamiliar is thus made intelligible by brief, on-the-hoof, definitions and explanations.

Non-scientists are also accommodated in these texts by the writer's management of cohesion. Cohesion depends on the semantic structure of a text and so on the reader's expectations and knowledge, particularly knowledge of lexical relations. However, because scientific texts rarely contain replacement or pronouns for cohesion, non-specialists may struggle to see connections across sentences (Myers, 1991).

Journalists, however, make these links explicit by using a variety of cohesive devices to serve as the basis for inferences about the meanings of any unfamiliar terms. In this extract from an article in *Scientific American*, for example, the writer is careful to ensure that the reader is able to recover the links describing the genetic causes of mental retardation. Through the use of repetition, conjunctive phrases such as '*which means that*', determiners (*the, those*), and synonyms, connections are specified and the passage becomes transparent:

> 9.   In humans, the disorder stems from a mutation on the X chromosome as a three-base sequence begins to repeat over and over in a section of the *fragile X mental retardation 1* gene (*FMR1*). The portion of the gene where this error multiplies does not code for a protein, which means that several repetitions of the sequence can occur without damaging the fragile X mental retardation protein (FMRP). People who have a gene with a sequence that is repeated 50 or fewer times are considered normal; those with fewer than 200 repetitions are carriers of the disorder. Individuals with more than 200 triplets, however, have disruptions to the promoter region of *FMR1* that block the gene from being transcribed into RNA and forming a protein, thereby prompting onset of the syndrome.

Clearly the 'naïve reader' is unable to learn the cultural system encoded in the language of science merely through reading scientific texts, but the representation of scientific knowledge in popularizations at least provides a basis for understanding the products of that culture.

A third way in which popularizations seek to engage with the incomplete knowledge-base of the non-specialist reader is to emphasize the credibility of the source of the information they report. In professional articles reliability is largely bestowed on findings by the writer's display of craft practices and expert handling of recognized research methods. Attributions to other scientists mainly function to align the writer in a particular camp or reward researchers who have conducted relevant prior work. Popularizations, on the other hand, bestow credibility on scientists through their *position* in an institution, only identifying particular scientists when they are directly relevant to the research being reported:

These examples illustrate something of this:

> 10. Scientists are just starting to identify a class of what they call vulnerability genes. In essence, they come in two forms: lucky and unlucky. 'If you have one version, you are relatively resilient in the face of stress', <u>says Brown University psychiatrist Ben Greenberg, who is collaborating with the Cleveland Clinic group</u>.
>
> (*Scientific American*, Nov 2007)

> 'We are now in a position to be able to generate patient- and disease-specific stem cells without using human eggs or embryos', <u>Shinya Yamanaka, leader of one of the research teams at Kyoto University in Japan, said in an e-mail interview</u>.
>
> (*Science News*, Vol. 172: 23, Nov 2007)

Instead of embedding new work in a community generated literature to demonstrate its relevance and importance, these texts use direct quotes to indicate the external origin of material in the current text and give credence to that material by drawing attention to the credibility of its source. In other words, it is journalism rather than science.

Not only is authority given to the research by underlining the status of informants, but scientists are often allowed to tell the story themselves through direct quotes, making extensive use of the reporting verb *say*, as in this example:

> 11. 'Human embryonic stem cells should not be considered only as sources in transplantation medicine; they can be used also . . . to create models for human genetic disorders', says study co-author Nissim Benvenisty, a geneticist at The Hebrew University of Jerusalem. 'This is the first example where we in this field learn something new about a human genetic disorder that we couldn't learn from the existing models'.
>
> (*Scientific American*, Nov 2007)

These options are hardly ever found in the article genre where imported material is overwhelmingly rewritten as a summary from a single source or as a generalization combining several different studies. In popularizations, then, science is both made intelligible in the characteristics of conversation and brought to life through the direct quotes of those involved.

iii.   Attitude and interactions

The use of direct quotes, researcher identification and a sense of immediate value all reaffirm the role of personal authorship in scientific
research which is usually absent in professional academic discourses.
In addition to the voices of researchers, however, the perspectives and
interests of journalism also intrude into the text, with popular articles
offering more emphatic claims about the findings of research and a
fuller expression of personal attitude than professional discourse.

As we saw in Chapter 4, hedges and other modal devices which
allow writers to comment on the factual status of propositions are key
features of research genres, indicating the degree of caution or assurance that can be attached to a statement. Writing for a peer audience,
academics must carefully handle their claims to avoid overstating their
case and risk inviting the rejection of their arguments. Hedges, then, are
crucial to negotiating knowledge claims with a potentially sceptical
audience, but scientists see their work as far more tentative and mediated than journalists, who take a very different view towards facts. For
the science journalist, hedges simply reduce the importance and news-
value of a story by drawing attention to its uncertain truth value.

As I noted above, the process of transforming research into popular
accounts involves removing doubts and upgrading the significance of
claims to emphasize their uniqueness, rarity or originality. Fahnestock
(1986) illustrates this by showing how the qualified conclusions from
an article in *Science,* reporting a longitudinal study of mathematical
aptitude, were transformed by two popular magazines. The original
research article looked like this (with hedges underlined):

> 12.   We favour the hypothesis that sex differences in achieve-
> ment in and attitude toward mathematics result from superior
> male mathematical ability, which may in turn be related to
> greater male mathematical ability in spatial tasks. This male
> superiority is probably an expression of a combination of
> both endogenous and exogenous variables. We recognize,
> however, that our data are consistent with numerous alterna-
> tive hypotheses. Nonetheless, the hypothesis of differential
> course-taking was not supported. It also seems likely that
> putting one's faith in boy-versus-girl socialisation processes
> as the only permissible explanation of the sex difference in
> mathematics is premature.

(Benowa and Stanley, 1980)

In *Newsweek* (Example 13) and *Time* (Example 14), however, this tentativeness is removed in favour of unmodified assertions which amplify
the certainty of the claims and, in so doing, the impact of the story:

170

13. The authors' conclusions: 'Sex differences in achievement in and attitude toward mathematics result from superior male mathematical ability'.

14. According to its authors, Doctoral Candidate Camilla Persson Benbow and Psychologist Julian C. Stanley of Johns Hopkins University, males inherently have more mathematical ability than females.

In glamorizing material for a wider audience, then popular science texts do not help readers to see how scientific facts can be questioned or modified removing hedges removes doubt.

It is also interesting to find these text littered with attitude markers, indicating the writer's affective responses to material, pointing out what is important and encouraging readers to engage with the topic. Unlike their role in research papers, however, these markers do not signal the writer's affiliation to shared disciplinary attitudes and values. Instead, they help to impart an informal tone and underline the accessibility of the material. The attitudes expressed are those which the interested lay reader might be expected to hold, rather than the writer:

15. Researchers have hit upon <u>an unusual way</u> to spin tiny propellers – set them on top of tiny bouncing bubbles.

    (*New Scientist*, Nov 2007)

    Algae <u>seems a strange</u> contender for the mantle of World's Next Great Fuel, but the <u>green goop</u> has several qualities in its favor.

    (*Popular Science*, Nov 2007)

    <u>Call it a renaissance, call it a revolution</u>; in the field of light microscopy, it is well under way.

    (*Scientific American*, Nov 2007)

Readers are drawn in and engaged by having attitudes attributed to them as the writer suggests what we might think on the basis of a community-endorsed common sense. Reaching out to the reader in this way, however, is rare in professional research articles which appeal instead to the presupposed understandings of the peer group.

Personal pronouns and questions are also far more common in the popular texts, where they perform a similar role of engaging readers in the issues:

16. <u>You may be</u> familiar with the examples of the evolution of drug-resistant bacteria or agricultural pests. Microbes and

171

pests may change the fastest, but they are not unique. <u>We see</u> rapid evolution most often where some force (<u>often us</u>) has given it a jump start by suddenly and dramatically altering an organism's environment.

(*Scientific American*, Nov 2007)

Solix must struggle for answers before it can sell a thing: Which species of algae will produce the most oil? What's the best way to grow it? And not least, how do you extract the oil from the algae once it's grown?

(*Popular Science*, Nov 2007)

Attempts to engage readers also lie behind the considerable use of similes and comparisons in this genre. Often writers use these to relate complex processes to more familiar events of our everyday lives, taking the reader's perspective to present the strange and exotic in the terms of the commonplace and unexceptional. Here a simile and a reference to a commonplace kitchen appliance work to better convey a biological process and the appearance of equipment for producing alternative fuel:

17. To get into the brain they must be shuttled across the blood–brain barrier by specialized transport proteins. Like passengers trying to board a crowded bus, amino acids compete for rides on these transporters. Not only does tryptophan have paltry representation among the passengers; it also competes with five other amino acids for the same transporter. Aced out by other amino acids, tryptophan thereby has a tough time hitching a ride to the brain.

(*Scientific American*, Nov 2007)

Two parallel tracks, each about 60 feet long, protrude from the snow like the twin runners of a giant upended sled. A washing-machine-size box studded with dials and blank displays sits at one end. Nothing moves, nothing glows, nothing hums. The future of alternative energy sits silent before me. This is what's going to make gasoline obsolete?

(*Popular Science*, Nov 2007)

In sum, science journalism provides an excellent illustration of the ways writers set out the same material for different purposes and readers. This is a discourse which establishes the novelty, relevance and newsworthiness of topics which might not seem to warrant lay attention by making information concrete, novel and accessible. Findings are therefore invested with a factual status, related to real life concerns, and presented as germane to readers with perhaps little interest in the ways that they were arrived at or in the controversies surrounding them. Readers, in fact, experience the academic world and its discourses as a succession of discoveries in the relentless advance of inductive science. In sum, science journalism works as journalism rather than science. It is written in ways which make the research accessible and allow a non-specialist audience to recover the interpretive voice of the scientist.

7.4 Conclusions

While often dismissed as mass-produced pseudoscience or misleading oversimplification, the discourse of popular science cannot be regarded as a single genre or dismissed so easily. Because of its widespread dissemination it is actually, most people's only encounter with academic research. As a result it inevitably exercises considerable influence on personal perceptions, popular opinion and public debate and so must be seen as key element of academic discourse.

Popular science is also of considerable importance to teachers, researchers in cultural studies, and those interested in the discourses of the academy. We have seen that popularizations take a variety of forms which can be located on a cline. At one end are the books which offer a celebration of scientific knowledge for an educated audience eager for prestigious knowledge. These are typically written by specialists or scientists themselves in a measured, literary style which situates research in historical and social contexts, elaborating controversy and disagreement while avoiding sensationalism. At the other end of the cline is the mass science journalism discussed in the previous section, emphasizing novelty, significance and immediacy to make research socially relevant, findings assured and benefits tangible.

In recontextualizing academic research for a wider audience, much popular science stresses the importance and value of findings and portrays research as an immediate encounter of a scientist with nature. Researchers thus become actors and the claim becomes a discovery event; jargon is evicted or roughly glossed; certainties replace tentativeness, and nouns regain their verbal status. Such a presentation therefore not only influences the ways science is understood, but also reconfigures its discourse, reminding us that science is a communicative activity conducted among human beings. For readers of popular science, investigators are real people conducting research, putting forward ideas and finding ways to support them, so that science once again becomes ideas to be discussed rather than information to be received.

173

8 Wider worlds

Much of this book has been concerned with the nature and role of academic discourse as it functions in the university: how it works to construct knowledge, disciplines, academics, and students. In focusing on its transformation into popular discourses, however, it becomes clear that the influence of academic discourse is not restricted to these contexts but spreads into the popular domain and into social debate. This closing chapter continues this discussion, pushing the context of academic discourse outwards from disciplinary communities into wider worlds. Here I briefly consider the impact of academic discourse on political and economic relations, on perceptions of science, and on international scholarship and publication.

8.1 Economic power and cultural authority

Academic discourses clearly possess considerable cultural and political clout. This is partly because of their prestige among an educated elite and the agenda-setting role of mass science in the media, but largely it is due to the control they afford over the physical and intellectual circumstances of our lives. For many people, such discourses represent access to reliable knowledge and its authority is underpinned by what it tells us about the world we live in and how these understandings are routinely transformed into practical benefits. Their power rests on both what they contribute to our material comfort and on an ideology which clearly demarcates them from the everyday discourses of politics, commerce, religion, or common sense. They embody a rationality apparently devoid of vested interest, emotional conviction or political and economic values. In this section I briefly consider these wider connections.

i. Academic discourse and economic power

One central reason for the power of academic, and particularly scientific, discourse is the control it provides over our physical environment through technology. This control lies at the centre of economic development and therefore at the heart of power in Western societies, where both government and private resources are ploughed into academic research. Lenoir (1997: 47), in fact, believes that disciplines are firstly political institutions whose main purpose is to assemble and channel the social and technical practices essential to the functioning of modern capitalism. This link is also clearly spelt out by Rose (1998: 237) in discussing the growth of science:

> Modern science would not have happened without the evolution of industrial capitalism. From Chaucer's Treatise on the Astrolabe, to the astronomy, mathematics and physics of Galileo, Descartes and Newton, the impetus and application of scientific discovery was in the maritime expansion of European trading and colonisation, and warfare between imperial powers. From Priestley to the present day, physical, chemical and geological sciences have developed in tandem with the beginnings, expansion and technologisation of mass industrial production, for which mercantile and imperial expansion provided the capital.

Academic work can only be supported in conditions of economic surplus and it is the allocation of this surplus which closely binds universities to their host societies. Increasingly, knowledge production has become ever more closely integrated with its application, driven by the emergence of global markets for knowledge. The intensification of international business competition has expanded beyond the capacity which in-house research can sustain and a new form of knowledge, evaluated by standards of applied usefulness, has replaced traditional academic knowledge based on standards of truth (e.g. Gibbons *et al.*, 1994).

A discourse of social utility, whether current or potential, has therefore come to dominate the academy so that the idea of research driven by disinterested curiosity now seems rather quaint. In straightened times where universities depend ever more on commercial sources of income, academics must pay their way by seeking 'consultancies' and funding from industry and commerce rather than governments and educational charities. This context of commercial interests and the bureaucratic imperatives of modern capitalism mean that many academics feel a conflict between quality audits and market pressures on one hand and cherished academic values on the other.

In this environment, disciplines can be seen as rival interest groups engaged in constant competition for power and resources. The discourses of different disciplines, and of research programmes within disciplines, stake out different definitions of reality and often compete to gain acceptance for them. The ability to conduct research, and the prestige that accompanies the publication of its results, is therefore often contingent on persuading powerful bodies in the non-academic sphere to provide resources, and as a result marketing norms have crept into university discourses (Fairclough, 1995). Through effective and well-organiseized political lobbies these promotional strategies have paid off handsomely. The hard sciences in particular have been very successful in articulating research with the priorities of government, military and business elites. Research in medicine, genetics, neuroscience, military and space technology, and 'big science' generally, requires massive public investment and a clear harnessing of research to secular goals.

Utility tends not to be a strong point of the humanities, however, where research is often too personal and context restricted to gain significant funding, but the growth of Higher Education and the media, has allowed history, philosophy, literature, and law to expand considerably. By promoting a strong academic image and a discourse of liberal scholarship in contrast to the relentlessly commercial goals of the sciences, these disciplines have been able to persuade governments of their usefulness and to actually expand their rates of publication and Doctoral students. The social sciences have increased their prestige in a different way, largely by engaging in policy-oriented research or by developing general laws of human understanding. Fields such as social work, business studies, marketing, and education have been extremely susceptible to commercial and political influences and even applied linguistics has become increasingly implicated in political and military objectives (e.g. Rampton, 1995).

Mammon has drawn closer to the academy, but the influence of political and commercial interests on academic practices should not be seen as a one way street. Science is as much a part of the zeitgeist of contemporary capitalism as commerce and can set agendas as well as respond to them. In the longer term this has a significant impact on how we understand scientific knowledge and the value that we place on it, leading to increased scepticism concerning the role of academics and of the objectivity of academic discourse itself.

ii. Ideology and authority

Academic discourses are not only related to the wider world through their support for industrial infrastructures, but also through the hegemonic perspectives they make available for understanding the world. These are prestigious and influential ideological systems, what Stanley Aronowitz (1988) calls the 'discourse of the late capitalist state':

> Science is a language of power and those who bear its legitimate claims, i.e., those who are involved in the ownership and control of

its processes and results, have become a distinctive social category equipped with a distinctive ideology and position in the post-war world.

These discourses now exert a considerable, although often unnoticed, influence on all aspects of our everyday lives. They have spilled out of the academy to become the dominant mode for interpreting reality and our own existence, shaping our world view and influencing control of both material and human resources. As Halliday and Martin put it

> Every text, from the discourses of technocracy and bureaucracy to the television magazine and the blurb on the back of the cereal packet, is in some way affected by the modes of meaning that evolved as the scaffolding for scientific knowledge. In other words, the language of science has become the language of literacy.
>
> (1993: 11)

The discourse practices of a powerful social group have, therefore, become a dominant influence in many walks of life, increasingly providing both a model for communication and a filter for perception. As we have seen, popular discourses have played a major part in disseminating schemata which facilitate a mechanically materialist view of the world directed to utility, but this is a discourse which reaches even further, influencing the ways we see ourselves and respond to our environment. Crowding out alternative perspectives, the dominant discourse is one of empiricism and universal laws which promotes a view of the world as composed of individuals passively subject to forces outside their control. In biology, for example, the doctrine of genetic determinism, that all human traits are encoded in our DNA from birth, puts the individual at the mercy of inescapable laws (Lewontin, 1991). Similarly, popular notions which suppress diversity to represent evolution as a fixed progression help construct an analogous picture of social and technological evolution as a march of uninterrupted progress to the present, justifying current political realities and humankind's rightful control over the physical environment (Gould, 1998).

In other words, scientific discourse is used for ideological purposes, justifying social relations by endowing those relations with nature's authority. The conventions of academic argument, the ways that research is discursively reconstructed for social agreement, draw on community values influenced by the ideologies and power relations which dominate socio-economic arrangements. For science's publics, as for scientists, what is accepted as true depends on the conceptual frameworks they employ – and these are social, not abstract intellectual constructs.

iii.   Understanding of science

In addition to shaping understandings of the world, academic discourses also fashion the ways we understand science itself. The public largely accepts science's claims, for example, that it offers unbiased insights into natural phenomena and beneficial pay-offs in terms of medicine, technology, and modern comforts. While not all disciplines have enjoyed the same status, the power of academic discourses has persuaded us to accept that the academy is deserving of state funding, that the curricula of schools and universities is best decided with their input, and that scientists should be autonomous and left free to police their own practices.

More generally, science is largely complicit in its misrepresentation to outsiders. As we saw in the last chapter, popular discourses support a definite, naively empiricist view of science that contradicts the picture embodied in scientific articles. This is also the view, moreover, which seems to inform representations of science in politics, commerce and secondary education (e.g. Sutton, 1996). To write science is to simply observe nature by proceeding from given questions to unambiguous answers, unencumbered by preconceptions, research decisions, or methodological setbacks (Myers, 1990: 189). Scientific knowledge is therefore made intelligible as everyday reasoning, disguising negotiation, personal interest, and social construction, and perpetuating unexamined myths about language operating to simply report external truths. The nature of academic language as speculative, interpretive, and theory-constitutive is lost as discourse is refashioned as reportage. Meanings, then, are not treated as socially contingent nor language as the means of exploring possibilities with others.

The integrity and neutrality of this discourse, however, is increasingly questioned and there seems to be a growing public disillusionment with the claims of science and the academy more widely. This is partly due to the close associations between academics and powerful interests, particularly in areas such as the development of genetically modified crops and weapons technology. In addition, public concerns about nuclear energy, genetic engineering, and the export of toxic waste, for example, have accelerated growing unease concerning science's destructive power and its apparent inability to control the forces which most threaten the quality of our lives.

A series of high profile academic fraud cases has further undermined confidence. In the last few years, for example, the Lawrence Berkeley National Laboratory in California admitted that one of its top scientists had fabricated the discovery of two new chemical elements and Jan Hendrik Schön, the rising star of nanotechnology at Bell Laboratories, was accused of fabricating the findings of up to 22 of his most recent published papers. Most celebrated and damaging, however, has been the case of Hwang Woo-Suk, professor of biotechnology at Seoul National University. Considered until recently as one of the pioneering experts in stem cell research, his claims in the journal *Science* in 2004 and 2005 to have succeeded in creating human embryonic stem cells by cloning were eventually shown to have been fraudulent. More insidious than this, and so harder to detect, are abuses which are coming to light where peer reviewing may be suspect due to the bias of referees. The problems are particularly acute as large numbers of scientists now work for organizations that are merely front groups for the fast food or pharmaceutical industries.

The power of the academy to provide knowledge regarded by the public as universal, objective, and socially beneficial seems seriously under threat as academic claims come to be more widely seen as socially contingent and dependent on political and economic patronage.

8.2 Global participation and academic discourse

The wider worlds in which academic discourses operate and interact with are not restricted to nation states and multinational corporations but include the global contexts of research and publishing. English is now unquestionably the language of international scholarship and an important medium of research communication for non-native English speaking academics around the world. Perhaps one in five of the world's population now speaks English with reasonable competence (Crystal, 2003) and the language has come to dominate the dissemination of knowledge. Universities in many countries now require staff to present at international conferences and, more crucially, publish in major, high-impact, peer-reviewed Anglophone journals as a pre-requisite for tenure, promotion and career advancement. These are the topics of this section.

i. Globalization of academic practices

Research shows that academics all over the world are increasingly publishing their research in English and finding these papers are cited more often. References to English language publications have reached 85 per cent in French science journals, for example, and English makes up over 95 per cent of all publications in the *Science Citation Index*. Swales (2004) observes that many leading European and Japanese journals have switched to publishing in English and this Anglicization of published research can also be seen in the dramatic increase in papers written by Non-Native English speakers appearing in leading English language journals. Many prestigious Chinese universities stipulate that their PhD students must have at least one paper accepted by an international journal before they can graduate, while the Chinese Academy of Sciences supplements the salaries of researchers who have published internationally. With libraries increasingly subscribing to online versions of journals, the impact of English becomes self-perpetuating, since it is in these journals where authors will be most visible on the world stage and receive the most credit.

The driving forces behind this global spread of English in academic life are complex and often tied to political and commercial interests, but one can view these developments in contrasting ways. On the one hand it is possible to see the growth of English as establishing a neutral lingua franca, embracing speakers of all languages and efficiently facilitating the free exchange of knowledge across the globe. In this view English empowers it's users as ever larger numbers of people can access the products of research and participate in networks which go beyond the local (Pakir, 1999). Alternatively, English might be regarded as a tool of linguistic hegemony and cultural imperialism assisted by governments, foundations, and private companies to cultivate markets for Western labour, products, and ideologies (e.g. Pennycook, 1994).

Despite having to jump the language hurdle, there is also evidence that the contribution of non-native English speaking academics to prestigious English language journals is actually increasing (e.g. Tomkins *et al.*, 2001; Wood, 2001). The main reason for this is that publication in international journals is no longer optional for many academics. Not only are they motivated to participate in this global web of scholarship and have their work widely read, but publication in English is now inseparable from the process by which prestige and credibility are assessed. Publication is not only important in tenure and promotion applications, but is also often central to good department reviews and high Research Assessment Exercise rankings in many countries. In other words, university funding is now often directly linked to individual publication lists as educational practices around the globe become ever more subject to administrative audit.

ii. Publishing in English

While the number of L2 researchers successfully publishing in international English language publications has steadily increased in recent years, it is likely that they represent a relatively small number of countries and elite institutions. In fact, there is a real danger that the hegemony of English may serve to exclude many L2 writers from the web of global scholarship (Gibbs, 1995), thus depriving the world of knowledge developed outside the Anglophone centres of research. So while all newcomers feel challenged by writing for publication, Non-Native English speaking researchers may feel particularly intimidated by the demands it makes on them. This is certainly the view of journal publishers and editors who have viewed the surge of NNES activity in the publishing arena with some alarm. This extract from an editorial in *Oral Oncology* is typical of this concern:

> An emerging problem facing all journals is the increasing number of submissions from non-English-speaking parts of the world, where the standard of written English may fall below the expectations of a scientific publication.
>
> (Scully and Jenkins, 2006)

As a result, publishers and universities have begun to offer mentoring and tutoring services to writers while referees and editors often provide a great deal of unsolicited language assistance.

As we saw in Chapter Four, L2 writers themselves similarly regard poor language skills as a major problem in drafting and revising academic papers, with Flowerdew's (1999) respondents, for example, reporting that they felt hampered by 'less facility of expression' and a 'less rich vocabulary'. But while language issues are often of greatest concern to editors and writers alike, the most serious barriers may be less linguistic than financial and physical, with the structural divisions between the advantaged Northern and disadvantaged Southern hemispheres creating the greatest inequalities (Wood, 2001). Canagarajah (1996), for instance, discusses how 'non-discursive' financial and physical aspects of the research and publication process can create difficulties for periphery scholars, with access to the literature, print quality, postal costs, and editor–writer interactions posing serious problems.

A central cause of difficulty for peripherally situated writers, then, is their intellectual and material 'isolation' from mainstream practices and disciplinary knowledge. Gosden (1992: 115) summariseizes the views of his sample of science journal editors in this way:

> The broad term 'isolation' covers many causes, for example: not carefully reading 'Instructions to Authors'; unfamiliarity with the journal and its academic level; not previewing previous literature well and relating to others' work, possibly due to a lack of literature/library facilities; a lack of awareness of what constitutes publishable research; and unfamiliarity with the broad (and unwritten) 'rules of the game'.

181

By focusing on scholarly writing as a situated practice and by examining the local interactions that occur in negotiating the passage of a paper to publication, discourse analysts have begun to unpack some of these rules. This has helped (i) to reveal how participation in the global publishing network functions as a mode of disciplinary learning for new scholars; and (ii) to provide EAP instructors with evidence-based descriptions of texts and processes so that these can be made explicit to novice researchers (Hyland, 2008b). The number of courses supporting junior researchers writing for publication have has grown enormously. Notwithstanding that the practices of publication and associated expectations differ markedly across fields, these focus principally on isolating key features of texts and making them explicit to writers. This not only involves raising awareness of the ways language works in disciplinary arguments and encouraging writers to reflect on their own practices (Swales & and Feak, 2000), but also providing them with strategies for analysing target publications and navigating the processes of submission and revision.

iii. Open access and global networks

Open access is a growing revolution in scholarly publication which has the potential to transform the isolation experienced by thousands of 'off-network scholars'. By making published research accessible to a massively wider audience, it promises to creatively restructure the dissemination of research, the involvement of researchers, and academic discourse itself. Open Access refers to journals which use a funding model that does not charge readers or their institutions for access. While it is commonly labelled 'author pays' to differentiate it from the traditional 'reader pays' model of journal subscription, it is usually those who fund the authors' research who pick up the bill. In fact, 'readers' are also mostly academic institutions, although what they pay with open access is likely to be substantially less than they pay at the moment. The 'losers' are the small but highly influential oligopoly of commercial publishers who account for the production of most scholarly journals.

While the main driver for this change has been unsustainable developments in the publishing industry in recent years, it is made possible by new modes of production and distribution which facilitate international scholarly collaboration and sharing. Scientific publishing, however, is a highly lucrative business worth $7bn a year, and so the open access movement depends on flourishing electronic journals outside the ambit of corporate ownership and pricing. Traditional publishing arrangements are based on an alliance between commercial presses and individual scholars, with a large pro bono contribution from the latter who write, referee, and edit articles and journals. From subscription rates and circulation numbers it has been calculated that under this model the scientific community currently pays about $4500 per article and with journal prices increasing faster than inflation, library budgets are unable to keep pace. All but a few libraries in elite universities and research centres are now able to provide access to the journals their staff and students need. For one third of the current cost, however, research articles could be made available to all, including academics in the developing world, instead of to a dwindling band of subscribers.

Open access experiments have flourished since the introduction of the internet and there are now at least two million peer-reviewed research articles freely available online. Most working paper archives and articles on personal homepages are free, for instance, as are collections in institutional and subject repositories, funded by the authors' research grants or institutional funds. *BioMed Central*, for example, makes nearly 200 open access journals in the fields of biology and medicine freely and permanently accessible online immediately upon publication and the *Public Library of Science* publishes electronic journals in biology, medicine, genetics, pathogens and other fields free to readers.[1]

Many of the bigger open access projects have been highly collaborative, drawing on both the communicative affordances of the internet and political commitments to the advancement and accessibility of knowledge. Notable among these are initiatives by the *Association of Research Libraries* and the *Open Society Institute*[2] although open access has also been actively encouraged by political bodies such as Western governments and the European commission, which believes that research funded by the European taxpayer should be freely available over the internet (Wray, 2006). The United Nations-sponsored HINARI (Health InterNetwork Access to Research Initiative) programme, for example, provides public institutions in developing nations with free or low-cost online access to 3,400 major journal titles in the biomedical and related social science fields, while Online Access to Research in the Environment (OARE) gives 100 of the world's least-developed nations access to over 1,000 peer-reviewed environmental science journals.

This obviously maximiseizes the chance of other researchers locating and reading articles and as a result goes some way to expanding the reach of global research networks and widening the participation of geographically and politically peripheral scholars. But while these initiatives enabled users to download 4.5 million articles in 2006, they offer only a partial solution to the access problems of the developing world. Many large low-income countries such as India, Brazil, China, Pakistan and Indonesia, for example, are currently excluded, largely, one supposes because these countries have significant research programs and so generate substantial income to publishers through subscriptions.

Clearly, many political and technical issues remain to be resolved before anything approaching truly global access will be possible. It is as yet uncertain, for example, how submission procedures, file transfers, editorial software, and article storage will be most effectively managed. Nor is it clear how the range of different cultural practices this expansion of research reporting will involve is will to impact on our conceptions of plagiarism, on processes of peer review, or on the conventions of academic discourse itself. Despite these uncertainties, the next decade is likely to produce major changes in international research, scholarly publication, and, as a consequence, academic discourse.

8.3 Conclusion and closing

My main purpose in writing this book has been to provide an overview and review of academic discourse: identifying the key concepts associated with this discourse, exploring its importance, and evaluating the research which informs our understanding of it. In doing so, I hope to have shown something of how communicative conventions influence academic practices. A major reason for making a study of academic discourse then, is that it allows us to unpack the assumptions such discourses carry about knowledge, about relationships, and about how these should be structured and negotiated. More than this, though, the study of academic discourses takes us beyond the academy to reveal their impact on how we comprehend and act in the world.

Philosophically, an understanding of academic discourse helps to undermine a naively empiricist view of knowledge. In other words it provides the tools to question research findings which are often presented as truths based on dispassionate observation, exacting methodologies, and informed reflection. Instead, it shows us that this is a privileged, historical, and agreed-upon set of procedural and rhetorical practices which imposes a single right way of explaining and talking about reality, making all others superfluous. By studying academic discourse then, we discover a form of persuasion rather than a guarantee of reliable knowledge. It weakens philosophy's claim to be the arbiter of pure reason and challenges science's right to speak for nature. An understanding of academic discourse therefore unpacks the connections between knowledge and the social practices of the academic community. It shows how particular genres and conventions play a privileged role in ratifying meanings and legitimizing the forms of interaction which produce conditions for agreement.

The study of academic discourse also helps to uncover the political and ideological dimensions of academic life. It helps illuminate, for example, that disciplines are sites of power and authority which influence differential access to resources for creating knowledge and which define discipline approved realities. It also helps show something of how powerful gatekeepers are able to define legitimate ways of conceptualizing and investigating problems and influencing how these can be publicly discussed in journals and at conferences. Power is revealed as the ability to expertly employ institutional discourses and academic discourses as the mechanisms for maintaining the positions of institutional elites.

More generally, the analysis of academic discourse shows that science is inextricably part of its wider social context. These connections are perhaps most clearly illustrated in the ways that new socio-political formations give rise to new ways of conceptualizing problems and new discourses of inquiry. The Copernican revolution, which represented a radical new view of the natural order, for example, did not involve new data or new technology, but a conceptual reconstruction only possible because of the changing class structure of sixteenth-century Europe. Similarly, Darwin's theories of biological evolution both borrowed from, and gave a strong impetus to, the mid-nineteenth century ideology of competitive individualism which encouraged free-trade and unfettered commercialism. Today, positivist and technicist beliefs dominate academic methods and discourses, sustaining a political orthodoxy which has little time for humanist and social values.

Academic discourse also provides insights into the connections between the academy and the economy. As we have seen in the discussion above, competition for global markets has created a demand for knowledge which outstrips the capacity of in-house research labs. Faced with expanding student numbers unmatched by government funding, universities are turning increasingly to commercial sources, which means that powerful interests are able to set agendas and determine the directions and terms in which research is conducted and discussed. The science parks in Europe, and large military projects with MIT, Berkeley, and Stanford in the USA, for instance, represent intensified interactions between industry and universities and the closer bonding of economics and knowledge production. More locally, university qualifications are demanded in ever increasing domains and the control of academic discourses has become essential for a career in almost every profession. Because of the connections with economic

185

development and production, then, academic discourses influence every level of education, technical training, and shop-floor manufacturing, establishing a workforce stratified by the access it has to such discourses.

Finally, and of most obvious utility, an understanding of academic discourse is important for the practical pay-offs it can have in raising students' awareness of academic literacy and inducting newcomers into academic and professional communities. The ability to create, comprehend, and appropriately respond to specialist texts is central to demonstrating learning, constructing disciplinary identities, displaying affiliation, and creating a persuasive argument. Therefore the more we know about what it looks like and how it works, the better we are able to help students and academics develop the advanced literacy competencies and insider knowledge involved in submitting an essay, preparing a conference paper, or crafting a manuscript for publication.

Most importantly in this regard, the study of academic discourse also helps us see that it is not a limited textual practice or the result of correctly following a set of predictable steps. Instead, it tells us that communication involves a creative balance between the expression of an individual perspective and the expectations of a disciplinary community, where language is used simultaneously to shape an individual identity, a disciplinary persona, and a convincing argument. We need to include in this understanding the individual's experiences together with a sense of self, of others, of situation, of purpose and – above all – of the linguistic resources to address these effectively in social action. Language is a basic resource for constructing our relationships with others and for understanding our experience of the world, and as such it is centrally involved in the ways we negotiate, construct, and change our understanding of our societies and ourselves.

In peeling the onion of context, we see that academic discourses have both a local and a societal relevance, and the former is often produced and understood in terms of the latter. We live in a world substantially influenced by the privileged discourses of the academy, and it is important for an understanding of this world that we are able to reconstruct the social contexts within which such discourses are produced and supported, and which they largely conceal. One conclusion which emerges from these pages is that academic discourse is not simply a labelling system for transmitting established information but an interpretive system actively used for generating new understandings in different genres, across different contexts, and for different purposes. The study of this system, I believe, reconnects academic activity with its users and takes us out of the lab and library and into the classroom, the conference hall, the newsstand and the home. Scientific language, like science itself, is an activity of human beings and should be seen in this wider context. Academic discourse is a social practice and inseparable from the lives and experiences of those who create, negotiate, contest and act upon it.

Notes

1. The Directory of Open Access Journals (http://www.doaj.org) currently lists 3000 journals with 170,000 articles covering a range of fields.
2. The Scholarly Publishing and Academic Resources Coalition is an initiative of the *Association of Research Libraries* and can be found at http://www.arl.org/sparc, while and the Budapest Open Access Initiative (http://www.soros.org/openaccess/) is promoted by the *Open Society Institute*.

References

Allison, D., Cooley, L., Lewkowicz, J. and Nunan, D. (1998). 'Dissertation writing in action: The development of a dissertation writing support program for ESL graduate research students'. *English for Specific Purposes, 17*(2), 199–217.

Allison, D. and Tauroza, S. (1995). 'The effect of discourse organisation on lecture comprehension'. *English for Specific Purposes, 14*(2), 157–73.

Aronowitz, S. (1988). *Science as Power: Discourse and Ideology in Modern Society.* London: Macmillan.

Atkinson, D. (1999). *Scientific Discourse in Sociohistorical Context.* Mahwah, NJ: Lawrence Erlbaum.

Bakhtin, M. (1986). *Speech Genres and Other Late Essays.* Austin, TX: University of Texas Press.

Bakhtin, M. (1981). *The Dialogic Imagination.* (ed. M. Holquist). Austin, TX: University of Texas Press.

Ballard, B. and Clanchy, J. (1991). 'Assessment by misconception: cultural influences and intellectual traditions'. In L. Hamp-Lyons (ed.), *Assessing Second Language Writing in Academic Contexts* (pp. 19–35). Norwood, NJ: Ablex.

Ballard, B. and Clanchy, J. (1988). 'Literacy in the university: an anthropological approach'. In G. Taylor, B. Ballard, V. Beasley, H. Bock, J. Clanchy and P. Nightingale (eds), *Literacy by Degrees* (pp. 7–23). Milton Keynes: Open University Press.

Bamford, J. (2004). 'Evaluating retrospectively and prospectively in academic lectures'. In J. Bamford and L. Anderson (eds), *Evaluation in Oral and Written Academic Discourse* (pp. 15–30). Rome: Officina Edizioni.

Bartholomae, D. (1986). 'Inventing the university'. *Journal of Basic Writing, 5,* 4–23.

Barton, D. (1994). *Literacy: An Introduction to the Ecology of Written Language.* Oxford: Blackwell.

Barton, D. and Hamilton, M. (1998). *Local Literacies.* London: Routledge.

Basturkmen, H. (2002). 'Negotiating meaning in seminar-type discussion and EAP'. *English for Specific Purposes, 21,* 233–42.

Bates, B. (2005). 'Public culture and public understanding of genetics: a focus group study'. *Public Understanding of Science, 14*(1), 47–65.

Baynham, M. (2000). 'Academic writing in new and emergent discipline areas'. In M. Lea and B. Stierer (eds), *Student Writing in Higher Education: New Contexts* (pp. 17–31). Buckingham: SRHE and Open University Press.

Bazerman, C. (1984). 'The writing of scientific non-fiction'. *Pre/Text, 5*(1), 39–74.

Bazerman, C. (1988). *Shaping Written Knowledge.* Madison, WI: University of Wisconsin Press.

Bazerman, C. (1993). Foreward. in N. Blyler and C. Thralls (eds), *Professional Communication: The Social Perspective* (pp. vii–x). Newbury Park, CA: Sage.

Becher, T. and Trowler, P. (2001). *Academic Tribes and Territories: Intellectual Inquiry and the Cultures of Disciplines.* Milton Keynes: SRHE and Open University Press.

Belcher, D. and Hirvela, A. (2005). 'Writing the qualitative dissertation: what motivates and sustains commitment to a fuzzy genre?' *Journal of English for Academic Purposes, 4*(3), 189.

Belles, B. and Fortanet, I. (2004). 'Handouts in conference presentations'. In I. Fortanet, J. C. Palmer and S. Posteguillo (eds), *Lingusitic Studies in Academic and Professional English* (pp. 63–76). Castello de la Plana: Publicacions de la Universitat Juame I.

Ben-Ari, E. (1987). 'On acknowledgements in ethnographies'. *Journal of Anthropological Research, 43*(1), 63–84.

Benbow, C. and Stanley, J. (1980). 'Mathematical ability: Is sex a factor?' *Science, 210*, 1262–64.

Benson, M. (1994). 'Lecture listening in an ethnographic perspective'. In L. Flowerdew (ed.), *Academic Listening: Research Perspectives* (pp. 181–98). Cambridge: CUP.

Bereiter, C. and Scardamalia, M. (1987). *The Psychology of Written Composition.* Hillsdale, NJ: Lawrence Erlbaum.

Berkenkotter, C. and Huckin, T. (1995). *Genre Knowledge in Disciplinary Communication.* Hillsdale, NJ: Lawrence Erlbaum.

Berliner, D. (2003). 'Educational research: the hardest science of all'. *Educational Researcher, 32*, 18–20.

Bhatia, V. (2002). 'A generic view of academic discourse'. In J. Flowerdew (ed.), *Academic Discourse* (pp. 21–39). Harlow: Longman.

Biber, D. (1988). *Variation across Speech and Writing.* Cambridge: CUP.

Biber, D. (2006). 'Stance in spoken and written university registers'. *Journal of English for Academic Purposes, 5*(2), 97–116.

Biber, D., Conrad, S. and Cortes, V. (2004). 'If you look at . . . : lexical bundles in university teaching and textbooks'. *Applied Linguistics, 25*, 371–405.

Biber, D., Johansson, S., Leech, G., Conrad, S. and Finegan, E. (1999). *Longman Grammar of Spoken and Written English.* London: Longman.

Biglan, A. (1973). 'The characteristics of subject matter in different scientific areas'. *Journal of Applied Psychology, 57*(3), 204–13.

Bizzell, P. (1982). 'Cognition, convention and certainty: what we need to know about writing'. *PRE/TEXT, 3*, 213–41.

Blakeslee, A. (1994). 'The rhetorical construction of novelty: presenting claims in a letters forum'. *Science, Technology, and Human Values, 19*(1), 88–100.

Blommaert, J. (2005). *Discourse.* Cambridge: CUP.

Bloor, M. (1996). 'Academic writing in computer science: a comparison of genres'. In E. Ventola and A. Mauranen (eds), *Academic Writing: Intercultural and Textual Issues* (pp. 59–78). Amsterdam: Benjamins.

Bondi, M. (1999). *English across Genres.* Modena: Edizioni Il Fiorino.

Bourdieu, P. (1975). 'The specificity of the scientific field and the social conditions of the progress of reason'. *Social Science Information, 14*(6), 19–47.

189

Bourdieu, P. (1991). *Language and Symbolic Power*. Oxford: Polity Press.

Bourdieu, P. and Passeron, J. -C. (1996). 'Introduction: language and relationship to language in the teaching situation'. In P. Bourdieu, J. -C Passeron and M. de Saint Martin (eds), *Academic Discourse* (pp. 1–34). The Hague: Mouton.

Bourner, T., Bowden, R. and Laing, S. (2001). 'Professional doctorates in England'. *Studies in Higher Education, 26*(1), 65–83.

Braine, G. (1995). 'Writing in the natural sciences and engineering'. In D. Belcher and G. Braine (eds), *Academic Writing in a Second Language: Essays on Research and Pedagogy* (pp. 113–34). New Jersey: Ablex.

Bridgeman, B. and Carlson, S. (1984). 'Survey of academic writing tasks'. *Written Communication, 1*, 247–80.

Bridgestock, M. (1998). 'The scientific community'. In M. Bridgestock, D. Burch, J. Forge, J. Laurent and I. Lowe (eds), *Science, Technology and Society* (pp. 15–3). Cambridge: CUP.

Brown, V. (1993). 'Decanonizing discourses: textual analysis and the history of economic thought'. In W. Henderson, T. Dudley-Evans and R. Backhouse (eds), *Economics and Language* (pp. 64–84). London: Routledge.

Bruffee, K. (1986). 'Social construction: language and the authority of knowledge. A bibliographical essay'. *College English, 48*, 773–79.

Bryson, B. (2003). *A Short History of Nearly Everything*. London: Black Swan.

Bunton, D. (1999). 'The use of higher level metatext in PhD theses'. *English for Specific Purpose, 18*, S41–S56 .

Burling, R. (1997). 'The Norwegian disputas'. *Anthroplognytt, 2*, 8–22.

Cameron, D. (1992). 'Not gender differences but the differences gender makes: explanation in research on sex and language'. *International Journal of the Sociology of Language, 94*, 13–26.

Canagarajah, A. S. (1996). '"Nondiscursive" requirements in academic publishing, material resources of periphery scholars, and the politics of knowledge production'. *Written Communication, 13*(4), 435–72.

Canagarajah, S. (1999). *Resisting Linguistic Imperialism in English Teaching*. Oxford: Oxford Universtity Press.

Canagarajah, S. (2002). *Critical Academic Writing and Multilingual Students*. Ann Arbor, MI: Universtity of Michigan Press.

Candlin, C. and Plum, G. (eds). (1998). *Researching Academic Literacies*. Framing student literacy: cross-cultural aspects of communication skills in Australian University settings. Sydney: NCELTR Macquarie University.

Carter-Thomas, S. and Rowley-Jolivet, E. (2001). 'Syntactic differences in oral and written scientific discourse: the role of information structure'. *Asp, 31*, 19–37.

Casanave, C. and Vandriick, S. (eds). (2003). *Writing for Scholarly Publication*. Mahwah, NJ: Lawrence Earlbaum.

Caulfield, T. (2004). 'Biotechnology and the popular press: hype and the selling of science'. *Trends in Biotechnology, 22*(7), 337–39.

Chang, Y. -Y. and Swales, J. (1999). 'Informal elements in English academic writing: threats or opportunities for advanced non-native speakers?' In

C. N. Candlin and K. Hyland (eds), *Writing: Texts, Processes and Practices* (pp. 145–67). London: Longman.

Clark, D. and Clark, S. (2001). *Newton's Tyranny*. New York: Freeman.

Cloitre, M., and Shinn, T. (1985). 'Expository practice: social, cognitive and epistemological linkage'. In T. Shinn and R. Whitley (eds), *Expository Science: Forms and Functions of Popularizations* (pp. 31–60). Dordrecht: Reidel.

Clyne, M. (1987). 'Cultural differences in the organisation of academic texts'. *Journal of Pragmatics, 11*, 211–47.

Coffin, C., Curry, M., Goodman, S., Hewings, A., Lillis, T. and Swann, J. (2003). *Teaching Academic Writing: A Toolkit for Higher Education*. London: Routledge.

Connor, U. (2002). 'New directions in contrastive rhetoric'. *TESOL Quarterly, 36*, 493–510.

Cooper, A. and Bikowski, D. (2007). 'Writing at the graduate level: what tasks do professors actually require?' *Journal of English for Academic Purposes, 6*(3), 206–21.

Coxhead, A. (2000). 'A new academic word list'. *TESOL Quarterly, 34*(2), 213–38.

Crane, D. (1972). *Invisible Colleges: Diffusion of Knowledge in Scientific Communities*. Chicago: University of Chicago Press.

Crawford Camiciottoli, B. (2004). 'Interactive discourse structuring in L2 guest lectures: some insights from a comparative corpus-based study'. *Journal of English for Academic Purposes, 3*(1), 39–54 .

Cronin, B. (2001). 'Bibliometrics and beyond: some thoughts on web-based citation analysis'. *Journal of Information Science, 27*, 1–7.

Cronin, B., McKenzie, G. and Rubio, L. (1993). 'The norms of acknowledgement in four humanities and social sciences disciplines'. *Journal of Documentation, 49*(1), 29–43.

Crystal, D. (2003). *English as a Global Language*. Cambridge: CUP.

Curtis, R. (1994). 'Narrative form and normative force: Baconian story-telling in popular science'. *Social Studies of Science, 24*, 419–61.

Cutting, J. (2002). *Pragmatics and Discourse. A Resource Book for Students*. London: Routledge.

Dawkins, R. (2006). *The Blind Watchmaker*. London: Penguin.

Delamont, S., Atkinson, P. and Parry, O. (2004). *Supervising the Doctorate* (2nd edn). Maidenhead: Society for Research into Higher Education.

Devitt, A. (1991). 'Intertextuality in tax accounting'. In C. Bazerman and J. Paradis (eds), *Textual Dynamics of the Professions* (pp. 336–57). Madison: University of Wisconsin Press.

Devitt, A. (1997). 'Genre as a language standard'. In W. bishop and H. Ostrum (eds), *Genre and Writing* (pp. 45–55). Portsmouth, NH: Boynton/Cook.

Doheny-Farina, S. (1992). *Rhetoric, Innovation, Technology: Case Studies of Technical Communication in Technology Transfers*. Cambridge, MA: MIT Press.

Donald, J. (1990). 'University professors' views of knowledge and validation processes'. *Journal of Educational Psychology, 82*, 242–49.

Dong, Y. R. (1998). 'Non-native speaker graduate students' thesis/dissertation writing in science: self-reports by students and their advisors from two US institutions'. *English for Specific Purposes, 17*, 369–90.

Douglas, J. Y. (1998). 'Will the most reflexive relativist please stand up: hypertext, argument and relativism'. In I. Snyder (ed.), *Page to Screen: Taking Literacy into the Electronic Era* (pp. 144–62). London: Routledge.

Dubois, B. (1980). 'Genre and structure of biomedial speeches'. *Forum Linguisticum, 5*, 140–69.

Dubois, B. (1987). '"Something on the order of around forty to forty four": imprecise numerical expressions in biomedical slide talks'. *Language and Society, 16*, 527–41.

Dudley-Evans, A. (1999). 'The dissertation: a case of neglect?' In P. Thompson (ed.), *Issues in EAP Writing Research and Instruction* (pp. 28–36). Reading: University of Reading, Centre for Applied Language Studies.

Dudley-Evans, T. (1994). 'Genre analysis: an approach to text analysis in ESP'. In M. Coulthard (ed.), *Advances in Written Text Analysis* (pp. 219–28). London: Routledge.

Faber, B. (1996). 'Rhetoric in competition: the formation of organizational discourse in conference on college composition and communication abstracts'. *Written Communication, 13*, 344–84.

Fahnestock, J. (1986). 'Accommodating science: the rhetorical life of scientific facts'. *Written Communication , 3*(3), 275–96.

Faigley, L. (1986). 'Competing theories of process: a critique and a proposal'. *College Composition and Communication, 48*, 527–42.

Fairclough, N. (1989). *Language and Power*. London: Longman.

Fairclough, N. (1992). *Discourse and Social Change*. Cambridge: Polity Press.

Fairclough, N. (1995). *Critical Discourse Analysis*. Harlow: Longman.

Fairclough, N. (2003). *Analyzing Discourse*. London: Routledge.

Ferris, D. (1998). Students' views of academic aural/oral skills: a comparative needs analysis. *TESOL Quarterly, 32*, 289–316.

Ferris, D. (2003). *Response to Student Writing*. Mahwah, NJ: Erlbaum.

Ferris, D. and Tagg, T. (1996). 'Academic oral communication: what subject-matter instructors actually require'. *TESOL Quarterly, 30*(1), 31–58.

Flowerdew, J. (1992). 'Definitions in science lectures'. *Applied Linguistics, 13*(2), 202–21.

Flowerdew, J. (ed.). (1994). *Academic Listening: Research Perspectives*. Cambridge: CUP.

Flowerdew, J. (1999). 'Problems of writing for scholarly publication in English: the case of Hong Kong'. *Journal of Second Language Writing, 8*(3), 243–64.

Flowerdew, J. and Dudley-Evans, T. (2002). 'Genre analysis of editorial letters to international journal contributors'. *Applied Linguistics, 23*, 463–89.

Flowerdew, J. and Miller, L. (1996). 'Lectures in a second language: notes towards a cultural grammar'. *English for Specific Purposes, 15*(2), 121–40.

Flowerdew, J. and Miller, L. (1997). 'The teaching of academic listening comprehension and the question of authenticity'. *English for Specific Purpose, 16*, 27–46.

Flowerdew, L. (2002). 'Corpus-based analyses in EAP'. In J. Flowerdew (ed.), *Academic Discourse* (pp. 95–114). Harlow: Longman.

Fortanet, I. (2004). 'The use of "we" in university lectures: reference and function'. *English for Specific Purposes, 23*(1), 45–66.

Foucault, M. (1972). *The Archeology of Knowledge*. London: Tavistock Publications.

Foucault, M. (1981). 'The order of discourse'. In R. Young (ed.), *Untying the Text: A Post-Structuralist Reader* (pp. 48–78). Boston: Routledge.

Francis, B., Robsen, J. and Read, B. (2001). 'An analysis of undergraduate writing styles in the context of gender and achievement'. *Studies in Higher Education, 26* (3), 313–26.

Frobert-Adamo, M. (2002). 'Humour in oral presentations: what's the joke?' In E. Ventola, C. Shalom and S. Thompson (eds), *The language of Conferencing* (pp. 211–26). Frankfurt: Peter Lang.

Fuller, G. (1998). 'Cultivating science: negotiating discourse in the popular texts of Stephen Jay Gould'. In J. Martin and R. Veel (eds), *Reading Science* (pp. 35–62). London: Routledge.

Furneaux, C., Locke, C., Robinson, P. and Tonkyn, A. (1991). 'Talking heads and shifting bottoms: the ethnography of seminars'. In P. Adams, B. Heaton and P. Howarth (eds), *Socio-Cultural Issues in English for Academic Purposes* (pp. 75–88). Hemel Hempstead: Pheonix ELT.

Gebhardt, R. C. (1993). 'Scholarship, promotion, and tenure in composition studies'. *College Composition and Communication, 44*, 439–442.

Gee, J. (1996). *Social Linguistics and Literacies: Ideology in Discourses*. London: Taylor and Francis.

Gee, J. (1999). *An Introduction to Discourse Analysis*. London: Routledge.

Gee, J. (2004). *Situated Language and Learning; A Critique of Traditional Schooling*. London: Routledge.

Geertz, C. (1973). *The Interpretation of Cultures*. New York: Basic books.

Geertz, C. (1983). *Local Knowledge: Further Essays in Interpretive Anthropology*. New York: Basic Books.

Gergen, K. J. and Thatchenkery, T. J. (1996). 'Organisational science as social construction: postmodern potentials'. *The Journal of Applied Behavioral Science, 32*(4), 356–77 .

Gibbons, M., Limoges, C., Nowotny, H., Schwartzman, S., Scott, P. and Trow, M. (1994). *The New Production of Knowledge*. London: Sage.

Gibbs, W. (1995). 'Lost science in the third world'. *Scientific American, August*, 92–99.

Giddens, A. (1984). *The Constitution of Society: Outline of the Theory of Structuration*. Cambridge: Polity Press.

Gilbert, G. and Mulkay, M. (1984). *Opening Pandora's Box: A Sociological Analysis of Scientific Discourse*. Cambridge: CUP.

Givon, T. (1995). 'Coherence in text vs coherence in mind'. In M. Gernsbacher and T. Givon (eds), *Coherence in Spontaneous Text* (pp. 59–116). Amsterdam: John Benjamins.

Glaser, B. and Strauss, A. (1967). *The Discovery of Grounded Theory*. Chicago: Aldine.

Goffman, E. (1981). *Forms of Talk.* Philadelphia, PA: University of Pennsylvania.

Goodchild, P. (2004). 'Clouds on the horizon'. *The Guardian*, July 2004.

Goodell, R. (1985). 'Problems with the press: who's responsible?' *Bioscience,* *35*(3), 151–57.

Gosden, H. (1992). 'Research writing and NNSs: from the editors'. *Journal of Second Language Writing, 1*(2), 123–39.

Gosden, H. (1993). 'Discourse functions of subject in scientific research articles'. *Applied Linguistics, 14*(1), 56–75.

Gosden, H. (1996). 'Verbal reports of Japanese novices' research writing practices in English'. *Journal of Second Language Writing, 5*(2), 109–28.

Gould, S. J. (1992). *Bully for Brontosaurus.* Harmondsworth: Penguin.

Gould, S. J. (1998). 'Ladders and cones: constraining evolution by canonical icons'. In R. Silvers (ed.), *Hidden Histories of Science* (pp. 37–67). London: Granta.

Griffith, B. C. and Small, H. G. (1983). *The Structure of the Social and Behavioural Sciences Literature.* Mimeo: Royal Institute of Technology Library, Stockholm.

Grimshaw, A. (1989). *Collegial Discourse: Professional Conversation among Peers.* Norwood, NJ: Ablex.

Hagstrom, W. O. (1965). *The Scientific Community.* New York: Basic Books.

Hale, G., Taylor, C., Bridgeman, B., Carson, J., Kroll, B. and Kantor, R. (1996). *A Study of Writing Tasks Assigned in Academic Degree Programs* (Research Rep. No. 54). Princeton, NJ: Educational Testing Service.

Hallack, G. and Connor, U. (2006). 'Rhetorical moves in TESOL conference proposals'. *Journal of English for Academic Purposes, 5*(1), 70–86.

Halliday, M. A. K. (1989). *Spoken and Written Language.* Oxford: OUP.

Halliday, M. A. K. (1994). *An Introduction to Functional Grammar* (2nd edn). London: Edward Arnold.

Halliday, M. A. K. (1998). 'Things and relations: regrammaticising experience as technical knowledge'. In J. R.Martin and R. Veel (eds), *Reading Science* (pp. 185–235). London: Routledge.

Halliday, M. A. K., and Martin, J. R. (1993). *Writing Science: Literacy and Discursive Power.* London: Falmer Press.

Hammersley, M. (2001). 'On Michael Bassey's concept of fuzzy genralization'. *Oxford Review of Education, 27*(2), 219–25.

Harris, J. (1989). 'The idea of a discourse community in the study of writing'. *College Composition and Communication, 40*, 11–22.

Hawking, S. (1988). *A Brief History of Time.* London: Bantam Books.

Hawking, S. (1993). *Black Holes and Baby Universes and Other Essays.* New York: Bantam.

HEFCE. (1999). *Performance Indicators in Higher Education in the UK.* Bristol: HEFCE.

Henry, A. and Roseberry, R. (1997). 'An investigation of the functions, strategies and linguistic features of the introductions and conclusions of essays'. *System, 25*(4), 479–95.

Hewings, A. (2004). 'Developing discipline-specific writing: an analysis of undergraduate geography essays'. In J. Ravelli, and R. Ellis (eds), *Analyzing Academic Writing: Contextualised Frameworks* (pp. 131–53). London: Continuum.

194

Hinkel, E. (2002). *Second Language Writers' Text*. Mahwah, NJ: Lawrence Erlbaum.

Ho, B. (2003). 'Time management of final year undergraduate English projects: supervisees' and the supervisor's coping strategies'. *System, 31*, 231–45.

Hoey, M. (2001). *Textual Interaction*. London: Routledge.

Hoey, M. (2005). *Lexical Priming*. London: Routledge.

Horowitz, D. (1986). 'What professors actually require of students: Academic tasks for the ESL classroom'. *TESOL Quarterly, 20*, 445–62.

Hovav, A. and Gray, P. (2002). 'Future penetration of academic electronic journals: four scenarios'. *Information Systems Frontiers, 4*(2), 229–44.

Huddleston, R. D. (1971). *The Sentence in Written English: A Syntactic Study Based on an Analysis of Scientific Texts*. Cambridge: CUP.

Hunston, S. (2002). *Corpora in Applied Linguistics*. Cambridge: CUP.

Hyland, F. (1998). 'The impact of teacher written feedback on individual writers'. *Journal of Second Language Writing, 7*(3), 255–86.

Hyland, K. (1990). 'A genre description of the argumentative essay'. *RELC Journal, 21*(1), 66–78.

Hyland, K. (1998). *Hedging in Scientific Research Articles*. Amsterdam: John Benjamins.

Hyland, K. (2001). 'Humble servants of the discipline? Self-mention in research articles'. *English for Specific Purposes, 20*(3), 207–26.

Hyland, K. (2002a). 'What do they mean? Questions in academic writing'. *TEXT, 22*, 529–57.

Hyland, K. (2002b). 'Directives: argument and engagement in academic writing'. *Applied Linguistics, 23*(2), 215–39.

Hyland, K. (2003). 'Dissertation acknowledgments: the anatomy of a Cinderella genre'. *Written Communication, 20*, 242–68.

Hyland, K. (2004a). 'Disciplinary interactions: metadiscourse in L2 postgraduate writing'. *Journal of Second Language Writing, 13*, 133–51.

Hyland, K. (2004b). *Disciplinary Discourses: Social Interactions in Academic Writing*. Ann Arbor, MI: University of Michigan Press.

Hyland, K. (2004c). *Genre and Second Language Writing*. Ann Arbor, MI: University of Michigan Press.

Hyland, K. (2004d). 'Graduates' gratitude: the generic structure of dissertation acknowledgements'. *English for Specific Purposes, 23*(3), 303–24.

Hyland, K. (2005a). 'Stance and engagement: a model of interaction in academic discourse'. *Discourse Studies, 6*(2), 173–91.

Hyland, K. (2005b). *Metadiscourse*. London: Continuum.

Hyland, K. (2008a). 'As can be seen: Lexical bundles and disciplinary variation'. *English for Specific Purposes, 27*(1), 4–21.

Hyland, K. (2008b). English for Professional Academic Purposes: writing for scholarly publication. In D. Belcher (ed.), *Teaching Language Purposefully: English for Specific Purposes in Theory and Practice*. New York: Cambridge University Press.

Hyland, K. and Milton, J. (1997). 'Hedging in L1 and L2 student writing'. *Journal of Second Language Writing, 6*(2), 183–206.

Hyland, K. and Tse, P. (2004). 'Metadiscourse in academic writing: a reappraisal'. *Applied Linguistics, 25*(2), 156–77.

Hyland, K. and Tse, P. (2007). 'Is there an "academic Vocabulary"?' *TESOL Quarterly,41*(2), 235–54.

Hymes, D. (1966). 'Two types of linguistic relativity'. In W. Bright (ed.), *Sociolinguistics* (pp. 114–67). The Hague: Mouton.

Hyon, S. (1996). 'Genre in three traditions: implications for ESL'. *TESOL Quarterly, 30*(4), 693–722.

Ivanic, R. (1998). *Writing and Identity: The Discoursal Construction of Identity in Academic Writing*. Amsterdam: Benjamins.

Ivanic, R., Clark, R. and Rimmershaw, R. (2000). '"What am I supposed to make of this?" The messages conveyed to students by tutors' written comments'. In M. Lea, and B. Stierer (eds), *Student Writing in Higher Education: New Contexts* (pp. 47–56). Buckingham: SRHE and Open University Press.

Jackson, L., Meyer, W. and Parkinson, J. (2006). 'A study of the writing tasks and reading assigned to undergraduate science students at a South African University'. *English for Specific Purposes, 25*(3), 260–81.

Johns, A. M. (1997). *Text, Role and Context: Developing Academic Literacies.* Cambridge: CUP.

Jones, C., Turner, J. and Street, B. (eds). (1999). *Students Writing in the University*. Amsterdam: Benjamins.

Jordan, R. (2002). 'The growth of EAP in Britain'. *Journal of English for Academic Purposes, 1*(1), 69–78.

Judson, H. (1995). *The Eighth Day of Creation: The Makers of the Revolution in Biology*. Harmondsworth: Penguin Books.

Kang, S. (2005). Dynamic emergence of situational willingness to communicate in a second language. *System, 33*, 277–92.

Kaplan, R., Cantor, S., Hagstrom, C., Lia, D., Shiotani, Y. and Zimmerman, C. B. (1994). 'On abstract writing'. *TEXT, 14*(3), 401–26.

Kaufer, D., and Geisler, C. (1989). 'Novelty in academic writing'. *Written Communication, 6*(3), 286–311.

Kelly, G. and Bazerman, C. (2003). 'How students argue scientific claims: a rhetorical–semantic analysis'. *Applied Linguistics, 24*(1), 28–55.

Kelves, D. J. (1998). 'Pursuing the unpopular: a history of viruses, courage and cancer'. In R. Silvers (ed.), *Hidden Histories of Science* (pp. 69–114). London: Granta.

Kent, T. (1991). 'On the very idea of a discourse community'. *College Composition and Communication, 42*(4), 425–45.

Killingsworth, M. J. and Gilbertson, M. K. (1992). *Signs, Genres, and Communication in Technical Communication*. Amityville, NY: Baywood.

Knorr Cetina, K. and Amann, K. (1990). 'Image dissection in natural scientific inquiry'. *Science, Technology and Human Values, 15*(3), 259–83.

Kolb, D. A. (1981). 'Learning styles and disciplinary differences'. In A. Chickering (ed.), *The Modern American College* (pp. 232–55). San Fransico, CA: Jossey Bass.

196

Krause, K. -L. (2001). 'The university essay writing experience: a pathway for academic integration during transition'. *Higher Education Research and Development, 20*(2), 147–68.

Kress, G. (1998). 'Visual and verbal modes of representation in electronically mediated communication: the potentials of new forms of text'. In I. Snyder (ed.), *Page to Screen: Taking Literacy into the Electronic Era* (pp. 53–79). London: Routledge.

Kress, G. (2003). *Literacy in the New Media Age.* London: Routledge.

Kress, G. and Hodge, R. (1979). *Language as Ideology.* London: Routledge and Kegan Paul.

Kress, G., Jewitt, C., Osborn, J. and Tsatsarelis, C. (2001). *Multimodal Teaching and Learning: The Rhetorics of the Science Classroom.* London: Continuum.

Kress, G. and Van Leeuwan, T. (2002). *Reading Images: The Grammar of Visual Design* (2nd edn). London: Routledge.

Kuhn, T. (1970). *The Structure of Scientific Revolutions* (2nd edn). Chicago: University of Chicago Press.

Kuhn, T. (1977). *The Essential Tension: Selected Studies in Scientific Tradition and Change.* Chicago: University of Chicago Press.

Kwan, B. (2006). 'The schematic structure of literature reviews in doctoral theses of applied linguistics'. *English for Specific Purposes, 25*(1), 30–55.

Lakatos, I. (1978). *Mathematics, Science, and Epistemology.* Cambridge: CUP.

Lantolf, J. P. (1999). 'Second culture acquisition: cognitive consideration's. In E. Hinkel (ed.), *Culture in Second Language Teaching and Learning* (pp. 28–46). Cambridge: CUP.

Larson, R. (1982). 'The "research paper" in the writing course: a non-form of writing'. *College English, 44*, 811–16.

Latour, B. and Woolgar, S. (1979). *Laboratory Life: The Social Construction of Scientific Facts.* Beverly Hills, CA: Sage.

Lave, J. and Wenger, E. (1991). *Situated Learning: Legitimate Peripheral Participation.* Cambridge: CUP.

Lea, M. and Stierer, B. (eds), *Student Writing in Higher Education: New Contexts.* Buckingham: SRHE and Open University Press.

Lea, M. and Street, B. V. (2000). 'Student writing and staff feedback in higher education'. In M. Lea, and B. Stierer (eds), *Student Writing in Higher Education: New Contexts* (pp. 32–46). Buckingham: SRHE and Open University Press.

Lemke, J. (1995). *Textual Politics: Discourse and Social Dynamics.* London: Taylor and Francis.

Lemke, J. (1998). 'Multiplying meaning: visual and verbal semiotics in scientific text'. In J. Martin, and R. Veel (eds), *Reading Science* (pp. 87–113). London: Routledge.

Lenoir, T. (1997). *Instituting science: The Cultural Production of Scientific Disciplines.* Stannford, CA.: Stanford University Press.

Lewenstein, B. (1987). 'Was there really a popular science "boom"?' *Science, Technology and Human Values, 12*(2), 29–41.

Lewin, B., Fine, J. and Young, L. (2001). *Expository Discourse*. London: Continuum.

Lewontin, R. C. (1991). *Biology as Ideology: The Doctrine of DNA*. New York: Harper Collins.

Lewontin, R. C. (1998). 'Genes, environment, and organisms'. In R. Silvers (ed.), *Hidden Histories of Science* (pp. 115–40). London: Granta.

Li, Y. (2006). 'A doctoral student of physics writing for publication: a sociopolitically oriented case study'. *English for Specific Purposes, 25*, 456–78.

Lillis, T. (2001). *Student Writing: Access, Regulation, Desire*. London: Routledge.

Lillis, T. and Curry, M. (2006). Professional academic writing by multilingual scholars. *Written Communication, 23*(1), 3–35.

Lin, A. M. Y. (2000). 'Resistance and creativity in English reading lessons in Hong Kong'. *Language, Culture and Curriculum, 12*(3), 285–96.

Love, A. M. (1993). 'Lexico-grammatical features of geology textbooks: process and product revisited'. *English for Specific Purposes, 12*, 197–218.

Luke, C. and. Gore J. (1992). 'Women in the academy: strategy, struggle, survival'. In C. Luke and J. Gore (eds), *Feminisms and Critical Pedagogy* (pp. 192–210). New York: Routledge.

McEwan, I. (2007). 'A matter of great human ingenuity'. *The Guardian,* 30 July, 2007 (podcast at http://blogs.guardian.co.uk/science/2007/07/we_can_celebrate_and_take_joy.html).

McEnery, T. and Wilson, A. (1996). *Corpus Linguistics*. Edinburgh: Edinburgh University Press.

MacDonald, S. P. (1994). *Professional Academic Writing in the Humanities and Social Sciences*. Carbondale, IL: Southern Illinois University Press.

Malfroy, J. and Yates, L. (2003). 'Knowledge in action: Doctoral programmes forging new identities'. *Journal of Higher Education Policy and Management, 25*(2), 119–29.

Martin, J. R. (1993). 'Genre and literacy – modeling context in educational linguistics'. In W. Grabe (ed.), *Annual Review of Applied Linguistics, 13* (pp. 141–72). Cambridge: CUP.

Martin, J. (2000). 'Beyond exchange: APPRAISAL systems in English'. In S. Hunston and G. Thompson (eds), *Evaluation in Text: Authorial Stance and the Construction of Discourse* (pp. 142–75). Oxford: OUP.

Martin, J. and White, P. (2005). *The Langugae of Evaluation: Appraisal in English*. London: Palgrave/MacMillan.

Mateos, M., Villaloìn, R., De Dios, M. and Martiìn, E. (2007). 'Reading and writing tasks on different university degree courses: what do the students say they do?' *Studies in Higher Education, 32*, 489–510.

Mauranen, A. (2001). 'Reflexive academic talk: observations from MICASE'. In R. Simpson and. J. Swales (eds), *Corpus linguistics in North America* (pp. 165–78). Ann Arbor, MI: University of Michigan Press.

Medawar, P. (1990). *The Threat and the Glory*. Oxford: OUP.

Miller, C. (1984). 'Genre as social action'. *Quarterly Journal of Speech, 70*, 157–78.

Miller, T. (1998). 'Visual persuasion: a comparison of visuals in academic texts and the popular press'. *English for Specific Purposes, 17*(1), 29–46.

198

Montgomery, S. (1996). *The Scientific Voice.* New York: The Guildford Press.

Moore, T. and Morton, J. (2005). 'Dimensions of difference: a comparison of university writing and IELTS writing'. *Journal of English for Academic Purposes, 4*(1), 43–66.

Morell, T. (2004). 'Interactive lecture discourse for university EFL students'. *English for Specific Purposes, 23*, 325–38.

Morell, T. (2007). 'What enhances EFL students participation in lecture discourse? Student, lecturer and discourse perspectives'. *Journal of English for Academic Purposes, 6*(3), 222–37.

Morita, N. (2004). 'Negotiating participation and identity in second language academic communities'. *TESOL Quarterly, 38*, 573–604.

Mulkay, M. (1976). 'The mediating role of the scientific elite'. *Social Studies of Science, 6*, 445–70.

Myers, G. (1990). *Writing Biology: Texts in the Social Construction of Scientific Knowledge.* Madison, WI: University of Wisconsin Press.

Myers, G. (1991). 'Lexical cohesion and specialized knowledge in science and popular science texts'. *Discourse Processes, 14*(1), 1–26.

Myers, G. (1994). 'Narratives of science and nature in popularizing molecular genetics'. In M. Coulthard (ed.), *Advances in Written Text Analysis* (pp. 179–90). London: Routledge.

Myers, G. (2000). 'Powerpoints: technology, lectures, and changing genres'. In A. Trosberg (ed.), *Analysing Professional Genres* (pp. 177–92). Amsterdam: John Benjamins.

Nelson, J. (1993). 'The library revisited: exploring students' research processes'. In A. Penrose, and B. Sitcoe (eds), *Hearing Ourselves Think: Cognitive Research in the College Writing Classroom* (pp. 102–24). New York: Oxford University Press.

Nesi, H. (2003). 'Editorial'. *Journal of English for Academic Purposes, 2*(1), 1–3.

Northcott, J. (2001). 'Towards an ethnography of the MBA classroom: a consideration of the role of interactive lecturing styles within the context of one MBA programme'. *English for Specific Purposes, 20*, 15–37.

Nwogu, K. (1991). 'Structure of science popularizations: a genre analysis approach to the schema of popularized medical texts'. *English for Specific Purposes, 10*, 111–23.

Nystrand, M. (1987). 'The role of context in written communication'. In R. Horowitz and S. J. Samuels (eds), *Comprehending Oral and Written Language* (pp. 197–214). San Diego, CA: Academic Press.

Onega, S. and Landa, J. E. (1996). *Narratology: An Introduction.* London: Longman.

Orlowski, A. (2006). 'BBC abandons science'. *The Register*, October 2006.

Orteza y Miranda, E. (1996). 'On book reviewing'. *Journal of Educational Thought, 30*(2), 191–202.

Pakir, A. (1999). 'Connecting with English in the context of internationalization'. *TESOL Quarterly, 33*, 103–14.

Paltridge, B. (2002). 'Thesis and dissertation writing: An examination of published advice and actual practice'. *English for Specific Purposes, 21*, 125–43.

199

Partington, A. (1998). *Patterns and Meanings: Using Corpora for English Language Research and Teaching*. Amsterdam: Benjamins.

Passell, L. (1988). 'Getting out the word: an insider's view of Physical Review Letters'. *Physics Today, 41*(3), 32–37.

Pearson, M. and Brew, A. (2002). 'Research training and supervision development'. *Studies in Higher Education, 27*(2), 135–50.

Pellechia, M. (1997). 'Trends in science coverage: a content analysis of three US newspapers'. *Public Understanding of Science, 6*, 49–68.

Pennycook, A. (1994). *The Cultural Politics of English as an International Language*. London: Longman.

Phillips, L. and Norris, S. (1999). 'Interpreting popular reports of science: what happens when the readers' world meets the world on paper?' *International Journal of Science Education, 21*(3), 317–27.

Pinker, S. (1995). *The Language Instinct*. New York: Harper Collins.

Plum, G. and Candlin, C. (2001). 'Becoming a psychologist: student voices on academic writing in psychology'. In C. Barron, N. Bruce and D. Nunan (eds), *Knowledge and Discourse* (pp. 238–66). London: Pearson.

Podgorecki, A. (1997). *Higher Faculties: Cross National Study of University Culture*. Westport, CT: Praeger.

Polanyi, M. (1964). *Personal Knowledge: Towards a Post-Critical Philosophy*. New York: Harper and Row.

Poos, D. and Simpson, R. (2002). 'Cross-disciplinary comparisons of hedging: some findings from the Michigan Corpus of Academic Spoken English'. In R. Reppen, S. Fitzmaurice and D. Biber (eds), *Using Corpora to Explore Linguistic Variation* (pp. 3–23). Amsterdam: John Benjamins.

Porter, J. (1992). *Audience and Rhetoric: An Archaeological Composition of the Discourse Community*. Englewood Cliffs, NJ: Prentice Hall.

Prior, P. (1998). *Writing/Disciplinarity: A Sociohistoric Account of Literate Activity in the Academy*. Mahwah, NJ: Lawrence Erlbaum.

Räisänen, C. (2002). 'The conference forum: a system of interrelated genres and discursive practices'. In E. Ventola, C. Shalom and S. Thompson (eds), *The Language of Conferencing* (pp. 69–94). Frankfurt: Peter Lang.

Ramanathan, V. and Atkinson, D. (1999). 'Ethnographic approaches and methods in L2 writing research: a critical guide and review'. *Applied Linguistics, 20*(1), 44–70.

Rampton, B. (1995). 'Politics and change in research in applied linguistics'. *Applied Linguistics, 16*(2), 233–56.

Ratzan, S. C. (2003). 'Editorial putting SARS in perspective: a communication challenge'. *Journal of Health Communication, 8*(4), 297–98.

Redner, H. (1987). *The Ends of Science: An Essay in Scientific Authority*. Boulder, CO: Westview Press.

Richards, S. (1987). *Philosophy and Sociology of Science: An Introduction* (2nd edn). Oxford: Blackwell.

Richardson, L. (2000). 'Writing: a method of inquiry'. In N. Denzin and Y. Lincoln (eds), *The Handbook of Qualitative Research* (pp. 516–29). Thousand Oaks, CA: Sage.

Ridley, D. (2000). 'The different guises of a PhD thesis and the role of a litera-ture review'. In P. Thompson (ed.), *Patterns and Perspectives* (pp. 61–75). Reading: University of Reading.

Robson, J., Francis, B. and Read, B. (2002). 'Writers of passage: stylistic features of male and female undergraduate history essays'. *Journal of Further and Higher Education, 26*(4), 351–62.

Rorty, R. (1979). *Philosophy and the Mirror of Nature*. Princeton: Princeton University Press.

Rose, D. (1998). 'Science discourse and industrial hierarchy'. In J. R. Martin and R. Veel (eds), *Reading Science* (pp. 236–65). London: Routledge.

Rost, M. (1990). *Listening in Language Learning*. London: Longman.

Rowan, K. (1989). 'Moving beyond the *what* to the *why*: differences in pro-fessional and popular science writing'. *Journal of Technical Writing and Communication, 19*, 161–79.

Rowley-Jolivet, E. (1999). 'The pivotal role of conference papers in the network of scientific communication'. *Asp,* 179–96.

Rowley-Jolivet, E. (2002). 'Science in the making: scientific conference presentations and the construction of facts'. In E. Ventola, C. Shalom and S. Thompson (eds), *The Language of Conferencing* (pp. 95–125). Frankfurt: Peter Lang.

Ruiying, Y. and Allison, D. (2003). 'Research articles in applied linguistics: moving from results to conclusions'. *English for Specific Purposes, 22*(4), 365–85.

Russell, D. (1991). *Writing in the Academic Disciplines, 1870–1990: A Curricu-lar History*. Carbondale, IL: Southern Illinois University Press.

San Miguel, C. and Nelson, C. (2007). 'Key writing challenges of practice-based doctorates'. *Journal of English for Academic Purposes, 6*(1), 71–86.

Scollon, R. and Scollon, S. (1981). *Narrative, Literacy and Face in Interethnic Communication*. Norwood, NJ: Ablex.

Scollon, R. and Scollon, S. (1995). *Intercultural Communication*. Oxford: Blackwell.

Scully, C. and Jenkins, S. (2006). 'Publishing in English for non-native speak-ers'. *Oral oncology, 42*(7), 753.

Shalom, C. (2002). 'The academic conference: a forum for enacting genre knowledge'. In E. Ventola, C. Shalom and S. Thompson (eds), *The Language of Conferencing* (pp. 51–68). Frankfurt: Peter Lang.

Shapin, S. (1994). *A Social History of Truth: Civility and Science in Seven-teenth-Century England*. Chicago: University of Chicago press.

Shapin, S. and Schaffer, S. (1989). *Leviathan and the Air Pump: Hobbes, Boyle, and the Experimental Life*. Princeton, NJ: Princeton University Press.

Shaw, P. (1991). 'Science research students' composing processes'. *English for Specific Purposes, 10*, 189–206.

Simpson, R. (2004). 'Stylistic features of academic speech'. In U. Connor and T. Upton (eds), *Discourse in the Professions* (pp. 37–64). Amsterdam: John Benjamins.

Sinclair, J. (1991). *Corpus, Concordance, Collocation*. Oxford: OUP.

Sinclair, J. and Coulthard, M. (1975). *Towards an Analysis of Discourse: The English used by Teachers and Pupils.* Oxford: Oxford University Press.

Singer, E. (1990). 'A question of accuracy: how journalists and scientists report research on hazards'. *Journal of Communication, 40*, 102–16.

Spack, R. (1997). 'The rhetorical construction of multilingual students'. *TESOL Quarterly, 31*(4), 765–74.

St John, M. J. (1987). 'Writing processes of Spanish scientists publishing in English'. *English for Specific Purposes, 6*, 113–20.

Starfield, S. and Ravelli, L. (2006). '"The writing of this thesis was a process that I could not explore with the positivistic detachment of the classical sociologist": Self and structure in New Humanities research theses'. *Journal of English for Academic Purposes, 5*(3), 222–43.

Storer, N. and Parsons, T. (1968). 'The disciplines as a differentiating force'. In E. B. Montgomery (ed.), *The Foundations of Access to Knowledge* (pp. 101–21). Syracuse: Syracuse University Press.

Street, B. V. (1995). *Social Literacies: Critical Approaches to Literacy in Development, Ethnography and Education.* New York: Longman.

Stubbs, M. (1996). *Text and Corpus Analysis.* Oxford: Blackwell.

Stubbs, M. (2001). *Words and Phrases: Corpus Studies of Lexical Semantics.* Oxford: Blackwell.

Sutton, C. (1996). 'Beliefs about science and beliefs about language'. *International Journal of Science Education, 18*, 1–18.

Swales, J. (1990). *Genre Analysis: English in Academic and Research Settings.* Cambridge: CUP.

Swales, J. (1995). 'The role of the textbook in EAP writing research'. *English for Specific Purposes, 14*(1), 3–18.

Swales, J. (1997). 'English as Tyrannosaurus rex'. *World Englishes, 16*, 373–82.

Swales, J. (1998). *Other Floors, Other Voices: A Textography of a Small University Building.* Mahwah, NJ: Erlbaum.

Swales, J. (2001). 'Metatalk in American academic talk: the case of *point* and *thing*'. *Journal of English Linguistics, 29*(1), 34–54.

Swales, J. (2004). *Research Genres.* Cambridge: CUP.

Swales, J. and Luebs. M. (2002). 'Genre analysis and the advanced second language writer'. In E. Barton and G. Stygal (eds), *Discourse Studies in Composition* (pp. 135–54). Cresskill, NJ: Hampton Press.

Swales, J. and Feak, C. (2000). *English in Today's Research World: A Writing Guide.* Ann Arbor, MI: University of Michigan Press.

Swales, J. and Malczewski, B. (2001). 'Discourse management and new episode flags in MICASE'. In R. Simpson and. J. Swales (eds), *Corpus linguistics in North America* (pp. 145–64). Ann Arbor, MI: University of Michigan Press.

Swann, J. (2002). 'Yes, but is it gender?', In L. Litosseliti and J. Sunderland (eds), *Gender Identity and Discourse Analysis* (pp. 43–67). Amsterdam: John Benjamins.

Tannen, D. (1982). 'Oral and literate strategies in spoken and written narratives'. *Language, 58*, 1–21.

202

Tauroza, S. (2001). 'Second language lecture comprehension research in naturalistic controlled conditions'. In J. Flowerdew (ed.), *Research Perspectives on English for Academic Purposes* (pp. 360–74). New York: Cambridge University Press.

Teo, P. (2000). 'Racism in the news: a critical discourse analysis of news reporting in two Australian newspapers'. *Discourse and Society, 11*, 7–49.

Thompson Corp. (2007). *ISI Web of Knowledge* [Web Page]. URL http://scientific.thomson.com/isi/.

Thompson, G. (2001). 'Interaction in academic writing: learning to argue with the reader'. *Applied Linguistics, 22*(1), 58–78.

Thompson, P. (1999). 'Exploring the contexts of writing: interviews with PhD supervisors'. In P. Thompson (ed.), *Issues in EAP Writing Research and Instruction* (pp. 37–54). Reading: University of Reading.

Thompson, P. (2005). 'Points of focus and position: Intertextual reference in PhD theses'. *Journal of English for Academic Purposes, 4*(4), 307–23.

Thompson, P. (2006). 'A corpus perspective on the lexis of lectures, with a focus on Economics lectures'. In K. Hyland and M. Bondi (eds), *Academic Discourse across Disciplines* (pp. 253–70). Bern: Peter Lang.

Thompson, S. (2002). '"As the story unfolds": The uses of narrative in research presentations'. In E. Ventola, C. Shalom and S. Thompson (eds), *The Language of Conferencing* (pp. 147–68). Frankfurt: Peter Lang.

Thompson, S. (2003). 'Text structuring metadiscourse, intonation and the signalling of organisation in academic lectures'. *Journal of English for Academic Purposes, 2*, 5–20.

Tomkins, R., Ko, C-Y. and Donnovan, A. (2001). 'Internationalization of general surgical journals'. *Archives of Surgery, 136*, 1345–52.

Toulmin, S. (1958). *The Uses of Argument*. Cambridge: CUP.

Toulmin, S. (1972). *Human Understanding, 1*, Oxford: Clarendon Press.

Tse, P. and. Hyland, K. (2006). '"So what is the problem this book addresses?" Interactions in book reviews'. *Text and Talk, 27*, 767–90.

Tse, P., and Hyland, K. (2008). '"Robot Kung fu": gender and the performance of a professional identity'. *Journal of Pragmatics, 40*(7), xxx–xx.

Turner, J. (2003). 'Writing a PhD in the contemporary humanities'. *Hong Kong Journal of Applied Linguistics, 8*(2), 34–53.

Valle, E. (1997). 'A scientific community and its texts: a historical discourse study'. In B. -L. Gunnarson, P. Linell, and B. Nordberg (eds), *The Construction of Professional Discourse* (pp. 76–98). London: Longman.

van Dijk, T. A. (1997). 'Discourse as interaction in society'. In T. A. van Dijk (ed.), *Discourse as Social Interaction* (pp. 1–37). London: Sage.

Ventola, E. (2002). 'Why and what kind of focus on conference presentations?' In E. Ventola, C. Shalom and S. Thompson (eds), *The Language of Conferencing* (pp. 15–50). Frankfurt: Peter Lang.

Vygotsky, L. (1978). In M. Cole, V. John-Steiner, S. Scribner and E. Souberman (eds), *Mind in Society: The Development of Higher Psychological Processes*. Harvard, MA: Harvard University Press.

Wallace, R. (1995). *English for Specific Purposes in ESL Undergraduate Composition Classes: Rationale*. Unpublished doctoral dissertation, Illinois State.

Wallace, C. (2002). 'Local literacies and global literacy'. In D. Block and D. Cameron (eds), *Globalization and Language Teaching* (pp. 101–14). London: Routledge.

Walsh, P. (2004). 'A complex interplay of choices: first and second person pronouns in university lectures'. In J. Bamford and L. Anderson (eds), *Evaluation in Oral and Written Academic Discourse* (pp. 31–52). Rome: Officina Edizioni.

Watson, J. D. (1980). *The Double Helix: A Personal Account of the Discovery of the Structure of DNA*. London: Atheneum.

Webber, P. (2002). 'The paper is now open for discussion'. In E. Ventola, C. Shalom and S. Thompson (eds), *The Language of Conferencing* (pp. 227–53). Frankfurt: Peter Lang.

Webber, P. (2005). 'Interactive features in medical conference monologue'. *English for Specific Purposes, 24*(2), 157–81.

Weissberg, B. (1993). 'The graduate seminar: another research-process genre'. *English for Specific Purposes, 12*, 23–35.

Wells, G. (1992). 'The centrality of talk in education'. In K. Norman (ed.), *Thinking Voices: The Work of the National Oracy Project*. London: Hodder and Stoughton.

Wertsch, J. (1991). *Voices of the Mind*. Cambridge, MA: Harvard University Press .

Widdowson, H. (2000a). 'On the limitations of linguistics applied'. *Applied Linguistics, 21*(1), 3–25.

Widdowson, H. (2000b). 'The theory and practice of critical discourse analysis'. *Applied Linguistics, 19*, 136–51.

Wignell, P. (1998). 'Technicality and abstraction in social science'. In J. Martin and R. Veel (eds), *Reading Science* (pp. 297–326). London: Routledge.

Wignell, P., Martin, J. and Eggins, S. (1993). 'The discourse of geography: ordering and explaining the experiential world'. In M. Halliday and J. Martin (eds), *Writing Science: Literacy and Discursive Power* (pp. 136–65). London: Falmer.

Wilson, D. (2002). *The Englishization of Academe: A Finnish Perspective*. Jyvakskyla, Finland: University of Jyvakskyla Language centre.

Wodak, R. (ed.). (1989). *Language, Power and Ideology: Studies in Political Discourse*. Amsterdam: John Benjamins.

Wood, A. (2001). 'International scientific English: the language of research scientists around the world'. In J. Flowerdew, and M. Peacock (eds), *Research Perspectives on English For Academic Purposes* (pp. 71–73). Cambridge: Cambridge University Press.

Woodward-Kron, R. (2002). 'Critical analysis versus description? Examining the relationship in successful student writing'. *Journal of English for Academic Purposes, 1*(2), 121–43.

Wray, R. (2006). 'Brussels delivers blow to Reed Elsevier'. *The Guardian*, 2 April 2006.

Wu, S. M. (2007). Investigating the effectiveness of arguments in undergraduate essays from an evaluation perspective. *Journal of English for Academic Purposes, 6*(3), 254–71.

Yakhontova, T. (2002). '"Selling" or "telling"? The issue of cultural variation in research genres'. In J. Flowerdew (ed.), *Academic Discourse* (pp. 216–32). London: Longman.

Young, L. and Harrison, C. (2004). 'Introduction'. In L. Young and C. Harrison (eds), *Systemic Functional Linguistics and Critical Discourse Analysis* (pp. 1–11). London: Continuum.

Ziman, J. R. (1974). *Public Knowledge: An Essay Concerning the Social Dimension of Science.* Cambridge: Cambridge University Press.

Author Index

Subject Index